born under the sign of jazz

Design: David Houghton

Printed by: Redwood Books Limited

Published by: Sanctuary Publishing Limited, The Colonnades, 82 Bishops Bridge Road, London W2 6BB

CD manufacture: Gramofonové Závody, Czech Republic

ISBN: 1-86074-194-0

born under the sign of jazz

under the sign of

randi hultin

English translation by Tim Challman

Acknowledgments

Acknowledgments must be given to William Carnevale, Jr – the American consultant who read the manuscript and gave us some really wise and instructive suggestions. I would also like to thank all my musician friends – or their families – who have so willingly given me permission to use some of the fine jazz atmosphere that they have created in Gartnerveien over the years. Rare and memorable jazz recordings have become a CD – one of a kind – which illustrates in a fine way why it is such a joy to have been born under the sign of jazz.

Randi Hultin
Oslo, November 1997

Dedication

Dedicated to my ex-husband Tor, who gave me the jazz bacillus, to my daughters Wivi-Ann and Christina, and to my grandchildren Camilla, Miranda, Samy, Naima and Jamil, all of whom share my love for jazz.

And to Fate, which allowed me to be born under the sign of jazz.

In memory of all the jazz greats who have left us, many of them close friends, and a very special person, Loret Miller Ruppe, American Ambassador to Norway 1989-93, who became a dear friend. She would have loved to have seen my book with an English title.

Christina, Randi and Wivi-Ann

Contents

CHAPTER 11

CHAPTER 12

CHAPTER 13

CHAPTER 14

CHAPTER 15

CHAPTER 16

CD Track Listing

1. Introduction from Randi
2. Pianist Sonny Clark plays 'Jeepers Creepers' 1954: 3.14
3. Comment from Randi
4. Jam session with Basie musicians Ernie Wilkins, Joe Newman, Eddie Jones, Freddie Green, plus Anthony Ortega, Tor Hultin, 1954: 6.35
5. Comment from Randi
6. Ernie Wilkins interview 1974: 1.50
7. Comment from Randi
8. Solo from Bjarne Nerem at the Basie jam, 1956: 2.23
9. Comment from Randi
10. Stuff Smith, 1965: 3.30
11. Comment from Randi
12. Zoot Sims, Einar Iversen, Roy Burns, Knut Ljung and Mikkel Flagstad: 6.00
13. Comment from Randi
14. Hampton Hawes, 1967: 7.23
15. Comment from Randi
16. Bill Evans interview: 2.20
17. Comment from Randi
18. Phil Woods sings/plays 1968: 1.54
19. Comment from Randi
20. Morten Gunnar Larsen plays 'Randi's Rag' for Eubie: 4.44
21. Comment from Randi
22. Kenny Dorham singing/playing his own 'Fairweather': 2.06
23. Comment from Randi
24. Jan Johansson plays 'Kors I Taket' by Østen Hedenbratt: 0.45
25. Comment From Randi
26. Reinhold Svensson plays piano on 'Tenderly': 4.04
27. Comment from Randi
28. Jan Johansson plays piano: 2.14
29. Comment from Randi
30. Finn Enger plays accordion for Paul Gonsalves: 2.20
31. Comment from Randi
32. Jaki Byard playing 'Oslo To Kristiansund To Molde': 3.56
33. Comment from Randi
34. Monica Zetterlund sings 'I Can't Give You Anything But Love, Randi', with Lasse Bagge, Carl Morten Iversen and Ole Jacob Hansen: 3.40
35. Comment from Randi
36. Bodil Niska and Einar Iversen play Tor's 'Ballad For Stan': 3.30
37. Comment from Randi
38. Phil Woods composing 'Randi' on piano and alto: 2.14

Private recordings by Randi Hultin (Copyright)

Meeting Sonny Rollins after many years in Oslo and London, 1996

Foreword

Randi Hultin is a legend. Her empathy for and love of jazz has endeared her to scores of musicians from the great to the near great to the journeyman player. And, I might add, to many other people in the arts who have enjoyed the friendship of this dedicated woman or have experienced her generous hospitality while travelling through Europe.

I'll never forget my first visit to Oslo and Randi's home. I was astounded by the names in her guest book and by all the stories of the impromptu jam sessions which seem to have been a regular occurrence!

This type of atmosphere is what has nurtured the rare art of jazz music and I'm sorry to say that such surroundings are becoming almost a thing of the past in this rapidly changing world.

So stay beautiful, Randi. We love you. Long live our Norwegian Angel of the Arts.

Sonny Rollins

Something About The CD

I was married for thirteen years to Tor Hultin, a very fine pianist, composer and arranger, and also a popular accompanist who toured all over the world with Josephine Baker in 1958/9. He also liked to play jazz, and from the beginning he tried to get me interested. It took him six years, but then we got our own small house and opened it for jam sessions at night, and I got really hooked. One of the first meetings with Norwegian and American musicians took place in 1953, after Lionel Hampton's band had played in Oslo. But then we had many visits from the Basie band, the Stan Kenton musicians, Dizzy Gillespie, Roy Eldridge, Stan Getz, Zoot Sims, and Ray Brown and Herb Ellis – who played bass and guitar for hours. We have also had visits from Paul Gonsalves and a lot of Swedish and English bands too.

In 1956 I started to write about jazz, and have done so ever since. When my husband left me and started to work with theatre music, I continued to have an open house for jazz. I also helped to get some musicians to Norway, like Keith Jarrett and the Charles Lloyd Quartet, Phil Woods and others. Keith has played real swing jazz on my piano and Getz, Dizzy, Zoot and Gonsalves have been jamming there. Trombonist Carl Fontana was one of the first to impress me. And many pianists have left wonderful tapes, like Sonny Clark, Hampton Hawes, Jaki Byard, Tommy Flanagan, Stanley Cowell, Adam Makowicz and Joe Zawinul. Guitarist Larry Coryell made his first trick recording on my old Tandberg tape recorder

Sonny Clark was twenty-two when he
played for me for four hours. Track 2

Joe Newman plays a swinging trumpet
solo with the Basie band. Track 4

Tor Hultin wrote 'Ballad For Stan' and jams
with the Basie band. Tracks 4 and 36

Phil Woods, composer of the beautiful
ballad 'Randi'. Tracks 18 and 38

with two tracks on both sides. Milt Jackson has been singing and playing piano, drummer Art Taylor loved to sing like Sinatra, accompanied on piano by his close friend, tenor player Johnny Griffin, and trumpeter Kenny Dorham also liked to sing and play the piano. Even Booker T and Stevie Winwood have recorded for me.

Some of my best friends for years have been numerous singers, like Sheila Jordan, Monica Zetterlund and Urszula Dudziak. Also Joe Williams, Charles Brown and Bob Dorough. Many musicians liked to sing, and some of them have even been filmed – like Max Roach, Chet Baker and Red Mitchell – all at the piano. A lot of Norwegian singers still get together at my house – Laila Dalseth, Karin Krog and Magni Wentzel; still

Johnny Griffin and Art Taylor, old friends and welcome visitors to Gartnerveien

eager to play jam sessions are the fine tenor players Totti Bergh and Bodil Niska; at the piano – like in the fifties – is pianist Einar "Pastor'n" Iversen, as well as Ole Jacob Hansen, Eyvind Olsen and Jan Horne on the drums, and Bjørn Pedersen playing the bass, as he has done with a lot of Americans at the Metropol Jazzhouse and with our oldest band, Big Chief Jazzband, since 1952. There is no longer the same need for jam sessions today, but in my house it still happens – like when the fine English tenor player Dick Morrissey showed up in 1996 as a big surprise.

In the sixties many musicians rehearsed at my home, or stayed there – like Clifford Jordan, Jimmy Heath, Art Farmer, and Phil Woods, who played with Norwegian musicians. Also Jan Garbarek rehearsed once for some concerts with another sax player, Marion Brown. After all these years I have hundreds of hours of fine jazz on tape, cassette, Super 8 and video. A lot of interviews have also been saved on the tapes – like with Sonny Rollins – when I first realised that I could also use my Tandberg for talking. It is sad to think of all the voices I have missed – like Bud Powell, John Coltrane, Coleman Hawkins, and Ben Webster.

One who really made a big impression, was Eubie Blake. He was ninety-four when he and his wife Marion came to visit me in Oslo. He

Sax player and Basie's great arranger,
Ernie Wilkins. Tracks 4 and 6

has left countless hours of his music, talking and singing on tape. He never learned to play his composition 'Randi's Rag', but one of Eubie's favourite pianists, Morten Gunnar Larsen, played it for him for the first time in my house (Track 20). From Eubie I also have more than 100 historic letters.

As mentioned, Einar "Pastor'n" Iversen (son of a clergyman), has been one of our leading pianists through the years and can be heard on the present CD with Zoot Sims in 1958, and with Bodil Niska in 1997. With Bodil, who plays saxophone in the female jazz group Girl Talk – featuring Elisabeth Walker on piano and Tine Asmundsen on bass – Einar plays 'Ballad For Stan', composed by my ex-husband Tor. Stan Getz loved the ballad, and played it at my house in 1960, together with Swedish pianist Janne Johansson. That same year Janne and the blind Swedish pianist, Reinhold Svensson, played for each other. Listen to tracks 24, 26 and 28.

Accordion player Finn Enger was often at our jam sessions, but the only solo existing on tape, is the one he played with Paul Gonsalves in 1958. Paul loved Finn's playing.

Stuff Smith also visited me many times, and one night, after playing at the Metropol in Oslo, he relaxed at my home, while I played old private tapes for him. Unfortunately he also wanted to play for my tape recorder, but since I had stopped playing piano when I met my husband – and had never played jazz – I couldn't accompany him. Suddenly I remembered that I had a small *Music Minus One* record, and was sure it should be played at forty-five rpm. Stuff – who was a little tired at five o'clock in the morning – never asked which tunes they played on the record, he just played. Four tunes in all. I have chosen the one where he first played the wrong tune, and we can also hear that the rhythm section is playing too fast. Neither of us noticed. Not even when he played 'I Got Rhythm'. But no one can say that Stuff doesn't swing on that fiddle!

Since then I have played the tape for Milt Hinton and Nat Pierce,

Zoot Sims played for hours with
Norwegian musicians. Track 12

Einar Iversen, leading jazz pianist in
Norway. Tracks 12 and 36

Mikkel Flagstad steps in for a tenor duet
with Zoot. Track 12

Hampton Hawes left a lot of beautiful jazz.
Track 14

Bill Evans talks about Bud Powell and Hampton Hawes. Track 16

Eubie Blake and Morten Gunnar Larsen. Track 20

Kenny Dorham played his 'Fairweather' for me first in 1964. Track 22

Janne Johansson and Reinhold Svensson met in 1960. Tracks 24, 26 and 28

DEXTER GORDON   **JOHN COLTRANE**   **BUD POWELL**   **BILL BASIE**   **EUBIE BLAKE**   **COLEMAN HAWKINS**

ANNE PHILLIPS AND BOB KINDRED
in association with
The St. Barts Playhouse

RANDI'S JAZZ

AN EVENING HONORING NORWAY'S RANDI HULTIN

—— ON FILM ——
First U.S. showing of documentaries
made from Randi's personal tapes,
films and photos. Intimate portraits of
America's greatest jazz artists as seen
through her eyes and heart. Rare
moments with Bud Powell, Louis
Armstrong, Eubie Blake, John Coltrane,
Stan Getz, Zoot Sims, Count Basie,
Sonny Rollins, Phil Woods, Clark Terry,
Joe Newman, Ben Webster, Charles
Mingus, Dizzy, Roy...

—— LIVE ——
RANDI'S FRIENDS:
Clark Terry, Clifford Jordan, Jackie
Byard, Phil Woods, Adam Makowicz,
The Leroy Williams Trio, Gene
Bertoncini, Michael Moore, Bob
Kindred, John Goldsby, Paul Meyers,
Bill Goodwin, and others.

**FOLLOWED BY AN
UNFORGETTABLE "JAM"
RECEPTION FOR RANDI**

Sunday, May 22nd
Monday, May 23rd
7:30

Show
$15

Show/"Jam" Reception
$30

St. Bart's Playhouse
Park Ave & 50th St.

Box Office:
212-751-1616 ext 219 between 12-6

Special Thanks To:
PAN AM, RINGNES BEER,
NORSK HYDRO SALES CORP., SONY,
NORWEGIAN INFORMATION SERVICE

For musicians and all lovers of jazz,
The evenings are in fact a tribute to one of the most beloved
figures in the world of jazz—Norway's Randi Hultin

The only tape existing of Finn Enger's jazz accordion. Track 30

Jaki Byard stayed for a fortnight and played a lot – of everything. Track 32

Monica Zetterlund, world famous jazz singer and actress. Track 34

Norwegian tenor player Bodil Niska plays Tor Hultin's 'Ballad For Stan'. Track 36

without knowing that they were the very ones who played bass and piano on this special record. They could easily understand why Stuff didn't like their fast tempo. The record should have been played at thirty-three rpm.

I think this CD will illustrate some of the fine musical experiences we have had at Gartnerveien for more than forty years. My interest in jazz has really given me a lot of friends forever.

WARM THANKS

Besides thanking all the musicians and their relatives who have allowed me to use the fine and special music on the CD, I must also thank Audio Virus LAB and Helge Sten for doing a fine job as Sound Engineer and for editing the music from my old reel tapes to DAT. Thanks also to musicians Frode Barth and Terje Gewelt for their help in producing the CD, and of course to Audun Strype for CD mastering at his studio in Oslo.

QUOTES ABOUT THE CD

From Louis Armstrong to Zoot Sims every jazz musician who has travelled to Scandinavia has become a friend of journalist Randi Hultin. I first met Randi in 1958 and joined the ranks of those musicians who made their way to her home in Oslo. Her warm hospitality was always in evidence whether your visit was for a few hours, or for a matter of days and weeks.

Listening to the CD that accompanies her book of personal memories is the aural equivalent of browsing through snapshots in a family album, each track evoking recollections of the great jazz legends who have relaxed and "partied" in her home. One seldom has the opportunity to hear these jazz stars in such informal circumstances, and it is a joy to vicariously "join the party at Randi's".

Dave Brubeck

23

I was really moved by the CD. Here are great musicians being happy and having fun in happy surroundings. There are some priceless moments here. A little of what it was like at Randi's.

Sonny Rollins

I have heard the best that anyone could offer in music right here in your house. I wish everyone understood music like you. Keep listening. (*From my guest book.*)

Stuff Smith

I feel really privileged to have been a part of the very important documentation that took place in your relaxed home. You are so important to the addition to our rich jazz history. I am sure the listening public will acknowledge your contributions are a blessing to have.

Tommy Flanagan

Photo: Berit Bolt

This CD presents some real treasures, like Phil Woods actually composing his ballad for Randi, plus Zoot Sims and Kenny Dorham – not to mention the great Scandinavian musicians, like the late Norwegian tenor player Bjarne Nerem, Swedish pianist Jan Johansson and, another high point, the new recording of 'Ballad For Stan', beautifully played by Norwegian lady tenor saxophonist Bodil Niska.

Scott Hamilton

CHAPTER 1

Randi's Jazz

It's 22 May, 1988 and I am standing on a stage in New York City. *Randi's Jazz* – thirty years of my life with jazz music, captured in four television programmes – is about to be shown on a large screen as part of "An Evening Honouring Norway's Randi Hultin". The place is St Barts Playhouse, the church with the adjoining hall that is often used for large jazz concerts. The church, dwarfed by skyscrapers on all sides, is located in midtown Manhattan.

I'm not nervous, just happy and bewildered. And full of reflections. My life has been a whirlwind of haphazard events. Never would I have believed that jazz was to play so significant a role or that the art form would create so many friendships for me. Or that I would ever see my story projected over a period of two days in the jazz capital of the world.

26

Ever since I boarded the plane on 17 May, things have happened quickly. I travelled first class and felt like a princess. In just two days, I've already been interviewed by several of the best known radio stations. The listeners were to be informed about the upcoming concerts while 'Randi's Rag' and other compositions were played on the air. Around town I have seen striking posters announcing *Randi's Jazz*, and when I examined the programme, I was surprised to read that in between the TV screenings, live music was to be played – compositions written for me and performed by my friends.

Outside St Barts Playhouse, things began to happen early. A jazz band was playing and people soon crowded around. Representatives from the Norwegian Information Service were standing there; several of my colleagues from the New York branch of Norsk Hydro appeared, and a host of American friends came from far and wide. Ted Curson showed up with a trumpet in hand; he had heard me on the radio. Guitarist Tal Farlow came from New Jersey – I had just talked with him in Sandvika, Norway, before I took the flight to New York.

I rise and go forward, mounting the stage. It feels strange to be standing on a New York stage. I am expected to tell a bit about myself, and in a way this seems easier to do in a foreign place and in a foreign tongue.

I remember when Miloud Guiderk staged *Jazz For Randi* in the Sandvika Theatre in 1981. I had to appear on stage then, too. Miloud had hired saxophonist Bjørn Johansen and Egil Kapstad's quartet, and he had flown in guitarist Rafaël Fays direct from Paris, to celebrate my twenty-fifth anniversary of jazz journalism. It was a fantastic experience. There were bouquets of flowers and speeches, and I was moved and grateful and even – for once – completely speechless. But here in St Barts

Photo: Frode Pedersen

In Molde, 1984

Photo: Sverre Bergli

On my "jazz staircase" at Gartnerveien, 1984

people expect me to say something, and so I do, with relish:

"It is an honour to be able to show these TV programmes in the USA. I have been so fortunate to have met many jazz personalities, and I want very much to share this with all of you. Jan Horne, who produced these programmes, has done an excellent job. And I am especially pleased that so many of my musician friends have come to play for me. Thanks also to Anne Phillips and Bob Kindred, who have invited me to New York and who have put all of this together..."

I share the front row with Adam Makowicz and friends of Eubie Blake. Jan Horne is also present for the occasion.

As the images begin to appear on the large screen, it is as if I relive my life with jazz once more. There are memories galore – encounters with well-known jazz musicians, private recordings, interviews, pictures and film clips. I feel that the audience sitting behind me is caught up in the moment; I can feel their response. The screening is new and unusual for the American audience.

My mind goes to Eubie Blake, the ragtime pianist who lived to be 100 years old. Had it not been for him, I would never have been in America. It was he who got me to come here for the first time, in 1978. Every time Norwegian radio plays the nine am vignette, I think of Eubie. His 'Memories Of You' is legendary.

Louis Armstrong was also a good friend. I'll never forget the night we went sleigh riding to Ullevålsether and everybody was bundled up in fur coats and woollen caps.

Louis was never a guest in my home. Neither was Duke Ellington, but I did meet him at close range, literally speaking. I have to smile at the thought. It happened at the Down Town Key club in Oslo, at a party for Ellington's musicians. The place was packed, and as I was passing the Duke, he accidentally came into contact with my chest and apologised, saying, "Excuse me – no, I mean of course, thanks!"

Quick witted as always.

At the same party was saxophonist Paul Gonsalves, veteran soloist with Ellington, and he had been a guest at my home – in Gartnerveien, Oslo. I'll never forget when he played sax together with Finn Enger on the accordion and Leif Eberson on guitar. Gonsalves is featured at the beginning of one of the TV programmes.

Adam Makowicz, July 1988

Up on the silver screen appears

Photo: Judith Kirtley

Jaki Byard came to *Randi's Jazz* in New York, 1988

pianist Bud Powell, whose acquaintance I first made at the Metropol Jazz House in Oslo – he was one of the great innovators of bebop, and he was a very special person. Some said he was schizophrenic, but for me he was nothing short of a genius. He was also a good friend. We had an unusual kind of bonding across the room from the moment he sat down at the club's grand piano. It was exciting listening to him. We knew his style from records, but suddenly here he was in the flesh, playing with Norwegian musicians. I had my camera with me, but I didn't want to wreck the ambience with brutal flashes. Instead I stood behind him and listened. Suddenly, as though he had eyes in the back of his head, he turned and said, "Aren't you going to take a picture of me?"

I was startled. During the intermission, he took me by the hand and asked if I would sit at his table. Ever since then, he always held my hand whenever we met.

In St Barts Playhouse, Bud Powell's son Johnny is seated with his wife and two children. Johnny was only seven when he was in Oslo. By now he must be about thirty-three. He is pleased to be able to see these films of his father; there isn't much he remembers from those years in Europe.

Between the TV programmes there is live jazz music. Several of my musician friends play melodies they have composed for me over the years. One of the first is Adam Makowicz who has composed a new melody for the occasion – 'Waltz For Randi' – which he will perform both days, between other concerts he is playing at Carnegie Hall with, among others, Benny Carter and Charlie Haden.

Pianist Jaki Byard shows up in the middle of the concert, having flown in direct from Oklahoma during a storm. When he gets to the podium, he asks if he can tell an anecdote. It's about Charles Mingus, with whom Jaki played for many years. "Can you remember that Mingus ate the whole lamb roast at your house?" Jaki asks. And then he plays a gorgeous ballad, 'Oslo To Kristiansund To Molde', which he had composed at my home in Gartnerveien several years ago.

Phil Woods was supposed to have performed his ballad 'Randi' himself, but he is out of town, so the tune will be played by another close saxophonist friend, Clifford Jordan. Tomorrow it will be performed by Jesse Davis – a young, promising musician. The coincidence here is that he has just taken his instrumental exam playing this very melody – I know that the song is well-known among college musicians in the USA.

Pianist Ted Rosenthal plays 'Randi's Rag', which was written by Eubie, and saxophonist Bob Kindred has rehearsed a beautiful version of 'Fairweather', given to me by Kenny Dorham. He also plays 'Beautiful Friendship' together with the Leroy Williams Trio.

After the concert, a lot of people come over and thank me for the films and recordings. Most of them have their favourites, and they are surprised over the intimate, private moments they've witnessed. Eubie Blake's friends are visibly moved. Many are curious about how I was able to have such close friendships with the American musicians.

On the second floor there is a jam session. I meet new friends and old, and have the pleasure of hearing Byard and Makowicz both play. Two of the world's best pianists and two of my best friends. A rare meeting. There is also an exhibition of my serigraphs – twenty

Duke Ellington and painter Inger Sitter in Oslo, 1971

drawings of jazz musicians – and food and drinks are being served. The atmosphere is lively.

But the fairy tale has not come to an end. Before I leave New York, there is a farewell party for me on Broadway, at the GianLuca Jazz Club. The place is packed and many Norwegian musician friends turn up – Carl Fredrik Størmer and Jørgen Næss, both studying drums in New York, and Urszula Dudziak, the Polish singer who got married in Gartnerveien. She has brought with her two Polish musicians that I have not seen since they were at the Metropol in Oslo during the1960s. Clifford Jordan appears also, and plays his own composition 'Impressions Of Scandinavia'.

It's all so overwhelming. So many new memories, I now have another album to add to my collection of sixteen guest books and numerous festival volumes. This one is filled with greetings and pictures from my visit to New York – "Four Days of Randi's Jazz-Filled Life".

Count Basie invited me to the VIP room in the concert hall to take a photo of him, Ella Fitzgerald and our Royal Highnesses, Queen Sonja and King Harald, 12 July, 1978

CHAPTER 2

The Young Artist

e didn't have a lot of money, but we always had things under control. Mum was really good at sewing, and a master at altering clothing. If anyone teased me about wearing hand-me-downs, I should just ask them if they have anything better to give me, said Mum. My confirmation dress, however, was new. It was black with silk stripes in every colour of the rainbow. Paid for in installments at Petrine Nielsen, it was so beautiful I'll never forget it.

I dreamed of becoming a full-time student somewhere, but ended up taking classes here and there. I had to help out with the finances at home. Besides, I was going to be a painter, so secretarial school had to do. It was a good idea to have something to fall back on, in case the painting didn't go so well. When I was fifteen years old, I could type, take shorthand, and had a diploma in basic accounting. Later I learned English stenography at night school.

I was selling fresh vegetables in Oslo at Young's Square (Youngstorget) for a neighbour when I got the message to meet for my first interview. I was wearing a big red hat that I'd bought with my own money, and like this, I showed up at the National Union of Mechanical Workshops. I was sixteen years old, and at this time jobs were hard to come by. Out of 147 applicants, I was chosen. It was pure coincidence...only because my name was Randi. The union president, Alf Bang, had a weakness for the name Randi because he'd had an excellent secretary for many, many years with the same name, but she was leaving.

Pappa, søster Eva og for au Randi

But I nearly didn't get the job. When I wrote the application, I had decided to change my name to Winnifred, my romantic middle name. I wrote as neatly as possible with ink and pen, but as I was signing "Winnifred", I splotched a big ink stain on the paper, and had to write the whole application over again. The second time I didn't think about what I was doing and of course signed "Sincerely, Randi Lindén". Of all the applicants, I was the only one named Randi.

I was the youngest employee, and earned seventy-five crowns a month, plus five crowns in inflation compensation. Now I could pay my way at home.

ANATOMY

President Bang soon discovered that I liked to draw, and had so much belief in me that he gave me every Thursday off so I could paint. He paid for equipment, transportation, and lessons with the painter Marit Nørregaard at Vindern. I studied there with his daughter, Karin Bang, who later became fairly well-known as an author. *Blues* is the title of one of her books, but it was our interest in jazz which brought us together again many years later. When she invited me to her home, I was very happy and proud to discover my first oil painting hanging on a wall of her living room along with other, more well-known Norwegian painters. I had given the painting to Alf Bang as a thank you for everything he had done for me.

Aged fifteen, in 1941

While I was working at the Union, I was accepted at night school at the Institute of Arts and Crafts. I was admitted directly into the second year level, upon Marit Nørregaard's recommendation. Classes started at four in the afternoon, but I was allowed to leave work one hour early in order to take extra classes in drawing with live models present. My first teacher was Carl von Hanno, who took a great interest in what I was doing. Maybe he was too kind, because after half a year, he said I could advance to third year level. The fact that I hadn't taken any anatomy classes didn't matter too much to him. It was more important that I learned to use a plumb line.

There was a year-and-a-half wait for a place in the third year class, and when I got in, I got Per Krohg as my teacher. He was very critical and could scare the wits out of the entire class when he came to discuss our work. He would swoop into the classroom and say, "I don't know why I bother coming here at all, none of you know how to draw." When he came to my charcoal drawing, he looked at me in exasperation and said, "Tell me something, have you ever even heard of anatomy? Down to second year level you go!"

I was completely in despair and started to cry.

"Stop that," Krohg commanded. "I can't stand it when women cry, I never know what to do."

I was allowed to continue at third year level, and the next time he came to class, I was standing there with an anatomy book in one hand and charcoal in the other...and Krohg was satisfied.

NORWAY'S WENCHE MYHRE

In addition to my job at the Union and night classes at the Art Institute, I took courses in First Aid at Ullevål Hospital. It was meant to be two weeks of theory and two weeks of practical training, but I found working at the hospital so interesting that they let me continue for six months, from seven to nine each day before I went to the office. As well as the early mornings, three nights a week I took extra classes

With Wenche Myhre, 1991

in drawing at Palle Storm's atelier. I was also a member of a painting club, along with Dad. It was in this group, the Oslo Painting Club, that I discovered Wenche Myhre, many years later.

Wenche was hired by the club to entertain during one of the larger annual meetings. She was thirteen years old and performed with her father and brother. I was so impressed by both her singing and her stage presence, that I asked her if she'd signed up for *The Top Ten*, a talent show arranged at Chat Noir every Saturday. She said that she'd sent in an application, but hadn't heard anything. I promised her I'd get her a spot. There was only one Saturday left of the talent shows, and I knew if she performed, she'd outdo everyone there. I called *Verdens Gang*, one of the national newspapers, who helped organise the contest, and asked them to find Wenche's letter. "She's one in a million," I told them. "She's got both a voice and stage presence."

Wenche won with ease and got a recording contract, but I never dreamed she'd become as famous as she did. I got a wonderful thank you letter and a box of chocolates after the talent show.

EMERGENCY PARAMEDIC

Just after the war had ended, I was called into service at Akershus Fort as an emergency paramedic. Now of course there was no emergency, but they needed people to help the soldiers coming from Sweden. First I became a stenographer, and not long after that I was made responsible for 125 girls my age, all eighteen or nineteen years old. I called myself "WA leader" and got my own chauffeur who drove me to and from work on a motorcycle. I had an enlisted uniform, officer's benefits, civilian wages, and lived at home, an excellent combination. In the evenings, I hung out a lot at the Allied Officers' Club in downtown Oslo, a meeting place for Norwegian and American military. They played a lot of jazz here and I remember Pete Brown playing drums, but I wasn't very interested in jazz at the time.

Everything was a little chaotic after the Liberation, but I eventually discovered that I had quite a knack for getting things organised. As WA leader, I wrote letters to schools and employers requesting that the girls be excused from their classes and jobs because they had important assignments to complete for the military. I also gave them letters stating that they should be allowed to ride for free on all public transport, and they were allowed to do so! They worked for free, so I thought this was perfectly justifiable. Nobody protested.

Later I was transferred to Solplassen, another military office complex, and became secretary to Lieutenant General Olaf Helset. He was a really nice boss. The Armed Forces Field Theatre had a rehearsal hall in the same building, and I remember one of the actors, Pelle Bjørgan, going to Helset to get a requisition for red wine. "I've got a sore throat," he said, "and I need medicine if I'm going to perform." He got his red wine.

When Helset was transferred to Lillehammer, I decided to transfer to Special Services at the Frogner Camp and the Armed Forces Field Theatre ended up there as well. Many well-known artists did their military service in the Field Theatre: opera singer Ragnar Ulfung, pianist Kjell Bækkelund and theatre director Arve Opsahl.

I MEET TOR

The first time I met Tor Hultin, he was selling sheet music and demonstrating pianos at Musikkforlaget, one of the largest music stores in Oslo. I went there quite often, but I never noticed Tor – not until he started his service in the army. Tor was stationed in Fredrikstad with an artillery regiment, and requested a transfer to the Frogner Camp when Arve Opsahl was theatre director. I was working as secretary to the Chief of Special Services for southeast Norway by then, keeping the books, doing set painting and writing cabaret sketches on the side. While Tor was in Arve's office, I was called in on the intercom.

"Wow, you got broads here too?" said Tor.

"Yeah, wanna see?" said Arve, and asked me to come in with some papers.

Tor has since insisted that he dreamed of me that night.

I was given the message to transfer Private Tor Hultin to the Frogner Camp as pianist for the Field Theatre. Friday, 13 September,

With pianist and husband Tor Hultin, 1947

1946, he was transferred. This is when I noticed him...because he was wearing the wrong uniform. "We wear field uniforms here," I said. "I'll get you a new uniform."

We were engaged on 19 October, a month later, in Lillehammer, during one of the Field Theatre's performances.

The first time I invited Tor home to meet the family, he must have thought we were pretty strange. Dad and I had rehearsed 'My Blue Heaven', a popular jazz piece, and we played it on piano and accordion. Tor listened politely and applauded just as dutifully. I've often thought about how polite he was that evening. I didn't know a thing about jazz, and our playing was probably less than good.

Painting on honeymoon, 1947

Tor had invited me to the Svend Asmussen concert, but I wasn't interested. The first jazz concert I finally went to was Don Redman's American Big Band at the Colosseum. I don't remember anything from that concert, not even the vocalist Inez Cavanaugh, who came to visit me at Gartnerveien twenty years later.

A couple of years before I met Tor, my family had moved from one room to two rooms and a kitchen on the east side of Oslo. But the idyll didn't last long. After Tor and I got engaged, he'd spend the night with me every time he missed the last bus to Grefsen, a not too infrequent event. My mum, who wanted things done properly, suggested we get married. We were to get one of the rooms! The wedding was on 19 April, 1947.

A few months later, we came home with a Steinway grand piano for which I'd borrowed the money at the office. Mum had to get rid of some of the furniture to make room for it, but she thought it went without saying that Tor should have a good instrument. Mum was amazing. So was Dad.

When I met Tor, I was taking drawing, tap-dancing and English classes, as well as piano and drum lessons. The drum lessons were supposed to help me stay on beat when I played the piano. For a while I also painted costumes for the Chat Noir. When Tor and I got married, we both left the army, and I thought about applying to the Arts Academy. But pretty soon I had to get a job again to help out with the finances. In September 1947 I was hired by Norsk Hydro, one of Norway's largest oil producers and fertiliser companies, where I worked until I retired in 1993.

It wasn't jazz that made me fall for Tor, it was the 'Moonlight Sonata', romantic as I was. He played it a lot better than I did, so I eventually abandoned my sheet music, and took up note pads instead. Tor began arranging and taught me how to write the different parts from the score. It was always exciting to hear the final product. Tor arranged all the dance music for The Temp Band, an act that played at various Oslo restaurants when the regular bands had a night off. They would play an hour and a half of concert music, the rest of the night taken up with dance music. It was during the dance portion that they tried to squeeze in as much jazz as possible. In addition they had to know various artists' original compositions for those restaurants that featured name acts. Tor, who didn't have an instrument to carry, always had to haul the suitcases – one for dance music and one for concert music.

WIVI-ANN AND CHRISTINA ARE BORN

Our first daughter, Wivi-Ann, was born in December 1948, and Christina was born in July 1952. At that point we were a family of seven people and a grand piano in two rooms and a kitchen. But it suited us fine. Tor worked at night, the rest of us worked during the day. Mum cooked meals, kept the house tidy and watched the kids. She was always evenly calm and content, and enjoyed spending time with Tor during the day. He's pretty entertaining and a great storyteller; he knew the art of dramatising even before he became the pianist for The Norwegian Theatre. Tor moved from his

Painting eggs

41

playing job at the Grand Hotel to one at Hotel Viking, where Ole Flagstad was music director. Ole was the father of one of our best saxophonists, Mikkel Flagstad, and the brother of opera singer Kirsten. Every time Ole was asked if he was the brother of the famous Kirsten Flagstad, he would answer firmly: "No, she's my sister."

In 1952, Tor started playing with The Spotlights at Hotel Viking, along with Per Nyhaug. Both Tor and Per wrote and arranged, and they were often broadcast live on the radio from Viking, as they were from many other restaurants. All the different orchestras in town began practically competing to see who could sneak the best jazz into their dance repertoire. The Spotlights were even voted best band in a "jazz poll" conducted by *Jazz Society* magazine

THE PRIMING SPARK

It took me six years to get interested in jazz, despite an enthusiastic, jazz-loving husband. Tor invited me to concerts, and played countless records: "Listen to that trumpet player, Randi, nothing else even compares!"

The trumpet player was Maynard Ferguson. I listened and listened until our one-year-old, Christina, crushed a whole stack of records by sitting on them. Big, shiny sixteen RPMs of Stan Kenton's big band that Tor had bought in New York. He had played piano on a boat to America in order to get to Birdland – the jazz mecca of New York. This was a common thing to do among jazz musicians during the fifties.

After a while I became somewhat impressed, and it was probably the "stratosphere trumpeter" who first sparked my interest in jazz. I eventually met both Ferguson and his family in Venice several years later, in 1969. In the meantime I'd heard many trumpeters who impressed me even more, although maybe not as high note artists.

Tor continued patiently playing records for me. At the same time he couldn't understand how I could whistle 'Tiger Rag' so well when I wasn't the least bit interested in jazz. Norwegian veteran Alf Søgaard's big band had recorded the piece, and I'd heard them at St Hanshaugen in the forties. I'd even gotten myself a seventy-eight of this orchestra playing 'Tiger Rag' – without giving a thought to the word "jazz".

The only Norwegians at Birdland – Scott Lunde at the piano, Knut Ljung on bass, Arnulf Neste on drums and Finn Enger on accordion

THE OSLOFJORD TO BIRDLAND

I mentioned that in the fifties, it was common among the city's musicians to take jobs on board one of the "America boats" in order to be able to experience one or perhaps two nights at Birdland – the famous jazz club "across the pond". It didn't make any difference that the ocean crossing took nine days.

One of the most enthusiastic Atlantic crossers was accordionist Finn Enger, also one of the best jazz performers on that instrument. In April 1956, he had a job with pianist Scott Lunde, an excellent swing player, the ever solid bass player Knut Ljung, and our leading jazz drummer at that time, Arnulf Neste. In a club in New York, they had heard Shirley Dean, a beautiful and talented accordion player, and they got her a job on board the Oslofjord. She had a good sense of harmony and was unrivalled as an improviser, says Scott Lunde.

PETRILLO ON BOARD

It was on exactly this same voyage that the Oslofjord was carrying a very celebrated VIP, the American Musicians Union's powerful chairman, James Petrillo – also a friend of Shirley. He thought the Norwegian quartet was so swinging that he offered them American citizenship and plenty of gigs. But first of all, they were to play a night at Birdland – the only Norwegian band ever to have that honour. According to Shirley, the audience response to the group's repertoire featuring tunes by Teddy Wilson and Benny Goodman was good. Shirley Dean was also the first to use the word "reefer" – something they smoked in America. This was new to us in the fifties. Whether Shirley still plays jazz accordion is doubtful. Scott said that she had retired to a cloister.

GARTNERVEIEN 6

My real interest in jazz wasn't aroused until jazz came into my living room – in 1953. By this time we'd built our own house at Høyenhall – at Gartnerveien #6 – and could invite musicians home. We built the house with the help of Tor's brother, and both Tor and I worked on it ourselves as much as we could. It was a single family villa turned into a duplex, ninety square metres each, with a living room measuring thirty square meters, a narrow kitchen, and three bedrooms on the second floor. It was a wooden frame house and everything was built according to the Housing Bank's rules and regulations. The walls of the stairwell up to the second floor eventually became covered with pictures of musicians, and of course the grand piano was placed in the living room. It all seemed like a castle, for a secretary married to a starving musician.

My most vivid memory from our first jam session, is that of an exasperated musician sitting in the kitchen with two fried eggs in his lap. He was starved, and these were the last two eggs we had left in the house. His two newly fried "easy overs" had landed right in his tuxedo-ed lap. The plate had slipped.

The unlucky musician was baritone saxophonist Oscar Estell, who was in Oslo with the world famous vibraphonist Lionel Hampton.

Gartnerveien 6 in 1953…

… and 1997

Photo: Tore Fredenlund

L-r: Henry "Lappen" Olafson on bass, Kristian Bergheim on tenor sax, Pete Brown on drums, Egil "Bop" Johansen on piano and Franco Cerri on guitar, August 1953

Oscar arrived at Gartnerveien quite late at night, along with some other band members. They had played two concerts at the Colosseum in Oslo. I hadn't been to either one myself and Tor couldn't go, because he was playing at the Viking. But the jazz photographer Tore Fredenlund had been there, and he's the one who came over with the Hampton band in tow.

Oscar Estell was also someone who managed to arouse my interest in jazz, because after we had staved off the worst of his hunger pangs with some Gouda cheese, he sat down at the piano. We were quite surprised that a saxophone player could play the piano that well. Today, of course, most jazz musicians can compose using the piano.

Oscar got things swinging, and the piano was surrounded by open-mouthed Norwegian musicians. Tor and Finn Enger were probably the most excited and Oscar had enough finesse to keep everyone completely enthralled. The guitarist Robert Normann, rarely seen at jams, was also there, as was, among the Americans, alto saxophonist Anthony Ortega. Another present was eighteen-year-old Mona Ørbeck who had been at the concert, and was herself a classical pianist. Little did she know at that point that she'd be getting engaged at Gartnerveien the following year – to Anthony.

Another one of the guests that night was Leo, Hampton's road manager and adopted son. He was the first one through the door, gallantly handing Tor his hat and cane. He must have thought Tor was the butler...until he turned the corner and saw our tiny living room. It was probably a pretty rare experience for them to be invited to someone's home when they were in Europe. This was one of the first jazz visits after the war, when the Hampton band came by train to Oslo.

Anthony Ortega didn't forget Mona Ørbeck. He came back to Oslo in 1954, and in February of that year they got engaged at Gartnerveien. By then Lionel Hampton had fired Tony, something many others would experience in the years to come. He had played for a studio recording in Paris, something Hampton didn't like.

"WHAT'S SHE SAYING?"

A couple of months later Mona and Tony showed up at Gartnerveien along with some other Norwegian musicians and ten members of the Basie band. The Count Basie Orchestra had had a concert at Folketeatret, and the jam session included, among others, trumpet player Joe Newman, baritone saxophonist Charles Fowlkes, trombonists Benny Powell and Bill Hughes, drummer Gus Johnson, sax player Ernie Wilkins, trumpeter Wendell Cully, bassist Eddie Jones, as well as the legendary guitarist Freddie Green. Green humbly seated himself in a corner in the entry way, and from here we could enjoy his famous guitar accompaniment close up. No other rhythm guitarist in the world ever had so much personality, and nobody has been able to replace him.

From that night I can also remember the kids waking up on the second floor. Wivi-Ann was now five, and Christina one, and Wivi-Ann

Photo: Tore Fredenlund

Ernie Wilkins
Mona Orbeck
Anthony
Orkega
Eddie Jones
Tor
Joe Newman
?Hisnes
Benny
Powell
Charles
Foulkes
Vertinna

Mars 54

Basie's musicians watched by Mona, Anthony, Tor and Randi, March 1954

wanted to come down to watch the musicians play. Her eyes grew round with amazement when she saw that several of them were dark-skinned, just like in the pictures she'd seen from Africa. "Mummy, they aren't wearing grass skirts, and look at those shoes! They're even shinier than Daddy's!"

After that, when night-time jam sessions became a common occurrence, there was seldom a reaction from the second floor. Every now and then they'd call for us, but then it was only to ask if there were any blacks downstairs. If there weren't, they would pull the covers back over their heads and go back to sleep. Christina got a lot of attention from the Americans because of her big blonde curls. Eddie Jones, Count Basie's bassist for several years and a guest at our home many times, always had to go up and say hello to her. The first time, however, I became a little perplexed. Christina stared curiously at this big strong bassist, and asked me quite unexpectedly, "Mummy, is he just as black under his clothes, too?"

48

"What's she saying?" Eddie asked me, but I was a little hesitant to translate, at least at that point.

"I'LL BOIL SOMETHING"

The first time the Basie musicians came to visit, I served hot dogs in our very tiny kitchen. I'll never forget the sight of all those tall musicians completely filling the room. We didn't have anything in the way of alcohol to offer them, and the musicians, who were somewhat thirsty, were wondering where their drinks were. I answered politely: "I'll boil something."

They looked at me funny, probably thinking something had gotten lost in the translation. After a while they began to play, and I got out our glass container and extension cords and put on a "brew" in the kitchen. My job was to monitor the fermenting process, even though I never tasted the stuff. I only used a teaspoon and matches to make sure the "percentage" was right. I'll never forget the reaction of Oscar Estell, the baritone saxophonist who had lost his fried eggs. He was so impressed with my moonshine brewing talents that he didn't want to leave Gartnerveien – not until I got the bright idea of giving him a soda-bottle full of hooch "to go". This was the only way he would even try to make it to the train station on time. There was Lionel Hampton, worried and watching the clock, but they made it only minutes before the train pulled out of the station.

L-r: Leo Moore, Lionel Hampton's adopted son, Oscar Estell and Finn Enger in front of the moonshine rig

Sonny Clark – one of our first visitors, from my guest book, January 1954

Basie's bassist Eddie Jones was also quite impressed with the taste. So impressed that he felt it for a week afterwards. As I've mentioned before, Birdland in New York was a popular place to go for Norwegian "ship musicians", and a whole band from Oslo went there once when the Basie band was playing. When the musicians heard that some of the audience members were from Norway, they asked the guys if they knew a pianist and a painter who lived in the hills by Oslo. The Norwegians understood that they were talking about Tor and me, and Eddie Jones asked them what on earth it was we'd given them to drink. It had tasted so good, but he'd been running to the toilet for a week afterwards! Our hospitality resulted in a free round of drinks for the Norwegian musicians.

In 1974, twenty years after the famous Basie visit, Ernie Wilkins, the Basie band's great arranger and composer, showed up in Oslo alone, to play with Norwegian musicians. I had the honour of having him as my guest at Gartnerveien for the week he was in Oslo. When I asked him what he remembered most from his first visit, he mentioned the unique drink we'd served him. He also remembered that there had been lots of snow, and that the band had thrown snowballs at the cab driver who picked them up that morning. It must have been quite a shock for the cabbie to see a group of towering black men come stumbling out of the house and start a snowball fight.

SONNY CLARK

Before the Basie band came to visit in 1954, we had a very special visit from the twenty-two-year-old pianist Sonny Clark, who was in Oslo for "Jazz Club USA". Billie Holiday was the big star, and Sonny played with clarinettist Buddy de Franco's quartet. The concert also included vibes player Red Norvo and his trio, and the world's most famous jazz critic, Leonard Feather, was Master of Ceremonies. An historical concert in Oslo.

After the concert Billie Holiday went home to a Norwegian saxophonist's house, and Sonny Clark, along with their drummer, came home with us. Sonny went straight over to the piano and played alone for two hours. He didn't use many more than six fingers, but

Einar "Pastor'n" Iversen

boy, did it swing. He was very inspired by Bud Powell, his great predecessor. There weren't many of us in the living room, and everyone stood around the grand piano in order to catch everything. He played 'Jeepers Creepers' and other standards, and it was great to listen to, but Sonny didn't say much, only two words in fact: "Art Tatum". That's what he answered when someone asked him who his favourite pianist was. Tatum has of course been the greatest mentor for many of the world's pianists.

Towards dawn – it must have been about four-thirty in the morning – they got a cab back to the hotel. But it wasn't long before the phone rang. Sonny wanted to come back because he thought the hotel was boring. It was after nine in the morning when he left.

RECORD FROM GARTNERVEIEN

I recorded Sonny's playing, of course, with my old Tandberg recorder, and Tor and I let some of our musician friends borrow the tape because we wanted everyone to hear how good he was. Someone apparently also copied the tape, because somehow it ended up in the US as part of *The Sonny Clark Memorial Album* put out by Xanadu Records. I wrote and asked how the company had gotten hold of the recording, and I was told that it had come from a collector in England.

Now – eighteen years later – when I contacted Don Schlitten, asking how he got the permission from Sonny's family, he said I was free to use part of his LP for my special CD, providing I write "By courtesy of Xanadu Records". It will surely please readers to listen to Sonny Clark's version of 'Jeepers Creepers'.

Sonny died only thirty-one years old, while at the home of the famous baroness in New York, Pannonica de Koenigswarter, otherwise known as "Nica". It was there that Charlie Parker died as well. Sonny had a short, but strong career, and managed to leave his mark. He had only been playing for a couple of years when he was our guest at Gartnerveien. Among other great accomplishments, he later recorded an album with saxophone player Dexter Gordon.

STAN KENTON

Stan Kenton's big band was the first jazz band recording Tor ever played for me, and I wasn't to hear the band live until ten years later. Not only did I hear the band, but several of the musicians came to visit at Gartnerveien as well. They were a very modern band at that time, and were known for their great arrangements. Our living room was packed with almost fifty people, as many Norwegians as there were Americans. Among the "natives" were pianist Kjell Karlsen and the famous comedian Rolf Wesenlund, who sat on the floor, actress Anita Thallaug with her husband, saxophone player Kristian

My drawing of Stan Kenton's concert in Oslo, 1956 – one of my first inspirations

Bergheim, cabaret director and jazz pianist Einar Schancke and the cabaret star Mary Anderson.

From that concert in Nordstrandshallen, I remember especially Carl Fontana's beautiful trombone solo in 'Polka Dots And Moonbeams'. But I didn't get to hear Ferguson on trumpet, who had played on the record Tor had played for me earlier. Instead Lee Katzman played trumpet. He was also at the jam later on, along with Carl Fontana.

Fontana wanted to play, but hadn't brought his horn, so he borrowed Gordon Nord's ancient trombone. What he played that night in our living room was to be my next big jazz experience. He had amazing tone and technique, and all of us were impressed. Gordon didn't even recognise his own horn.

The concert had also made a big impression on me and I was a new convert. But there was one individual in particular who didn't like Kenton's modern arrangements, and this was the critic who signed his column "Munk" in the daily newspaper *VG*. He wrote that the Kenton band was boring. He had fallen asleep, he said, and had longed for

Armstrong and Lionel Hampton during the evening. This got me really mad, and without telling Tor, I sent in an angry letter to *VG*: "Dear Munk, get out of the monastery and with the times. Didn't you hear the great arrangements, or had you maybe fallen asleep? Leave any reviews of Kenton to someone who can appreciate modern jazz."

These were my first printed words on jazz, and they caused a big stir among the musicians who came to jam at Gartnerveien a few days later. Several had cut out the letter and were dying to know who had the initials "RWH". They thought the letter was funny, but most of them agreed – most of them, that is, except trumpet player Rowland Greenberg. "Have you seen the letter about the Kenton band in *VG* today? What a joke – I agree with Munk," Rowland said. "Kenton doesn't swing at all."

None of them had realised that "RWH" stood for Randi W Hultin.

PRESS DEBUT

My pianist husband wanted me to get interested in jazz, and I did – from the first time musicians came through our door in 1953. It's difficult to explain how one becomes interested in jazz, because it's an emotional thing. But when you first get the bug, there's no turning back. The understanding and appreciation of the music only grows.

After three years I had become so interested that I made my debut as a jazz reporter in *Filmjournalen* and *Morgenposten*. When musicians first started visiting us, I always had my sketch pad with me both at home as well as at the concerts. My first drawings of musicians were printed in 1955 in *Verdensrevyen*, in which Karl Otto Hoff wrote about jazz. The drawings led to my first article in *Filmjournalen*. Jazz reporter Tor Lauritzen came to a jam at our house, and wanted to introduce me in the paper as hostess and illustrator. That was in April, 1956. A month later, on 17 May, the Swedish bassist Georg Riedel was to play in Oslo, and Lauritzen asked me if I could bring my sketch pad with me to the Penguin, one of the most popular jazz clubs at the time. Later I invited them to a jam session, and Riedel came along with some Norwegian musicians. Since Lauritzen never showed up, I decided to write a little myself, and that's when it all started. Georg Riedel was the subject of my debut.

I wrote for *Filmjournalen* for several years, the first two for free. The first concert I reviewed was trombonist Kid Ory and his aging band at Nordstrandshallen. I wrote that the American government should pay them such a big pension that they wouldn't have to tour. They were so old, and I was incapable of appreciating their originality.

I continued to write for *Filmjournalen* and other magazines, and the same year I started writing for *Morgenposten*. I wrote for the "young adult" section, and among other things, I got to interview Eartha Kitt – my first interview in English. I was visiting Stockholm and went to Berns, where she was going to perform, to set up an interview. She agreed to meet me after the evening performance. She was hot stuff, but didn't think too highly of journalists. I wasn't particularly nervous. Since I was writing for *Morgenposten*, nobody could stop me.

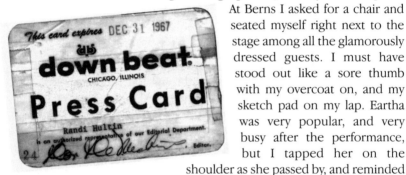

At Berns I asked for a chair and seated myself right next to the stage among all the glamorously dressed guests. I must have stood out like a sore thumb with my overcoat on, and my sketch pad on my lap. Eartha was very popular, and very busy after the performance, but I tapped her on the shoulder as she passed by, and reminded her about the interview. The drawings were all finished. She asked me to wait, and she disappeared again. I went to look for her, and found her with some friends at one of the tables. In the end, I got my interview. She was very arrogant, and I was probably pretty annoying. I hadn't planned what I was going to ask her about, and wasn't prepared enough to conduct a good interview in English.

Later I got a job as correspondent for the Swedish magazine *Accordionjournalen* which came about via a jam session with accordionist Andrew Walter and his musicians. A couple of years later I became correspondent for the Swedish edition of *Show Business* – again because someone who worked there was at a jam at Gartnerveien. A string of coincidences. At a party in Oslo I met Sverre Østen, who did lay-out for the society magazine *Nå*, and he asked me if I'd consider doing my own column for them. Having two years of *Filmjournalen* behind me didn't hurt.

GOING ABROAD

I had written a bit about the jazz scene in Sweden, but the first time I really went abroad was in 1960, to Switzerland, to visit a friend in Basel. There wasn't too much jazz there, just "spaghetti bands", as I called them. At a café I met a young guy who knew about a jazz pianist in Basel. "You have to meet him, he sells cars during the day," he told me.

It turned out to be George Gruntz. I'd brought tapes from various jams in case I should run into someone who was interested in jazz, and was soon invited over to George's. He mentioned that he arranged jazz for Lugano radio, and I seized the opportunity to get him to arrange for a big band in Oslo. I had been asked to be on the look-out for possible arrangers, but the leader couldn't pay more than twenty-five Norwegian Crowns (three or four dollars) for each arrangement. George arranged his own composition 'Sabrina's Dance' in 5/4, which got immediate approval from the big band.

But George never got any money. The leader had to collect money from the boys in the band first, he said. With a big band it shouldn't be too expensive for each to chip in. When Kjell later wrote to Gruntz for a new arrangement, Gruntz answered that he could forget the money for the first piece, but that from now on each arrangement cost forty dollars. Kjell thought this was simply unheard of.

Needless to say, Gruntz eventually became a world-famous big band leader. He has played as a soloist and with his big band in Molde, and with his Concert Big Band he toured the globe in 1997, celebrating its twenty-fifth anniversary. He has put out several albums, and from 1973, and for some years after, he replaced Joachim Berendt as head of the jazz festival in Berlin. Following my visit to Basel, I did an article on "car salesman and pianist" George Gruntz, and sent it along with various pictures to *Dagbladet*. It was printed the summer of 1960 and filled most of the music section. Gradually they printed more and more of my material, and although I never had a contract, I worked continually for *Dagbladet* for twenty-three years, up until

1983. At this point I was given my own column in *Aftenposten*, and wrote for them until the end of 1990.

So I've been writing about jazz since 1956, and in addition to newspaper columns, I've been a correspondent for lots of foreign jazz magazines. I've written for *Down Beat*, the world's most prestigious jazz magazine, since 1962. And I also led my own jazz news programme for NRK radio for twenty years.

I've also written for *Jazz Forum*, the magazine of the International Jazz Federation, since 1969. My name is listed as foreign correspondent in many magazines. In Norway I've had jazz columns in the magazines *Pan*, *Lyd & Bilde* (Sound And Image), *Kulturguiden*, and *Hva Skjer* (What's Happening). When the Norwegian Jazz Society's *Jazz-Nytt* was revamped in 1987, I was offered my own column called "Randi's Jazz". I've also contributed to several books: *Møte I Musikk*, an American book on Coltrane *Chasin' The Trane*, various encyclopedias and textbooks, as well as *Jazz I Norge*, which came out in 1975.

My writing even led to a change in my main job at Norsk Hydro. A secretary since 1947, I became editor of the company's magazine, *Hydro Oslo*, in 1970 until my retirement in 1993. Professionally as well as for fun, jazz has certainly changed my life.

CHAPTER 3

Count Basie

Count Basie in Oslo with the Norwegian Royal Guard

In 1956, several of the Basie musicians came to visit again. I can remember standing in my house recording, with the mike in my hand, when I suddenly heard a change in the bass line behind me. Eddie Jones had slipped in the porch entrance and had taken over the bass from the Norwegian player – usually there would be three or four bassists hanging out waiting for their turn. Trumpet player Joe Newman came too, but wasn't feeling well, so he sat on the floor and played when he got the urge to contribute. He was operated on for an ulcer a few days later.

With Count Basie in Antibes, 1961

"The Count" himself was a little worried about Newman. Later on that night he showed up, and sat on the stairs that led to the second floor. At that point Bjarne Nerem, one of the leading tenor players in Norway, and Joe Newman were playing together, and Basie was impressed with the Norwegian. It felt strange all of a sudden to have one of the world's best-known big band leaders sitting in the stairwell. In the living room Joe Williams was singing the blues – there was barely enough room for his voice in there. The beautiful ballad 'Tenderly' practically made the walls vibrate, and that was without a microphone. They weren't the only celebrities present that night, though. Cabaret artist Mary Andersen, who was living in Oslo at the time, was also there. She and Williams sang duets which was quite an experience. When we asked Basie if he wanted to sit in at the piano, he said the guy who was playing was doing a good enough job – that "guy" was Tor. "I prefer to listen," Basie said, and stayed in the stairwell all night.

He never came into the living room, not until several years later when he came to spend his day off at Gartnerveien, while the rest of his band were wandering around the city of Trondheim. Count Basie, or William ("Bill") Basie, became a good friend. His big band created a style that has inspired bands all over the world. He himself played piano in a very unique way, streamlined, effective, and with a swinging beat.

My next encounter with Basie and his band after Oslo was at the festival in Antibes. There he carried my recorder and camera bag for me. I remember we wandered into the casino, where Basie wanted to try his luck. He was quite a gambler, and known for it too, but when he tried getting in to the fashionable gambling hall, the answer was no. Members Only.

Italo Bertolotto, Joe Newman and Bjarne Nerem, 1956

"Well, tomorrow you're gonna have to let me in, 'cause I'm playing here," Basie said. He was giving a concert there the following night.

IN THE BATHROOM

In Antibes, Basie and the band stayed at the big, swanky Grand Hotel, whereas I booked a small, inexpensive boarding house, Les Pergolas. I liked it there, because I had a kitchen with cooking facilities. The only

The equestrian Sonny Payne in Antibes, 1961

problem was that there was no dark corner where I could develop my film. The bathroom was flooded with sunlight during the day, and at night by the lights from the night clubs. There was a tiny room in the basement, but if I were to use that, the owner had to stand in front of the door so it wouldn't swing open. She was big enough to block the sunlight, but the whole arrangement seemed cumbersome. When I described my situation to Count Basie, he immediately offered me the use of his own bathroom.

"Bring your darkroom equipment over to my place," he said. "I'm never there during the day anyway. But for God's sake, don't spill any chemicals. I don't want to get thrown out."

I moved my developing equipment, and eventually my typewriter, too, over to Basie's hotel room. He left orders at the reception that I should be given a key, and that I could order what I wanted from room service, on his bill. As the films were hanging to dry on the balcony, I wrote my articles for the Norwegian daily, *Dagbladet*, with the incredible view of the Mediterranean serving as extra inspiration. Looking down over the balcony, I would frequently see the Basie musicians in the hotel swimming pool. The drummer, Sonny Payne, loved horses and was always waiting for the opportunity to rent a horse at some nearby stable, complete in full riding attire. It must have been incredibly hot wearing riding pants, boots, and a heavy jacket, but he loved to parade around like that. I told him I wouldn't believe he rode until I saw it, and Sonny just laughed.

"I'll let you know," he said with a smile.

AN AUDIENCE WITH RAY CHARLES

That same year in Antibes, the blind singer and pianist Ray Charles and his big band were also in town. I'll never forget the night they were playing at the casino restaurant. I couldn't afford a ticket to the concert, so I found myself a free seat out on the terrace. It was a beautiful night, and as Ray Charles was singing the ballad 'Ruby, My Dear', I could hear the waves of the Mediterranean lapping onto the shoreline in a slow tempo – perfect brush accompaniment. All of a sudden I felt someone's arm around me. It was the Swedish tenor player Bernt Rosengren, who also had a free seat.

Another time, when the Basie band played in the park at Juan-les-Pins, I was standing there listening right next to Ray Charles. We stood so close together, in fact, that when he tapped the rhythm against his thigh, his hand would tap me at the same time. This didn't create any special contact between us, though, since he couldn't see me. His road manager, however, promised me an interview with Ray Charles at his hotel.

When the audience had been arranged, Sonny Payne came and announced that he'd found a horse, and that I had to come with him to the "ranch". Eager to get pictures of this grand occasion, I asked the manager if I could postpone the interview with Ray Charles until the following day. This was fine with him, because another lady journalist, from Finland, had also requested an interview. She took my place that day, and this resulted in an instant love affair between her and Charles. It was so consuming that she unhesitatingly left her husband and children in Finland to follow him. Charles was also married at the time. I never did get that interview with him, because they left a day early. I always felt responsible for this new romance because if I hadn't gone with Sonny Payne that fateful day, the beautiful Finnish journalist would never have had her interview with Ray Charles and two marriages might have been saved.

BASIE ADOPTEE

In 1962 I was adopted as a member of the Basie band. They were giving a concert at Liseberg in Gothenberg, and Count Basie gave me a big welcome when I arrived. This was one of those fantastic occasions when the audience could dance to the Count Basie Orchestra. The next day I was to join the Basie bus to Uddevalla. It was Basie's birthday – 21 August – he was fifty-eight years old, and the band had planned to announce this on stage. However, they were somewhat let down by the boss himself, who showed up for the event in his everyday outfit. Everyone else was wearing a tuxedo. "Where the hell's your tux?" his road manager asked him.

"I thought you had it," said Basie. "But who cares what I'm wearing anyway?"

It was somewhat comical seeing the whole band in tuxedos, while Basie himself was wearing a plaid jacket, striped pants, and his famous cap. When he set the beat for their first number that evening, the piece he'd announced never came – instead the band opened with 'Happy Birthday'. Basie looked like he didn't even know it was his own birthday, he was so obviously surprised. And I don't think the band has ever been that undisciplined, before or since.

Basie played better than ever that night, he was in his element, and as usual when someone in the band was playing particularly well, nods of approval came from the others in the Basie family.

During the same tour of Sweden, I had dinner with the Count at a restaurant, and at the table next to us, there were a couple of young kids who were waiting to get a few words with him. When they finally came over to the table, they had their questions ready: "When did you take over Benny Moten's orchestra?"

"You got your history all wrong, young man," Basie said. "I didn't take over, but I played with Moten."

"Who's bigger, you or Duke Ellington?" the younger one asked.

After a little pause, Basie smiled: "The difference between me and Ellington is the same as the difference between me and your fellow countryman, the boxer Ingemar Johansson. Duke is like Ingemar."

A DAY OFF IN OSLO

Every time Basie played in Oslo, he wanted me to keep him company at the hotel. Telling him I had to go home to write a review never had much of an effect.

"You can do that at the hotel," he'd say, "I won't bother you." He called the reception himself and asked them to get me a typewriter and the review would be written in the hotel reception.

In his room, Basie would listen to the radio and watch TV at the same time, and wanted a translation of everything. He'd stare in fascination, even if the TV programme was about the preservation of

Basie at Gartnerveien, 1977

Norwegian farms. Everything was interesting. At the same time he could ask who the vocalist was on the radio at the moment. He ate all the time, often two dinners a day and then sugar-free chocolate afterwards. He was a diabetic.

Speaking of eating, I can remember everything he ate once when he spent his whole day off at Gartnerveien in 1977: hot dogs with roquefort cheese and rye crackers with cold cuts. Everything tasted good to him and he looked like he really enjoyed himself. That day I introduced him to my VCR. He didn't know such a thing even existed. I asked him if he wanted to watch a movie, and put on a video starring Gregory Peck and Charles Laughton.

"How on earth did you know that these are my best friends?" he said. So I asked him if he wanted to see Bud Powell. But when the sounds from Bud's piano came out of the TV set, Basie looked at me in surprise:

"What kind of TV stations do they have here in Norway, that actually play good jazz and show that good a movie?"

I explained a little about video cassettes and recording, but it took some time before he'd believe me: "You mean I can watch one channel, and record from another at the same time?"

"Yes, and you can get your very own tomorrow, if you want to," I told him. "Especially since you love TV so much."

During his visit I also played him a video recording from the Kongsberg Jazz Festival, where Thad Jones conducted a big band of Norway's top musicians. I had one musician specifically in mind, trombonist Frode Thingnæs, because I had a feeling Basie might be interested in a new trombonist. His reaction was as I'd expected:

"Who's that trombone player, can you call him?" he asked me. "I'll steal him, take him with me to America."

Unfortunately Thingnæs was on vacation in Spain, and the two never did meet, but Basie never forgot Frode's playing. "He's a good arranger, too," I told him. "He'd be perfect for the Basie band."

When I met Basie one year later in New Orleans, he'd bought his own VCR.

TWO FRIENDS TALKING

I interviewed Basie several times, both for *Dagbladet* and for radio, but usually we were just two friends talking. The question he hated the most was, "Why do they call you 'Count'?"

"I myself just say Basie," he said. "There is only one Basie, I don't know of any others."

He told me he did as little as possible during his spare time. "I go for walks, watch TV, but I don't play. I don't even have a piano at home, only an organ."

Basie lived in Freeport in the Bahamas, and even though he didn't play during his spare time, he loved living the life of a musician. "Playing is the most important thing in my life," he said, and at that point he was over seventy. Even a heart attack didn't keep him off the road. "It's not because I have a band to keep together. Even if I'd played the bass drum, I'd keep touring."

One time when I asked him how he got interested in jazz, he laughed. "The word 'jazz' didn't even exist when I started playing, at that time they were only talking about ragtime."

"Did you hear Eubie Blake?"

"Actually not until I became an adult. Then I saw his show

Chocolate Dandy on Broadway, with Josephine Baker. I love Eubie," Basie said, "he's fantastic."

When Basie visited me that day off, Eubie had planned on coming up from Denmark right afterwards. Eubie felt quite flattered when Basie called him in Copenhagen and told him: "Randi has made her own pond in her backyard and named it after you: 'Eubie Blake Lake'."

BASIE "THE HEALER"

I also got to experience some of Basie's other talents. One time when I took the band bus to Njårdhallen here in Oslo, he blurted out, all of a sudden: "Keep your eye on the driver, he's gonna drive the rear view mirror to pieces." I of course wondered what on earth he was talking about, but as we approached the musicians' entrance, the mirror did break.

During one of his visits I told him that I had a lot of pain in my shoulders and I'd had a stiff neck for several weeks.

"I'll fix that," Basie said. I laughed and thought he was joking, but when he put his hand on my neck, I have to admit I felt a special heat. And I actually got better. Did he have talents as a "healer"? One thing's for sure: when Basie said something, no matter how absurd it may have sounded, he meant it. Brief and concise, the same way he led his orchestra. One finger in the air, and the band was playing.

He was maybe a little superstitious, because he'd never walk on the stage without chewing gum in his mouth.

One of the last times he visited Oslo, the audience stood outside and waited by the musicians' entrance. He was picked up by a limousine, and all the way from Château Neuf down to the hotel, people waved to him from the sidewalk. I felt like I was in the company of royalty – and, of course, I was.

CHAPTER 4

Jamming At Gartnerveien

T here's really not enough room for big bands at Gartnerveien, but there have been plenty of them in our living room nonetheless – with and without instruments. The Basie musicians have been several times, as have members of the German Kurt Edelhagen band, who showed up in November, 1954 after playing a "Hit Parade" at Folketeatret, with the singer Catarina Valente.

The next big session was with Malte Johnson's big band from Gothenburg, when they played at Chat Noir. Some of their musicians – including the Norwegian pianist Ivar Wefring and trombonist Andreas Skjold – came to our home with vocalist Sonya Hedenbratt and took part in a great jam evening.

Later, I had visits from Frank Foster's big band, Thad Jones and Mel Lewis with their musicians, and the Clark Terry Big Band. Most of them had to sit on the floor, because a thirty square-metre living room is not designed for big bands. Still, we had a lot of fun. Either the musicians themselves would play, or I would bring out some old, private jazz recordings or a jazz video. Even before we could buy the videos, I think there was more jazz shown on European television than was shown in the USA. It seemed so, at least.

GUITAR AND BASS

In February, 1956, Jazz At The Philharmonic played in Oslo for four

L-r back row: Harald Wibeto, Ray Brown and Tor Hultin; middle row: Karl Otto Hoff, Åse Wentzel, Illinois Jacquet, Pete Brown, Arne Hermansen, Per Nyhaug (covered), Kare Aslaksen and Ragnar Robertson; front row: Herb Ellis, Øystein Ringstad and me

days, and the musicians had plenty of opportunity to relax. A photographer, Tore Fredenlund, brought Dizzy Gillespie to Chat Noir to hear the singing group The Monn-Keys. Later there was a big party at actor Per Asplin's home and both Dizzy and Ella Fitzgerald were there. I stopped by the Viking, where Tor was playing with The Spotlights, and in the audience I found bassist Ray Brown and guitarist Herb Ellis. They obviously dug the band, and Tor was pretty excited.

"See if you can get the guys over to our place," he said.

I went straight over to the table and introduced myself, and asked them if they wanted to come home with us – it probably seemed like a pretty strange proposition. Who knows how I convinced them, but Ray said they would come along for a little while.

I also asked the bassist and guitarist from The Spotlights to join us, because of course we hoped to set up a session. Ray and Herb were tempted when the others showed up with their instruments, and ended up playing alone on the bass and the guitar, for four hours. I recorded everything I had room for on the tape. We were pretty broke at the time, so I did everything I could to save tape, including recording at slow speed. It turned into an unforgettable evening. There were only a few musicians there, and everyone hovered around the two Americans performing their encore at Gartnerveien. Ragnar Robertsen was there as usual, and he sat in on a couple of tunes, something Ray Brown has talked about several times since. He always asked about that fine clarinet player, and Ragnar has always been one of my personal favourites.

Later on that night saxophonist Illinois Jacquet showed up along with some Norwegian musicians. Everyone listened intently to the bass and guitar, except Illinois, who was pretty loudmouthed so we had to keep hushing him, and eventually he slumped down next to me on the couch. He put his arm around me in a more than friendly way, and at that point the host had had enough.

"Out of my house!" yelled Tor.

Illinois just giggled, but pulled himself together. The tape recorder was on all night long, and we've gotten a lot of enjoyment from this recording. It sounds just as good today, and I know it by heart, note by note.

AT BEPPE'S

As mentioned, the JATP musicians were in Oslo for several days, and on one of those days they were invited to the home of Beppe Lykke-Seest, an avid jazz fan whose father was an oil company director and had a huge house. Beppe was allowed to invite all of the JATP home, plus some Norwegian musicians. I think they even sent out written invitations. Tor and I were invited, maybe because we knew Ray and Herb, but they never arrived. I myself came straight from a skiing party arranged by Norsk Hydro, and was still wearing my ski outfit. When I got to Beppe's, I was greeted at the front door by his parents, who were dressed formally – it was a tuxedo affair. They had bought lobster and whisky, and his father commented on how quickly it all was being consumed. Of course it was, with sixty hungry and thirsty Norwegian musicians there. They weren't used to such luxuries at jams, at least not at Gartnerveien.

Photo: Tore Fredenlund

At this 1956 jam session, Ray and Herb played for four hours. Åse sang while Illinois watched

The only American who came was Illinois. Very quietly. When he saw Tor he hid his face in his hands and said, "Sorry, I was a little drunk last time."

RAY BROWN

The next time Ray Brown came to visit he came alone. He'd brought his bass, but didn't want to play. JATP was in town again, and Ray couldn't for the life of him understand why the phone was ringing off the hook the entire time.

"What do you say to everyone who calls? Is this some kind of switchboard?"

After a while the doorbell started ringing too, and one by one our steady jam musicians showed up. What everyone was calling about was of course to see if there'd be a jam, and I'd told them all yes. Later on that night even Stuff Smith, the world's leading jazz violinist, came by, and that was a big surprise. He brought a whole case of beer with him; he chattered and played, and made himself heard throughout the house. He liked hanging out with the Norwegian musicians.

Ray eventually said good night, but had probably hoped for a visit from Ragnar Robertsen. He has visited us several times, without his bass and we've often dined together at the Continental, where he used to stay when he was here with the Oscar Peterson trio. One time when he came to visit, he told me he'd lost his bow at a jam session in Sweden, and I played detective until I found it. As a thank you, he sent me six albums he'd played on, among them one by the Peterson trio which featured a track called 'Flamingo'. On this song Ray played a solo with his bow which I thought sounded pretty out of tune. I mentioned this the next time I saw him, suggesting that Norman Granz should have dropped that track because it was embarrassing. Ray got annoyed, took out his bass and bow, showed me which strings he played, and started playing. He told me his hands had been moist during the outdoor concert, and that this often made it sound out of tune.

"That's not what I'm talking about, I meant the whole track should have been cut," I said. But Ray kept playing for me, children's songs and jazz, with his bow and bass.

"Is it in tune now?" he asked. He played for so long that we barely made it in time to the concert at Nordstrandshallen.

On one of his visits, after a concert at Club 7 with The LA Four, he played the piano. And very well, I might add. Since then we've had breakfast in Warsaw, and met again in Holland, when Maastricht had its first jazz festival in 1990, as an extension of the North Sea Festival. He also played in an excellent quartet at the Cosmopolite in Oslo with Niels Lan Doky, Billy Hart and Bobby Hutcherson and it was good to hear Ray's warm bass tones – more personal than anyone else's.

Later he came to Vossa Jazz and Sandvika in 1996 – the year that both he and I turned seventy years old – with a trio featuring the ever youthful Benny Green, a fascinating pianist, whom I first heard in 1986. He was in Oslo at the time with Betty Carter, playing together with bassist Michael Bowie and drummer Winard Harper. They came home with me afterwards and played blues four-handed. All of them young and promising. Benny has impressed me more than once – with Art Blakey in London, New York and Warsaw, and on the anniversary tour with Ray Brown which proved to be an exciting cooperative venture

Mikkel Flagstad playing on a tenor which was a gift from his aunt, opera singer Kirsten Flagstad, in the fifties

between Benny and Ray, who is thirty-seven years older. It is strange to think that when Ray first guested Gartnerveien – along with Herb Ellis – he was only twenty-nine. He's been at the top of his career for all these years and is still a deeply respected musician. I've also met Herb Ellis again after the memorable jam session in 1956 – at Clark Terry's wedding in Texas, and on a jazz cruise aboard the SS Norway.

"TO SOFIE STREET"

Musicians did a lot of weird things during the fifties, and seemed to have their own sense of humour. Maybe it was a sign of frustration from having to play dance music at restaurants instead of getting to play jazz, because no-one could make a living playing jazz; there were no grants or stipends and jazz was almost a luxury. This may explain all the strange behaviour, like the times when musicians showed up unannounced outside our door in the middle of the night. One time we found a "roadblock" complete with blinking lights on our stairs. Then we knew the Humla band was close by. The "Death Squad" on their red scooters – Børsum, Neste, Flagstad, and Einar "Pastor'n" (The Preacher) Iversen.

Another time I was getting ready to go to work and looked out of the window to see what the weather was like. That's when I noticed that the front yard was filled with street signs and flags: "New magazines out this week", "To Sofie Street" and at the gate there was one which read "Norwegian League of Master Hairdressers". When I came down, I found even more things outside the door – a window and a drain pipe that read "Greetings from the Chain Gang". On the window it said: "This was taken from Carsten Byhring's bedroom." Byhring was a Norwegian actor.

I woke up Tor, who preferred to sleep in after I'd gone to work. He didn't appreciate the "joke" as much as I did when he saw how the yard had been decorated. He had a feeling he knew who the kleptomaniac was, and called the jazz singer in question. His mother answered the phone and told Tor that her son had just gone to bed.

"He'd better get over here right away," Tor said. "The police are here." Which wasn't true, but that got the guy out of bed and the signs collected – including the window, which belonged to Byhring's neighbour.

Thinking of Byhring reminds me of another actor who actually stayed with us for four days: Arvid Nilssen. Tor had met him on the street and invited him home. He was in good shape and on the wagon and was a constant source of entertainment. He was drinking only water and every time he got himself another glass, it was with great style:

"You have wonderful water here in Høyenhall, I think I must help myself to some more!"

Speaking of "having more" reminds me of yet another episode, when sculptor and opera singer Hans Aarhus was staying at Gartnerveien. He knew we were making dandelion wine because the container was bubbling away in the kitchen, but it was only two days old when this incident occurred. Tor was going to work in the evening and had gone into the bedroom for a nap. Hans had been downtown, but suddenly showed up at our place along with composer Fliflet Bræin, having walked all the way. They had already had a few beers, and wanted more, but they were broke. Then Hans remembered the wine, and told Fliflet about the chemical reactions going on in our kitchen. It must have been quite a hike up all those hills, from Stortingsgaten downtown all the way up to Høyenhall, but when they arrived, they went straight into the kitchen. By the time I got in there, Hans was standing with his back to me pouring what one day would have been wine into a saucepan.

"Are you crazy," I said, "that's practically swamp water."

"Be quiet," said Hans. "Are you turning into a prude?"

"You're gonna get sick," I told him.

But before I got the chance to say anything else, Fliflet had already finished off a whole glassful. "That's an extraordinary wine," he said, "might it be possible to get another glass?"

I practically flew up the stairs to wake up Tor, who was slightly annoyed. "I'm not getting up yet," he said.

"Hans has started on the wine," I said, which got him up in a hurry, but there wasn't much left by now. Two weeks later we were awakened by cacophonous serenading outside our window from two thirsty musicians – one sang and the other played the fiddle. The fiddle cracked, it was so cold outside.

"Can we have some dandelion wine?"

Of course we let them in, we even fed them. They were from the Bristol band, and it was October, 1956.

THE JAM-HAPPY FIFTIES

When I go through the guest books from the fifties, I come across several jam sessions a month, even though there weren't necessarily any big concerts in town. There weren't many jazz clubs, so there really was a need for a place to get together. There were a few jams at Penguin, our Sunday club, and musicians working at the big restaurants in Oslo were always interested in playing jazz. There were several well-known jazz musicians in each band, for example, saxophonist Mikkel Flagstad, and the pianist "Pastor'n" Iversen, not to mention Tor's colleagues in The Spotlights.

1956 was the year The Spotlights had a car accident. They were going to give a couple of concerts in Vestfold one Sunday, and I had a strange feeling when Tor left that day. They didn't get very far, before the van, filled with musicians and instruments, veered off the side of the road as the driver was blinded by sunlight. They fell fifteen feet, and landed upside down and people who had witnessed the accident didn't think anyone had survived, according to Tor. But most of them suffered no more than shock, although Tor broke his collar bone.

Vibes were rarely seen at jams, but in August 1957, we had as many as three vibraphonists visiting, plus a film maker named Albert Owesen. I don't know if he was just looking for ideas, or actually planning on filming, I only know that it was a big deal when he came. Unfortunately the vibe players were stopped by the police, undoubtedly on suspicion of driving while under the influence, in an area called Grønland, on Oslo's lower east side as they made their way to Gartnerveien. They called from the police station and said they had been arrested. It was in the middle of the night, and the rest of the party was sitting there waiting. In addition to the three vibraphonists Per Nyhaug, Jon Svendsen and Sven Olofson, the place was packed with Norwegian musicians who couldn't wait to play. I finally called the police station and asked them to send the vibes home to us. "We need it, they're filming," I said.

The vibes showed up in no time. Jon Svendsen owned this set, and strange things happened once Jon had left it at our place, to be picked up later. The evening after the jam, I was home alone and wondered if I dared to try to play it. I'd always wanted to play vibes, and now that I was alone, nobody'd even hear me. As soon as I'd played only my very first notes, I heard a sharp male voice on the radio, which I thought was turned off.

"This is the police, we're outside Gartnerveien 6!"

I was so shocked I immediately dropped the mallets. Who had reported my vibes debut? In fact the police were on the trail of a burglar, and the police radio had accidentally been picked up by my innocent little radio. That was the first and last time I ever played vibes.

PHONE CALL FROM THE COPS

Many have wondered how it's possible to have jam sessions in one half of a duplex, and I can understand this. Tor and I shared the house with his brother, and how much jazz they heard, I have no idea. They never said anything, probably always hoping that we were planning to move. Our kids rarely woke up in the middle of the night, and our maid was a heavy sleeper. It's strange: if you play good music, without any extra noise, people don't wake up very easily if they've already gone to sleep. I think that was part of the secret. We started when most of the neighbours had already been sleeping for two or three hours, and we never used any loud PA systems.

When my brother- and sister-in-law moved to Paris for a couple of years, we got "substitute" neighbours. That was worse. He was a lawyer, she a doctor – and they had a daughter. When we were introduced to the new couple, I mentioned that we often had music parties, and they thought that was just great. "We love music," they said. I didn't have the heart to tell them that our music consisted of jazz only and that our parties were in the middle of the night. We continued to live the way we always had, and our relationship with our neighbours seemed both pleasant and harmonious. Until, that is, November, 1957.

Tenor player Arvid Grahm Paulsen, 1956

One night, after a club job, we experienced an historical jam session. Tenor player Arvid Grahm Paulsen, also known as "Acid Paul", was in town, along with several other Norwegian jazz veterans. We hadn't seen Paul in over half a year and he'd been touring Northern Norway, or as he put it, he'd been touring with a circus of musicians, artists, an elephant, four monkeys, six ponies, and a clown. But he had got so sick in Narvik that they ended up rushing him to the hospital, and straight onto the operating table. When they opened his stomach, they simply closed it again. There was little they could do. He was laid up in the hospital for two months and after that he came to Oslo.

Paul was unusually sober when he arrived, and played fantastically. Paul at his best was an experience for anyone, and we were really pleased when he wanted to come over to our place. Also at Gartnerveien were guitarists Robert Normann, Leif Eberson and Frank Aasen, violinist Frank Ottersen, drummer Pete Brown, accordionist Finn Enger, saxophonist Kristian Bergheim and bassist Kjell Gustavsen. The names all belong to Norwegian jazz history, and this became an unforgettable session in many ways. We sat there as if hypnotised while Paul played 'Body And Soul' with a tonal quality that few could equal. As usual, I was holding my recording microphone, when the phone rang. It was the neighbour.

Arvid and Rowland Greenberg at the Metropol Jazzhouse, 1957

"Enough is enough! We've put up with this music for a long time, but now it's got to stop – they've got laws for this!"

I was of course disappointed, but understood his point of view. It was just so strange that they'd lived there for six months without saying anything. It was probably because he'd been at a Christmas party, and had had enough to drink to get up the nerve.

"We'll stop," I said, but honestly, I couldn't interrupt Paul right in the middle of 'Body And Soul'. As soon as the song was over I told everyone about the call from the neighbours. As a result, violin, guitars, saxes, drums and bass were packed without a protest. In the meantime Tor had come home again. He was trying to get rid of the flu and went straight to bed.

The phone rang again, and this time it was Bryn Police Station. They'd had a complaint and wanted to talk to the man of the house. I asked what it was about. "Everything's quiet here now," I said, "no drinking, no fighting, but we've just had a wonderful experience."

Everyone in the house was quiet as a mouse while I was talking.

"I realise it's difficult for the police to understand why we play music in the middle of the night, but I couldn't interrupt 'Body And Soul'. There's a musician here visiting us who we haven't heard in a long time, and besides, I think the neighbour went a little overboard. He could have waited until the song was over."

"I would have loved to have been there myself," said the policeman, "but next time warn the neighbours."

On New Year's Eve, the neighbours came over to make peace, and not long after that, the jam sessions were on again. For months we just had bands over to listen to records, and then – in April, 1958 – the Good Friday and Easter Sunday jams took place.

MARY ANDERSON

Tor played at Chat Noir for a while and told me about a fantastic American singer who was performing there – Mary Anderson. She had a beautiful face, but was otherwise a little too full-figured, but this was capitalised on: when she stood on the stage, they illuminated first her face, then the rest of her body, wearing a tight knit dress. She sang really good jazz, and became a regular at Gartnerveien.

Her first visit was in March, 1956, after a jam session at the Big Chief in Majorstuen. Mary often came over with Norwegian and Swedish musicians, and as I mentioned before, sang duets with Joe Williams when the Basie band was visiting. She has also played drums in our living room; she was always full of surprises. I'll never forget when she turned thirty, and showed up on our doorstep at two in the morning, with several actors from Chat Noir. I was just on my way to

Photo: Tore Fredenlund

L-r: Eddie Jones, Tor, Bjarne Nerem, Mary Anderson and Joe Newman

bed, when the doorbell rang. There was Mary with an armload of firewood she'd picked up outside our house.

"Let's get a fire started, we're having a party. I'm thirty!"

It didn't take many minutes to turn the living room into a cabaret stage. The actors asked for knives, forks and wooden spoons – everything I could find in the kitchen, because they were going to "operate". I've never seen a funnier doctor sketch. One of the guests had his head operated on, with a ridiculous running commentary from Arvid and Dan. After the operation, it was run through again and explained with quite an impressive vocabulary. I couldn't possibly have gotten upset with Mary for coming over unannounced.

That was one of the few times no-one played jazz. I guess it was more like a cabaret improvisation. Of course, it wasn't only jazz musicians who visited Gartnerveien, although almost. One night we had a visit from "Hjallis", ice-skater Hjalmar Andersen. He lived at the Viking Hotel, and he and the band had become good friends. He'd been driven up to Gartnerveien by his skating colleague Roald Aas, and when they got near our house, they asked a couple of kids on our street where number six was.

"It's that white house over there, but don't play so loudly!" they said. They probably realised there was something familiar about the two in the car. There was no jazz that night, but lots of good stories.

BRUBECK

In 1958, on a visit to Sweden, I got to know Dave Brubeck and the rest of his world-famous quartet: Paul Desmond on alto-sax, Gene Wright on bass and Joe Morello on drums. Brubeck is an excellent pianist and one of the most well-known American jazz musicians ever, renowned as quite an innovator in the use of time signatures. His quartet stayed together for almost twenty years and one of the group's biggest hits is undoubtedly Desmond's 'Take Five'.

I joined the tour bus for a short tour and was entertained the whole

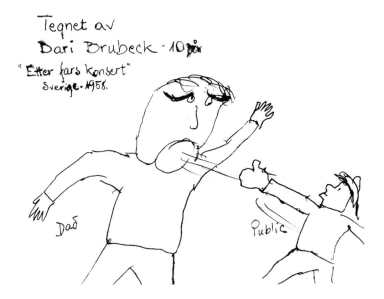

"After Father's Concert" – a drawing by Dari Brubeck, aged ten, in Sweden, 1958

way by Brubeck's kids. He has five children, and the two oldest were touring with him, as well as Iola, of course. She's phenomenal, a loving wife and perfect mother. She helps Dave with music, texts and secretarial work. I can't think of a more harmonious marriage. Ten year old Dari, or Darius – named after Darius Milhaud – was the greatest entertainer on the bus. He gave interviews and did drawings of his father.

"Here's Dad at a concert. Can you see the audience throwing tomatoes at him?" said Dari. He told me that he played trumpet, drums and piano: "But I don't think I'll be the next Dave Brubeck."

Years later I met Dari – and his wife – by which time he was playing electric piano. His brother Chris has played trombone with Daddy Brubeck in what began as the "house" band which was together when I met them in Sweden.

Along with the Brubeck musicians I stopped by Nalen in Stockholm, Sweden's most famous jazz club, and the evening eventually turned into a jam session, with Paul Desmond and Swedish saxophonist Arne Domnerus. I also said hello to Norwegian drummer Egil "Bop" Johansen, who has been in Sweden since 1953.

Monica Zetterlund made her debut at Nalen that night. Before she showed up in Stockholm, she had sung with Ib Glindeman's Danish big band, but at Nalen she was accompanied by Swedish

Monica Zetterlund's drawing of me, 1958

Dave and Iola Brubeck at Gartnerveien, 1996

83

Monica, John Hendricks and Phil Woods in Molde, 1968

musicians plus Egil "Bop", and received a lot of justifiable attention. I asked Egil what her name was. "Beats me," he said.

Trumpeter Donald Byrd also had his debut at Nalen at the same time as Monica, and has been another of the live-in guests at Gartnerveien. He was one of the first to write a piece for me – 'Randi', recorded by Norwegian Radio Big Band. Monica has been my guest several times, and in 1996 I had the pleasure of introducing her from the stage both at a festival in Lillehammer and in Fredrikstad. A beautiful friend, and a great singer and actress.

The Brubeck quartet came to my home after a concert in 1968 in Njaardhallen. Gerry Mulligan was in the group by then, having taken over from Paul Desmond. Bassist Jack Six, drummer Alan Dawson and his wife, and of course Dave and Iola, were all there, and I turned the evening into a spontaneous Bengt Hallberg occasion, suddenly getting the urge to play his record from NDR, where he turned 'Dinah' upside down in a humorous arrangement for a large workshop-band.

Mulligan was bent over laughing, and I had to play the record several times. Later I asked Hans Gertberg in Germany to send each of them a copy of the record and every time I met Mulligan after that, he talked about it – "It's almost worn out now." The quartet wanted to hear everything I had of Hallberg, so the Swedish pianist really had an attentive audience that night.

Iola and Dave Brubeck are always the first to send out Christmas cards every year. I've met Dave and Iola, and several other members of the family in various places. Once, at the jazz festival in Nice, Brubeck stood in line to buy creole food for me; a true friend. I felt this the last time they were in Oslo as well. He gave a concert at the Cosmopolite in May, 1996, and the place was packed with old and new fans. Mulligan had played the same venue the year before, and I heard him again some months later on board the SS Norway. An Englishman filmed the concerts, which were to be Gerry's last, and through a friend, I got a copy. Brubeck saw the film at my home and took a copy to Franca, Gerry's widow, who was preparing her own documentary. Gerry and Allan Dawson died only one month apart – twenty-eight years after both were guests at Gartnerveien. A strange coincidence.

JAMMING WITH ZOOT SIMS

When tenor player Zoot Sims played in Oslo with Benny Goodman's big band, there was, not unexpectedly, a jam session that night, too. However this time I didn't want too many people in the living room. I knew a party was being arranged at a restaurant near the concert hall, Nordstrandshallen, so that's where I sent the band's young drummer – Roy Burns. I told everyone who asked me if there would be a jam, to follow Burns. Meanwhile I invited Zoot alone and asked Roy to catch up with us.

Zoot Sims completing a crossword, Sandvika 1968

Zoot Sims had a lot of fans among Norwegian saxophone players. Along with Stan Getz, Zoot was one of the famous "Four Brothers" from Woody Herman's orchestra. Zoot listened to some of my private recordings when he came over. I offered him Aquavit, and after a while he wanted to play. The question was, could I get a hold of any musicians?

I called Tor and asked him to bring home musicians and instruments as soon as he finished working. He managed to bring Jon Svendsen and a newly purchased snare drum. The problem was just that Jon had never played drums. He was an accordionist and vibraphonist, and had only bought the drum because he wanted to start practising. But, since we didn't have a drummer in the house, he made a debut he'll never forget – in the company of Zoot

Zoot at Sandvika in the eighties

Sims. I remember there was a lot of confusion when the jam first started, mostly due to key signatures and language.

"A flat," said Zoot, and Tor had to play the blues in several different keys before he finally got it right. Eventually Zoot would just play a few bars, and then they were fine. We weren't quite accustomed to American terminology in 1958.

In the end they jammed all

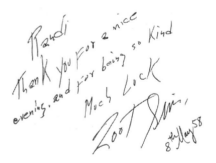

night, and Zoot's playing was unforgettable. I can still hear him and see him in my mind the way I saw him that night from the doorway into the living room. Zoot sat in the same spot for hours, without putting down his horn. He'd ask for a light for his cigarette, and for more drinks and I remember his cigarette was almost stuck between his fingers when he played. I had to put out several so he wouldn't burn himself, because Zoot was obviously feeling comfortable and in the mood to play.

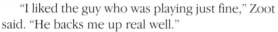

A little later that night Einar Iversen came, and I told Zoot that now he could play with our leading jazz pianist.

"I liked the guy who was playing just fine," Zoot said. "He backs me up real well."

We noticed a big difference when Einar took over, though, but I can understand Zoot's point of view, because Tor played well that night. He has always been a good orchestra musician, and has always preferred to play accompaniment rather than solos.

After a while Jon Svendsen was relieved by young Burns, who had finally found his way to Gartnerveien. He made an impression with his incredible brush accompaniment in our living room.

Mikkel Flagstad showed up while the jam was at its most intense. At the time I was standing with the microphone in my hand and my back to the door, when all of a sudden I heard another saxophone. Mikkel blended in with the rest of them immediately, and traded fours with Zoot. It sounded great, and Mikkel was obviously pleased with himself.

"I could hear it was Zoot Sims playing even before I opened the door," said Mikkel. "That sound is unmistakable. It's fantastic to be able to play with a jazz musician like that."

One of Norway's leading jazz singers, Laila Dalseth, impressed the musicians at Molde, 1976. L-r: Red Mitchell, Zoot Sims, Walter Norris and Red Rodney

A MAN OF FEW WORDS

Zoot and I sat in the kitchen for a while after the session was over and I drew a portrait of him, while he told me about his family. His parents were circus artists, and all the kids were musicians. His brother Ray, the trombone player, was the only one, aside from Zoot, who was well known. "I've grown up with theatre and music," Zoot told me. "My parents played, danced, tapped and juggled. I myself started on the drums and clarinet, and I toured for the first time when I was fifteen."

The next time I met Zoot was in Copenhagen. He was playing in Jazz Under The Stars, along with a constellation of other top names, among them pianist Red Garland. When I met Zoot at the hotel, I doubted he'd remember where he'd seen me before. It's not easy to keep track of everyone when you travel from country to country all the time, but the first thing he told me was that he'd talked about me when the plane had passed over Oslo.

The day after the concert I dined with Zoot and Garland, and I can remember Garland sending his steak back because it was too raw.

"I'm not exactly a cannibal, either," he said.

Zoot and I laughed, because the comment seemed even more sardonic considering that Garland was black.

Zoot Sims played in Molde several years later, with trumpeter Red Rodney. I remember well how impressed he was when Laila Dalseth sat in on a couple of numbers. She did a good job as usual and few singers in Norway can compare with Laila at her best. The next and last time I met Zoot, he was playing in Sandvika with his "tenor brother" Al Cohn; a very good concert. Zoot was a man of few words, however his playing compensated. He expressed warmth and feeling through his tenor. He became a friend for life, and is one of the musicians I miss the most. Always straightforward and honest, he died of cancer in March, 1985. A few years later, Red Rodney died. Both men jazz legends.

GETZ, DIZZY AND ELDRIDGE

Only days after Zoot Sims' visit, it was time for Jazz At the Philharmonic again, with Ray Brown, Stan Getz, Dizzy Gillespie, and Roy Eldridge, among others. This was in July, 1958, and as usual, I had eaten with Ray at the Continental Hotel, and went backstage to meet him after the concert. He didn't want to come over because he was too tired, but he asked Stan Getz if he would go along.

"Go home with Randi and play for her," Ray said.

Roy Eldridge asked if I was the one named Randi. He'd heard about our jams and wanted to come over. In addition, Dizzy Gillespie was ready with his trumpet, however, when we left the dressing room at Nordstrandshallen, he was "just gonna get a couple of girls", and Ray disappeared. Getz just stood there with his hands in his pockets and waited. Finally I told Dizzy there was a beautiful, young, blonde girl waiting at home in the living room. What I didn't tell him was that she was the babysitter, and that she was very pregnant. I didn't want to wait any longer, and besides I had to get home to open the door. The

Dizzy at Gartnerveien early one morning

Above and right: After the jam session, Dizzy got a lift to the hotel from Einar Iversen and even tried to drive his scooter, July 1958

Norwegian musicians always showed up when there was a big concert in town, regardless of whether or not they were invited, so someone had to be there to let them in.

Finally we got a cab. When Dizzy got to our place, he'd forget about the blonde and would join the jam, I figured, and that's exactly what happened. There was a non-stop stream of people arriving at the house, and all of them musicians, so I couldn't say no to any of them. But after a while I got a little concerned.

Stan Getz wanted to play, but realised that he'd forgotten his saxophone which had been sent directly to the airport along with all the other instruments. That's when I got the idea to call Mikkel Flagstad at Humla and ask him if we could borrow his tenor while he switched to clarinet for the rest of the night.

"What are you up to now?" he said.

I hesitated a minute. "Stan Getz is here, he's the one who needs the tenor."

There was a long pause, and then he said, "Randi, I'll send the sax immediately, and then I'm coming as soon as I can."

Getz was Mikkel's greatest idol, and I can just imagine how the rest of the evening must have been for him, with Mikkel standing there

with the clarinet in his mouth thinking about the man who at that very moment was playing his saxophone.

People kept coming until there were almost sixty. It was summer and nice and warm out, but I didn't dare open the windows and doors because of the volume. I had to hold the recording mike, and at the same time keep an eye on the door. One time the doorbell rang, and a woman I'd never seen before was standing there.

"Is Truls here?" she asked.

"Don't know any Truls," I said.

"There he is," she said, and ran past me into the living room. Nobody knew this couple, so they had probably just followed the crowd from Nordstrandshallen. When Tor came a little later, another woman opened the door.

"I'm sorry, there's no more room here," she said.

"But it just so happens that I live here!" said Tor.

People sat on the stairs and on the floor. Tor disappeared into the kitchen and left the piano to Sigurd Jansen. "Atom Jørgen" – Svein Erik Gaardvik – played drums, and there were several bassists.

The kitchen eventually filled up as well, and this is where Eldridge was to be found, along with Tor and a few others who were playing poker. Roy let Dizzy do the trumpet playing. With a thirty square-metre living room, and a kitchen half as large, it's no wonder we felt like it was getting a little crowded. But nobody was being noisy, they were all listening to the music. We didn't have much in the way of

Dizzy and Sheila Jordan in Oslo in the early seventies

drinks either, but people seemed content. I recorded all night long. I only had one microphone, so I had to keep moving it from soloist to soloist. When they were playing four bars each, I was pretty busy.

After a while it got so crowded I couldn't even see the musicians. People made room for me so that I could get closer to Dizzy, but when he saw me, his thoughts probably turned to the ever elusive blonde.

He went upstairs and was on his way to the maid's room where the babysitter was sleeping, when he met Tor. Tor had no idea about the vague promises I'd made, and of course got pretty upset.

"You have no business going in to her room," he said.

"I like you," said Dizzy, as he tickled Tor under the chin and strolled back downstairs. Then he sang scat back-ups to 'The Champ', from one of his albums, a number that's now become famous.

Later, when I looked into the maid's room to make sure everything was okay, I had to laugh. On the bed was our babysitter, with her mountainous stomach sticking straight up, and under the bed was the sleeping photographer Fredenlund, with his cameras strewn all over the floor – not surprising, considering there were people all over the place. This was probably the only place where it was possible to sleep. In the kids' room, the girls were sleeping soundly in their bunk beds, and in our bedroom people were sitting and chatting. Sixty people have to go somewhere when the living room is full.

When the party started breaking up, the Humla band started their scooters. Mikkel Flagstad had offered to drive Stan Getz to the hotel, so Getz was given a helmet, and by then Fredenlund had woken up again and was back taking pictures.

He got even luckier with photo subjects when "Pastor'n" was about to drive Dizzy home, because Dizzy insisted on trying the scooter himself first. He'd never even been near a scooter before, but with his bowler hat on, camera and chess board around his neck, and trumpet case in hand, he started. He revved the motor, and the scooter rose vertically. Dizzy was thrown into the air, but managed to land on both feet.

Then they were off. Mikkel didn't drive directly to the hotel, but swung by Vindern, and "borrowed" a bottle of expensive cognac from his father. A bottle his father had been saving for several years.

"Nothing's too good for Stan Getz," Mikkel said, "and that's probably the only time I'll ever have the honour of driving him anywhere on my scooter." He couldn't bring himself to drive straight to the hotel.

AT STAN GETZ'S HOME

I've met Roy Eldridge, Dizzy Gillespie and Stan Getz several times since, and Stan eventually felt like family.

During the autumn of 1958, around the same time I met Zoot Sims in Copenhagen, I took a trip over to Malmö in Sweden to hear violinist Svend Asmussen. Outside the concert hall I bumped into Stan Getz with his Swedish wife Monica. I said hello and asked if he remembered me. With sixty other people at a party, it can be difficult to keep track of who the hostess is. He remembered not only me, but the entire house. He introduced me to Monica, and then started telling her in detail about the pictures on my walls.

"You'll have to come and visit when we move to Copenhagen," said Stan. "We've rented Professor Fisker's house from 1 October, in Kongens Lyngby."

Monica was from Lund – born von Silverskiöld – and shocked her entire family when she went so far as to marry an American jazz musician. She had met Stan when she was studying in the States. Now they had a little girl together, Pamela, and she had also taken over responsibility for Stan's three older children from his previous marriage, Steven, David and Beverly. "When I married Stan, I got three more kids practically in the mail," she joked.

The Asmussen concert took place just a couple of days before Stan and Monica were to move to Denmark, so I told them about Montmartre in Copenhagen, a club where they had modern jazz every Wednesday. Stan remembered all of this later. He had an amazing memory, and proved it several times during the thirty-three years we knew each other. I'd gotten extra time off from Norsk Hydro, Tor was on tour with Josephine Baker, and I didn't want to miss the opportunity to visit Monica and Stan. They didn't know Copenhagen any better than I did, so I helped them find their way around the neighbourhood. The first evening there, Stan all of a sudden blurted out, "It's Wednesday! You mentioned a jazz club, so if Monica can get a babysitter, we can all go there."

At Montmartre there was a big reaction in the audience when they recognised Stan Getz. Max Brüel was playing, and I can also remember an older gentleman who came over to our table and introduced himself as "President of the Stan Getz fan club".

Monica and I smiled. Jazz musicians rarely have fan clubs, and this same gentleman wanted to have a talk with Stan. After what seemed like ages, Stan came back and told us that he'd agreed to a gig on 31 October with Ib Glindeman's big band.

Stan became a true Dane for a couple of years, and a regular at Montmartre. The night we were there, we were driven home by Brüel, who lived in the same direction. I remember he told us that he too was Jewish, like Stan. "But no one can tell," Max said.

"You should never be ashamed about being Jewish," said Stan.

PAUL GONSALVES

On 5 November 1958, we had another unforgettable jam session. Duke Ellington's orchestra had given a concert in town, and saxophonist Paul Gonsalves, one of the band's leading soloists, came over to our place. He brought the band boy and road manager, and was really in the mood to play, although he stayed in the kitchen for a long time to begin with, where Finn Enger played accordion for him. Paul was impressed.

My drawing of Paul Gonsalves, 1958

"You can come to America whenever you want," he said.

Finn played jazz and folk music equally well. Although they were having a nice time, the guests in the living room were waiting for Gonsalves. "Pastor'n" was playing the piano, Arne Styhr – who'd become my brother in law – played bass, and Karl Otto Hoff played drums. But a problem arose when Gonsalves wouldn't play until Finn joined in on accordion and "Pastor'n" wouldn't play if there was going to be an accordion: accordion at a jam was unheard of. Twenty-one-year-old Eivin Sannes saved the night when he took over at the piano for one hell of a debut. The accordion and sax played great together, and Leif Eberson played some really swinging guitar together with Gonsalves, who ended up playing not only *more* solos at our house than he had at the concert, but also better ones. Jams like that just don't happen anymore.

CHAPTER 5

At Josephine Baker's Home

I n August and September 1958, Tor was on tour with the fantastic singer Josephine Baker, playing piano along with Eilif Holm on guitar, clarinet and vibes, Ole Kristian Salater on bass and guitar, and Jon Svendsen on vibes, accordion and drums. Very well rounded musicians, all of them.

At this point Josephine Baker had adopted nine children, and one of them, the Finnish Jari, was with her on tour. The tour opened in Norway at Momarken, in pouring rain, followed by six performances at the New Theatre. Every day of the performance the front rows were filled with actors – everyone wanted to study Josephine, one of the world's leading cabaret artists. She could talk for ten minutes about falling snow – in English or in beautiful French – and keep us spellbound. Her songs were unique, she had incredible stage presence and charm, and she even managed to do something personal and unique with songs like 'La Vie En Rose', 'Cha-Cha-Cha', or 'J'Attendrai'.

Her creations were also tasteful: "Costumes: Dior" and "Perfume: Chanel". When she first played in Norway, she wore nothing but bananas. But there was plenty more than just bare breasts over her banana-skirt: Josephine had style and taste. On stage she looked like she was thirty-five, backstage she seemed quite a bit older. She was never reserved on stage, and danced like a teenager, even though she was at the time fifty-two years old.

"I could have danced all night," she'd sing, with her dazzling smile, and while she danced, with her back to the audience, she would make faces at Tor and whisper that her feet were killing her.

Tor and the band got to play at all kinds of great places with Josephine, and they got excellent reviews everywhere. After Mysen and the New Theatre, they toured much of Sweden and Finland. Tor got quite used to the stage after a while, and Josephine was very pleased.

But the first time he ever met her, he was really nervous. They had a rehearsal after the press conference, and when Josephine called out the key, Tor didn't hear what she'd said. I was paying close attention, and although I was probably just as nervous, I managed to catch what she'd said and passed it on to Tor.

The infamous journalist Veronica, from *Aftenposten*, had stayed on after the press conference, and glanced over at me while asking loudly and clearly: "What's that woman doing here? Doesn't she review rock 'n' roll?" Veronica was known for her sharp tongue and aggressive pen, but she was right about my having reviewed a couple of rock concerts. The following day in *Aftenposten* we read this about Josephine: "She is being backed on tour and at the theatre by Randi Hultin's orchestra!"

JOSEPHINE AND TOR

After the tour with Josephine, Tor was back at Hotel Viking, when Josephine suddenly showed up and said she wanted him back on tour – alone. "For six days," Tor assured me. But of course it turned into more. After a few days in Finland, Tor called and told me that Josephine's husband had asked him to continue for a couple of months. He had said that Tor was one of the best accompanists she'd ever had. I didn't doubt that they liked his playing, he's a born accompanist – he's got a good ear and is flexible. And as a rehearsal pianist, he has always been highly in demand by singers, actors, and dancers.

I swelled with pride when Tor called. Of course he had to go. But what about a substitute, what about the band uniforms they were supposed to order – in fact, what about the whole job at Viking?

"You can handle that, you're phenomenal, Randi," said Tor, and I

Josephine on stage

Josephine and Tor in Turkey, 1959

got even prouder. "Just call the manager Grieg Martens and ask him about everything."

"What about a band leader? Or songs?" I asked.

"You can fix that, and ask if I can get a leave – but I have to know within the hour," said Tor, and with that he hung up the phone forgetting to tell me where he was.

I recommended a band leader, and was promised both uniforms and a leave for Tor. I was all excited to tell Tor, but where was he? And what about his passport? It was a good thing he was travelling with a famous woman, because all I had to do was call a couple of theatres in Helsinki and ask where Madame Baker was playing. They were in Kotka.

Tor travelled from Finland to Switzerland, Greece, Poland, Yugoslavia, France, Italy – in short, they covered half the globe and altogether the tour lasted seven months. I got a lot of letters, but not a lot of money. He had never been very good with finances, and Josephine was probably taking advantage of his gratitude and excitement over getting to tour. The job was fun, educational and a real adventure, and Josephine probably didn't have that much money herself, what with nine children and an entire village to support, people of different nationalities who took care of her château and other properties in Les Milandes. That was expensive, and she had a lot of mouths to feed. The château hadn't been as popular for tourists as she had expected. It was in the south of France, by the Dordogne river, and it was difficult to get there.

Tor was in Switzerland the first time he invited me to join the tour, but the plans were cancelled at the last minute. "But listen, Randi, Josephine has invited you and the girls to come and celebrate Christmas with us at the château," he wrote. "Isn't that nice?"

A TRIP TO FRANCE

I was expected to accomplish this, cost what it may and although Tor had promised to send travel money, it never arrived. "You'll get the money when you get here," he wrote. That would have been fine with me, because up to that point in time I had not yet seen any of the money Josephine owed him.

We were to meet in Paris, where Tor's oldest brother lived. When we left, I was flat broke and had to borrow money for the trip from my company. We travelled at the least expensive rate, and the kids were fantastic. Wivi-Ann, who was then almost ten, and Christina, who was six, sang on the train the whole way down. First to Hamburg, and then to Gare du Nord in Paris – where Tor was not waiting to meet us. Instead we were met by my brother-in-law Rolv, who hadn't heard from Tor either. Finally, a couple of days later, he called from Rome at two o'clock in the morning and instructed us to take the train that left that very morning at the crack of dawn – the day before Christmas Eve.

"Josephine's brother will meet you in Dordogne," he said.

I couldn't bring myself to wake Tor's family, so we left a little later the next day. It was a stressful trip with two small daughters and lots of luggage. In addition, I spoke French badly. I had learned how to say "Where does the train leave for Les Milandes?", but I hadn't figured on so many different railroad platforms and such complicated answers from the French. Whenever they didn't understand me, I tried saying "Joséphine Baker – quelle direction?" – and it was unbelievable how much better they understood if I pronounced the name with an exaggerated French accent. Everyone seemed to know who Joséphine was and in which direction her castle was. She was a popular lady.

The train trip went well, but I can remember that there was flooding in several places because the weather had been very mild that Christmas. We changed trains in Libourne and Le Buisson, and got off at the little station in Castelnaud-Fayrac. During the last stretch of the journey I didn't even have tickets; the place was probably not even on the map back home in Norway. When the conductor asked for our tickets, I replied with only "Non comprendre" and he finally gave up asking. Josephine's brother stood waiting with an ancient truck loaded with milk pails and other items. We communicated by finger language, and I tried to ask for Monsieur Tor, but apparently he and Josephine had not yet arrived.

FAIRY TALE CASTLE

The château dated from the sixteenth century and it was a real fairy tale castle – three restaurants, two hotels, a theatre, a cinema, tennis and golf, and its own chapel. All the streets bore the name or titles of Josephine's songs. She also had a souvenir shop where we could buy various gift items emblazoned with "Les Milandes" – the name of her own private village. There were two swimming pools – one for the adults and one for children. The park was full of sculptures. The château itself, which was perched on a hill, was illuminated at night and in case of problems Josephine had her own electrician in her employ. In the cellar there was a museum with wax figures of Josephine at different times of her life – from the time she first sang for her sisters and brothers at the age of six, from her wedding in 1947,

Josephine Baker's castle in Les Milandes, South France

and from her audience with the Pope in Rome. She also had a room full of monkeys and rare birds. Tor said that they had dragged around animal cages during the whole tour – in addition to gifts and accumulated shopping items. It must have been a sight each time they checked into a hotel – usually the Hilton.

The children and I were each given our own room in the castle and we were told to dine in the finest restaurant. Each room was equipped with a bath, and one of the guest baths was so luxurious that Josephine later decided to deposit parts of it in the local bank – the parts that were solid gold. The bath was decorated with black tiles, and the joint compound between these tiles was pure gold. The monogram "Jo & Jo" was everywhere – an abbreviation for Josephine and her husband, Joe Bouillon, a violinist and orchestra leader. It was he, too, who crawled around on his hands and knees and put together the toy train set for the children's Christmas. A whole room had been decorated for the children. My own kids quickly made

Josephine with her adopted children, Christmas Eve 1958

themselves at home, and they were soon happily in the company of Josephine's multi-ethnic adoptees. Nobody had any communication problems.

Late Christmas Eve, Madame and Tor showed up in the midst of the festivities. It was late at night when we finally sat down at the table, and it was really late for our children to be eating a meal. We were served mussels – something that none of us liked – but Josephine was catering to a visiting stepbrother, and he was fond of mussels. Even Wivi-Ann's plateful – including the mouthful she had carefully spit out – was consumed with gusto by the stepbrother.

Josephine's nine adopted children – her "rainbow children" – were woken up and dressed in identical bathrobes. Each was given his Christmas stocking with candy that Tor and Josephine had bought in Rome. I was given a lovely housecoat – also from Rome. The rainbow children were thrilled to see Josephine again, and it was a lovely sight to see them wandering around the Christmas tree while Tor played the piano. He played on a grand that had belonged to Franz Liszt and was lavishly ornate.

"WHAT ABOUT THE MONEY?"

The next day I asked Tor to ask Madame if he could have some of the money she owed him as I had to pay for the train tickets and other expenses. Tor went to talk to Josephine, and after several hours he returned.

"Wow! You should hear that girl sing! I'd like to take her back to Oslo with me."

"What girl?"

"The Spanish maid."

"But what about the money?"

"The money? Oh yeah, Madame is still sleeping."

So I just had to wait, but I was starting to get nervous. It was no fun being broke.

That evening Tor, Josephine and her husband, along with a number of other French performers, went to Algeria to entertain the troops there. Tor travelled under the code name "Vernér", on a mission that was not totally free of dangers – according to Tor. The bus they rode in was bombarded with stones. It was war time.

Josephine's husband, Joe Bouillon, prepares the electric train set for the children

While Tor was away we visited Josephine's half sister, Margareth, who also had adopted a child. They lived in a separate house, where chocolate cake and other goodies were set out during the Christmas holidays. Music of Mahalia Jackson was played all day long, and Wivi-Ann and Christina sang Norwegian songs for our new friends. Josephine's half brother Rickhard had eleven sons and fifteen grandchildren – all of whom lived nearby. Josephine supported them all.

Tor and Josephine were not back before the day after Christmas –

Tor at the grand piano that once belonged to Franz Liszt, alongside two electricians, 1958

when we were to entertain the local villagers – with the priest, the mayor, and *Paris Match* magazine in attendance. I would be there, too, with my borrowed Flexaret camera.

PHOTOGRAPHIC DEBUT

I had a smashing debut as a photographer, truly. Little did I know before I left that I would cover three whole pages in *Nå* magazine, and the publishers of *Nå* certainly didn't expect that either. They had instructed me to hire a local professional photographer – but of course they didn't know Tor, and they didn't know the location of the castle. To follow instructions would certainly have led to an even earlier divorce, and besides, the château was so remote.

I really did not want to ask if I could start shooting with my flashbulbs. This was, after all, a private party. But I was permitted to photograph whatever I liked, and so I first visited the children in their room.

As people began to enter the hearth room for the party, I reminded Tor to ask Josephine about the money, so that I could eavesdrop. Fortunately I already had a return train ticket, but it would have been nice to be able to buy some food, too, not to mention all the other necessities.

"Madame," Tor was grovelling, "do you think that I can have my fee for the Algeria tour yesterday?"

"Algeria? But Tor – that was charity. You must know that."

I understood at that point that there would be no payment for Tor. Instead, I resolved to borrow from his family in Paris, and I was infinitely grateful to them when they agreed.

The party at the castle was most pleasant, although I was a bit taken aback by the priest getting "tipsy" and running around pinching the servants' behinds. Still, Wivi-Ann and Christina thought it was marvellous to see their father again and that day there was a great table of desserts, too. The whole atmosphere was one of cheer and good will. Tor, who was

My impression of Josephine, 1958

dubbed "court pianist" by the villagers, played once more on Liszt's piano and attracted many attentive listeners, including the wife of the "court pianist". The next day, Tor and Josephine went to Turkey, and I felt pretty much abandoned, standing there in the courtyard, waving goodbye. I cried, too. We hadn't seen much of each other during the past few days.

After Tor left for Turkey, the rest of the family returned to Norway, but *en route* we stopped a few days in Paris, where I had my films developed in a photo shop. I had taken thirty-nine pictures, and all of them were sharply in focus. I borrowed a typewriter, and the story was sent home to surprised colleagues at *Nå*: darned if that girl didn't manage to get some good shots with that amateur camera of hers. When I arrived in Oslo, the article was already in print.

BUZZING AROUND PARIS

Since I was in Paris, I wanted to visit the jazz clubs I knew, and the first one on my list was the Blue Note, because Stan Getz was playing there.

He hadn't yet come when I arrived, but I had the time to wait. I went upstairs to find the ladies' room and was addressed by a handsome young man.

"What's a woman like you doing alone in a jazz club?"

"I'm here to listen to Stan Getz."

"I don't think so," said the guy. "Where do you come from?" he asked, going on to say that Norwegian women were beautiful.

"It looks like there are handsome men here, as well," I said, "but maybe we should introduce ourselves?" I introduced myself and asked him his name.

"Nico Buninc."

"Oh, so you are the pianist from Holland who just made a record with Dizzy Reece and Lennart Jansson?" I asked. Buninc looked astounded, and he was even more shocked when I got a warm welcome hug from Stan Getz a little later. Nico accompanied me around Paris to various jazz clubs the next day. Later he sent me letters from the United States, and we kept in touch for many years. He played with Charles Mingus, and he was also the first to tell me about Ornette Coleman, his white plastic saxophone and his historic concert with trumpet player Don Cherry, at which he had been present. At the time, I wasn't aware of either, but later both Ornette and Cherry became my good friends.

On the way home, the children and I stopped in Copenhagen and spent the night with Monica Getz and her children. "Did you see if Stan got any money?" Monica asked.

I had to laugh: "It doesn't seem to matter who we are married to – one musician is just like the next one, whether his name is Tor or Stan!"

JOSEPHINE'S TENTH CHILD

Tor worked for Josephine Baker until April, 1959 when he decided to come home. They had been in Caracas, Venezuela, where they both were arrested because Josephine had decided to adopt her tenth child. She wanted an Indian boy, and the child was chosen, but as Tor carried the child off the plane they were arrested. The authorities had cruelly told the boy's mother that Josephine intended to slaughter the child and drink his blood. Josephine was very upset, but the next day she gave a charity concert in Maracaibo, and when the concert was over, an Indian chieftain in the audience rose to his feet and said that if Josephine would follow him, she could take with her as many children as she wanted. The next day they drove for hours into the desert and, in a remote straw hut, they finally chose a fourteen-month-old boy named Mara. The boy was frightened, but Josephine managed to calm him. "She really had a way with children," Tor said. When Josephine died, she had twelve adopted children. One of them had been rescued from a garbage container in Paris.

Tor came home in April, and bassist Ole Christian Salater drove the children and me to Fornebu to meet him. The first thing I asked Tor about was money – as unromantic as one can get. According to his letter, he had sent 400 kroner from Luxembourg and 1,000 from Caracas, but I had been waiting in vain for several weeks.

"Randi, that is just like you. Aren't you happy I'm home?" Tor said. "Here, you can have these eighty kroner I have. And with that he gave me a hug and a big gorgeous bouquet of flowers.

"But how did you send the money, then, Tor?"

"In an ordinary letter, of course. If I'd sent it registered mail, everyone would have known there was money inside."

JOSEPHINE'S TAX LETTER

While I visited Tor in Josephine's château, I mentioned that he should apply to submit a delayed tax return, but of course he thought this was unnecessary. He was not even in the country. We received tax due notices, both of us, since Tor was assessed on previous annual income – and that was unfair, especially since I hadn't had any income at all. Tor himself didn't earn very much, but the tour was educational and exciting. I asked

Paris, October 28, 1959

Mr. NESTOR
c/o Tor and Randi HULTIN
OSLO

Dear Mr. Nestor,

     Mr. Tor Hultin was with me in France, Italy,
Switzerland, Finland, and Algier. In the places where
he worked with me, he received 76.000 Frs in 1958
because he took the trip mostly to visit these countries
and to study, to improve his capacity in his profession.

     From the 76.000 Frs that he received from me,
he had to pay his food and hotel expenses etc.. and I
took care of his taxes and transportation wherever this
was necessary but the most of the time, he was a guest
in my castle; Therefore, had no expenses whatsoever and
was not working either.

     I hope that this information will give you
satisfaction and will clarify Mr. Hultin's situation
during the time he was away from Norway.

Sincerely yours,

Josephine Bouillon-Baker

**Josephine Baker's
letter to the tax office
on our behalf, 1959**

Josephine Baker to write exactly that to Secretary Nestor, of the
Norwegian Internal Revenue. It helped. Our tax was reduced.

CHEZ JOSEPHINE

When I was in New York in 1993, I was invited to the exclusive Chez
Joséphine restaurant in Manhattan, on Forty-Second Street, owned by
one of Josephine's many adopted sons, Jean-Claude Baker. We had
been in contact earlier while he was writing his book about Josephine.
It was an experience to see the restaurant, which was adorned wall-to-
wall with Josephine memorabilia. In 1996 the establishment
celebrated its tenth anniversary. Another of Josephine's adoptive sons
– Jari – helps at the restaurant, which is frequented by well-known
actors, jazz musicians and, of course, gourmets.

CHAPTER 6

Legendary Louis Armstrong

E arly in February 1959, Louis Armstrong came to Oslo to give a concert at the local arena, Nordstrandshallen, a visit that was to become historic in more ways than one. I was still working for the weekly pictorial magazine *Nå*, where the editorial staff had been discussing different ideas for some special event the next time a jazz group came to visit Oslo. "Since you know so many musicians," said one of my colleagues, Knut Skaar, "couldn't you invite Louis Armstrong on a sleigh ride – a traditional Norwegian *kanefart?*"

"That sounds next to impossible," I said, knowing full well how many invitations he constantly received from all over the world – invitations he usually turned down. A jam session, I thought, would be completely out of the question because of his contract with the concert promoters.

From the moment the suggestion was made, however, I felt challenged. I could always give it a try and I knew Peanuts Hucko, the clarinet player in Louis's band, from when he had visited my house when he was in town playing with Jack Teagarden. I decided to write to him, and after a few letters back and forth between the two of us, I wrote directly to Louis. I explained to him about the *kanefart*, how a caravan of horses and sleighs, decorated with torches and jingle bells, would take us through the woods and countryside at night, to a party. Then I drew a picture of him with a woollen hat in the midst of snow and glitter. I also included some flattering remarks about his wife, who

Photo: Tore Fredenlund

Louis and I got typical Norwegian food at Ullevålseter

I had just seen in a recent photo. This may have turned the trick, as I was sure she read his mail.

On Sunday, before the concert, Peanuts called to say that Louis had accepted the invitation. "I can hardly believe he's going along with this," he said. I called the editor, Kjell Lynau, at his home, and we agreed to have a meeting in the morning, before I went to my regular job in Norsk Hydro. Lynau became very excited and started to plan a grand party. He wanted speeches, formal seating arrangements at the table, etc, but I protested: "Let's make the party as private as possible. Let the people sit wherever they want, preferably allowing them to walk around. We may well have Norwegian foods, girls in national costumes, and our famous actor Alfred Maurstad playing our national fiddle, the harding fiddle. But first and foremost, the theme has to be jazz. We also have to provide all of them with warm clothing and some brandy along the trail. I'd rather not take the responsibility for the band members catching bad colds."

I offered to find musicians who would play for free. Who wouldn't want to play for Satchmo? I made sure I chose musicians who played the same instruments as the guys in Armstrong's band. I felt sure that they would want to borrow the instruments, once they became inspired.

Little by little, Lynau left all the party planning to me, while my colleague, Knut Skaar, took care of the practical arrangements of renting horses, sleighs, torches and also the place where the party was to be held, in Ullevålseter, a restaurant located in the woods just outside Oslo.

When Armstrong arrived at the airport, he was greeted by a Dixieland group, Big Chief Jazzband, playing 'Struttin With Some Barbecue'. Naturally, I was present, and I didn't have to ask for Louis because he immediately called out, "Where's Randi?" The following day, Veronica, the aforementioned journalist in the Norwegian daily, *Aftenposten*, wrote bitingly in her column: "A journalist

Louis wanted to try the skis

from our weekly colour press was clinging to Armstrong. She must have been planning for her magazine to scoop an extra edition."

This was practically the case, because the front page and another four pages inside the magazine had been earmarked for coverage of this event. Not one newspaper, however, got advance knowledge of the arrangements that were to take place after the concert.

SLEIGH RIDE

I had brought with me a big sack full of mittens, scarves and sweaters that I distributed to the band members. Everyone wanted to come along, except the singer, Welma Middleton, who was very sceptical about going on a sleigh ride in the middle of a sub-freezing night.

Norwegian trumpeter Rowland Greenberg gave Louis a warm welcome in ice cold weather

"Louis is coming," I said.

"You mean Pops has agreed to come? Then I'm going too!" And so I outfitted her, too. She was indeed a generous-sized woman.

As we rode the bus out to the suburbs where the horses were waiting, Louis was entertaining us with tall stories. There was no damper on his spirit – he was being hilarious. As soon as we arrived, we were served hot toddy – *gløgg* – from a big kettle. Then everybody dressed up in fur coats and red wool hats. It was an historic procession that set off into the woods. All the sleighs were decorated with bells and the passengers bore flaming torches.

Along the route, we were greeted by accordionists playing tunes to create a Norwegian atmosphere, while tough-looking "lumberjacks" flagged us down, offering swigs from their flasks. As we approached Ullevålseter, we noticed that the big ski jump nearby was illuminated with floodlights that my colleague had managed to borrow from the army. The setting was beautiful. Norwegian trumpet player Rowland Greenberg was standing in a snowbank playing his horn, which really

Louis has borrowed Alfred Maurstad's harding fiddle, while the famous actor himself is trying to play trumpet

impressed Louis. He kept wondering how anyone could play in such freezing cold. Why don't his lips get stuck to the mouthpiece?

Suddenly, a ski jumper came zooming down the hill, and then one after the other, others kept coming off the jump, the last one a boy only nine years old. Louis's big round eyes got even bigger, as did Lucille's. It was obvious that she loved the whole adventure, although she was a little taken aback when Louis said that he would like to try the hill! He talked to the little boy and, in jest, asked to use his skis. He patted the horse, a Norwegian fjording, which also impressed him.

As we walked in the door at Ullevålseter, we were greeted by ladies dressed in national costumes, and a marvellously decorated table. A huge moose head was placed in the middle of the table, surrounded by an abundance of Norwegian culinary specialities. Armstrong and his crowd did not hesitate in helping themselves to the food.

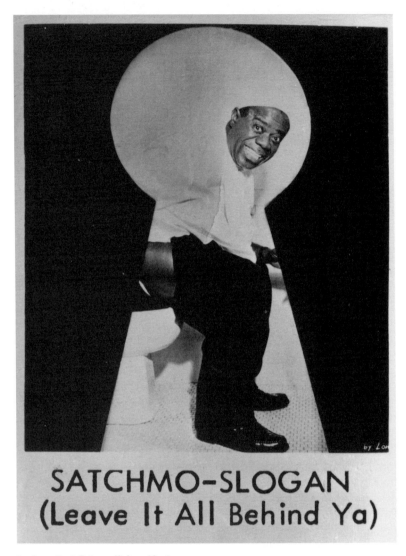

Louis on the toilet – a gift from him to me

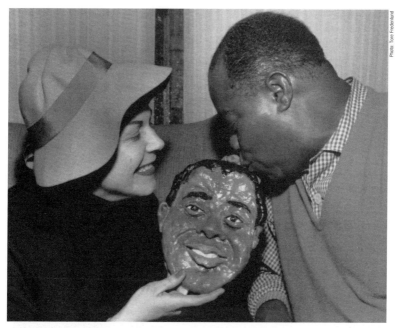

Photo: Tore Fredenlund

Louis in clay, which I made the night before the concert in Oslo, 1959

LOUIS IS HAVING A BALL!

On stage, the Norwegian musicians Rowland, Pete Brown, Kjell Gustavsen, Arne Hermansen and Tor Braun were getting in the groove. Armstrong and the others were very appreciative of the music. It really hit the spot. Everybody was having a great time. Seating arrangements would have been totally out of place, because people were walking around, sitting down wherever they pleased.

Hello

Glad to see you.

Yours

Louis Armstrong

(Satchmo)

After a while, Alfred Maurstad brought out his fiddle and played Norwegian folk music, including 'Fanitullen', the way only he could do it. This impressed Louis and his musicians, and later Louis decided to attempt the fiddle himself. This provided the photographer, Tore Fredenlund, some exceptional opportunities, especially when Maurstad borrowed the trumpet from Rowland. "You see, Mrs Hultin, I used to play in the school band, but I'm probably a little rusty," he said.

By and by, our American guests became a bit itchy, and before long they had taken over the instruments. Welma and Louis even sang some duets.

Lucille Armstrong was standing on the table in order to hear better. She was clapping her hands, beaming. "Louis is having a ball," she ex-claimed, "or else he wouldn't be playing like that. Actually, he's not allowed to play after the shows, but he doesn't seem to care about that now."

That evening Louis came over several times, thanking me for having persuaded him to come along. "This is a lot of fun," he said, and he and Lucille were the last ones to leave Ullevålseter that night. Louis had also been talking to Rowland Greenberg – among other things, about mouthpieces for trumpets. Would Rowland like Louis to send him a mouthpiece? Later on, when it arrived by mail, Rowland could hardly believe his own eyes.

As we were about to leave, I asked Welma if she wanted a cab. "No thank you," she said, "I want the same horse and the same driver as before. This was fun!"

It was almost morning when we got back to the city. The pianist Billy Kyle and several others wanted to play some more. I sent them off to my house, while I made a short stop at *Nå*'s office to do the article about the party. It was urgent, because the magazine was due out in two days.

I'll never forget the reactions when it appeared in print, with Louis on the front page with the Norwegian fjording horse and the young ski jumper. The article must have surprised quite a few people.

I later read an interview with Billy Kyle in *Melody Maker*, retelling the sleigh ride episode. I also have proof positive that the experience meant something very special to Louis.

With Louis and his band in Antibes, 1967

"RANDI, WHERE ARE YOU?"

The next time I met Armstrong was in Antibes in 1967. This was the last time he visited Europe and a full eight years after the sleigh ride. It wasn't easy to get in to see him because he was not in good health, and the managers who were trying to protect him from the press had confined him to the dressing room behind the stage. I had made a layout of the photographs from the trip to Ullevålseter, and I asked his valet to take it to Louis.

There must have been at least two hundred journalists and photographers lined up hoping to catch a glimpse of the jazz legend. Imagine everyone's surprise when Louis suddenly appeared and called out: "Randi, where are you?" I was immediately let through the crowd, and we had a very cordial reunion. There were a lot of new musicians in the band, so Louis told them all about his fantastic experience in Norway. He told them about the ski jumpers, and about how Rowland played the trumpet in the freezing cold. He had not forgotten a single detail.

Present in the dressing room was the best known jazz photographer in France, Jean-Pierre Leloir. He was allowed everywhere at the festival in Antibes. Louis demanded that Leloir take a picture of the two of us. I have written to Jean-Pierre several times and requested this picture, but he has never replied. Perhaps he hadn't any film left in his camera that day? I asked the band boy to take a couple of pictures with my camera as well. They didn't turn out well, but they are still nice keepsakes.

Louis asked if I could have dinner with him the next day, but I was unfortunately unable to do so. I was travelling in a car with Karin Krog and Johs Bergh, and we were leaving for Paris the following day, before the close of the festival. I was very sorry that I had to decline that invitation.

Later, I received a letter containing humorous pictures, with captions. In addition, he sent an advertisement for a laxative. Was he possibly the first musician to be sponsored by a pharmaceutical company? The letter was mailed to me at Norsk Hydro. It was marked "Special Delivery" in Louis's characteristic handwriting.

When I met Louis in Antibes, Lucille was ill and had stayed at home. When I saw her fifteen years later at Eubie Blake's ninety-ninth birthday, she looked quite touched when we discussed the sleigh ride.

"Louis always talked about that trip to Norway as one of the highlights of our life," she said.

CHAPTER 7

On My Own

T he jam sessions continued while Tor was away with Josephine
Baker, along with other entertaining diversions like the sleigh
ride with Louis Armstrong. It was on the way back from our
Christmas visit to Josephine's castle that I had met Stan Getz at the
Blue Note in Paris and now – 25 February that same winter – Stan
was coming to Oslo on tour. He was due to give a concert in the
University auditorium, but while his band – including pianist Janne
Johansson – booked into the Bristol Hotel, Stan preferred to stay at
my house. After both concerts we had a terrific jam session.

When Tor came home after the tour with Josephine, he started
playing with The Globetrotters at Sundøya for a time, but
eventually returned to his old position at the Viking Hotel. Not
many months passed before he met another woman. She wasn't
especially interested in jazz, and basically she was my antithesis. It
was a sordid affair, and I had an awful time accepting this. Tor
moved out 21 November, 1959. Wivi-Ann was ten and Christina was
seven years old.

As the years went by, however, Tor's Irene and I have become
close friends. We share our children and grandchildren, and the kids
have created a bond between us. Wivi-Ann married in England and
Christina in Tunis – both of them with musicians. Wivi-Ann's husband
of twenty-seven years was drummer Spike Wells.

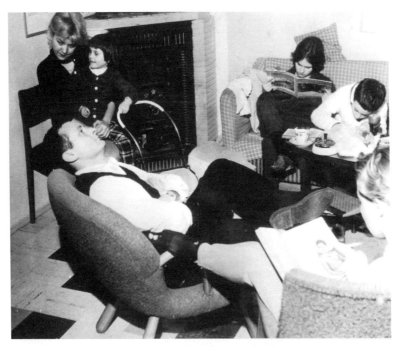

Stan Getz, Helen Merrill and Monica with the children, Christmas 1959

HELP FROM STAN GETZ

It was hard in the beginning, when Tor moved out. After all, we had been married for thirteen years and had many common interests. In the beginning, I got a lot of generous support from Stan Getz – not that he was actually aware of it. I was tempted to get out of the house, so I went with Stan on a little tour of Tønsberg and Drammen before his next University concert on 18 December. As Stan and I came off the train in Tønsberg, we were filmed at the station by a guy who asked if I was "Mrs Getz".

"Of course," joked Stan, and then we danced together a bit for the photographer. We thought he was from the local jazz club. But a couple of months later, while I was shopping for a new TV in Oslo, the salesman claimed he had seen me on television dancing with a famous saxophonist. I had a good laugh. It must have been a sight. On our return to Oslo, we went to the Grand Hotel, because it was there that fourteen-year-old Magni Wentzel was singing, and I wanted Stan to hear her. He was very impressed.

Just before the concert at Oslo University, Monica Getz arrived from Copenhagen with the kids – Steven, David, Beverly and Pamela – and singer Helen Merrill with her son Allan. Helen was going to make her debut in Norway by singing at the concert, then all of them were going to celebrate Christmas with me. Gartnerveien is nicely located near a number of parks, so on Christmas Day Monica went off to try the ice skating rink, and Stan went along to watch. .

Steven and Allan were eleven years old – like my own Wivi-Ann – and they fought over her like cats and dogs. Wivi-Ann got a lot of love letters from Stan's oldest son. He even gave her a ring. Before

Our children at Christmas, 1959. Clockwise from the left: Alan Merrill, Steven Getz, Wivi-Ann, Christina, David Getz and Beverly Getz

Christmas, I went shopping with Helen, who needed help buying ski equipment. She and the Getzes were planning a trip to Bolkesjø Tourist Hotel, and Wivi-Ann was invited to come along. A lengthy illustrated article appeared in *Dagbladet*, with a picture of Stan on skis. He'd only put them on for the picture.

The next time I saw Stan, he was at the Metropol with Swedish pianist Janne Johansson.

THE METROPOL AND OTHER CLUBS

Metropol Jazz House was opened on my birthday, 9 January, 1960, and it was one of the most prestigious jazz clubs Norway has ever seen. It was located in Akersgaten and later became a gay bar, but from 1960 to 1965 it was a first-rate jazz club that was regularly visited by living legends – the same players who played Gyllene Cirkeln (The Golden Circle) in Stockholm and Montmartre in Copenhagen. The Metropol also had a restaurant on the premises, and the club was not only frequented by jazz fans and musicians, but also by regular business people, as well.

One would invariably meet acquaintances there. The bandstand was just inside the door, up the steps to the right. Those who were really keen used to stand on the stairs, but I preferred to sit on the sofa located behind the bandstand.

We have had many clubs in Oslo since the 1950s. In fact, at one time there were nine of them. One of the oldest was the Big Chief Jazz Club in Majorstua, which opened its doors in 1953. It was open every Sunday, and became frequented even by Queen Sonja in her younger days. The club presented mainly older, traditional jazz, a style which has never lost its popularity. Another well-known club in the fifties was the Penguin, in Norabakken, also open every Sunday. A couple of hours before the dance music began, there would be a jam session, and it was here that we would often discover new, upcoming talent. I was present for one of Karin Krog's first performances there. The audience consisted of well-dressed, well-groomed young people. At the same time, it was a hangout for jazz musicians.

In the sixties, we had a very special jazz cellar in Gamlebyen school, where the very young musicians used to gather. A pianist

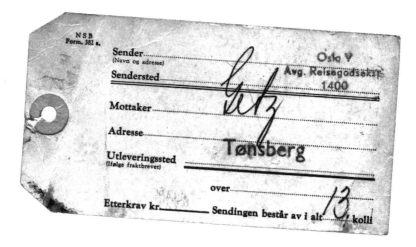

A parcel tag from Stan Getz's Norwegian tour, 1960

named Arild Wikstrøm used to teach "jazz school", presenting jazz and poetry to the audience like a guru of jazz. Gamlebyen Jazz Club was also frequented by saxophonist Jan Garbarek, drummer Jon Christensen and bassist Arild Andersen – all of whom are world class musicians today. They undoubtedly gleaned a lot of inspiration in that club, at a time when musicians in general were probably better than they are today at visiting the jazz venues.

In Club 7 we eventually built up an established jazz clientele, especially after the club moved to Munkedamsveien. Actually, there were just as many jazz giants featured here as there had been at the Metropol, and they also had rhythm and blues.

"Club 7" became a catchword. It was here that we found a "second home", a place where we could meet old friends and make new ones, where we could watch theatre and films, or where we could simply read. Club 7 even had its own particular Norwegian dialect and you could actually identify the established club members by the way they talked. I'd love to relive those days at Club 7, just as I would love to go back to Jazz Alive – our jazz night club – which was located at Solli Square on Drammensveien. Or any of the other clubs – Studentbyen in Sogn, or The Beehive. There have been many fine jazz clubs, but often

125

only short-lived. No-one earns a lot of money running a jazz club.

BENGT HALLBERG AND KJELL BÆKKELUND

Swedish pianist Bengt Hallberg was the first internationally recognised jazz star to visit the Metropol, in January 1960. Three years later, he came back and played a whole week there. Not surprisingly it was packed every day, but then he is one of the world's greatest jazz pianists and always attracts a large audience. In December the same year, he was back again to do a radio series with the Norwegian classical pianist Kjell Bækkelund and together they opened the *Contrast* programme series of the Norwegian Broadcasting network. There appeared to be a difference of opinion on whose task was harder.

"It's no problem for Hallberg," Bækkelund said, "because as a jazz player, he doesn't have to play anything more difficult than he knows he can handle. It's harder for me – I have to play the classical music that's written."

"Why is it then," I asked, "that Bengt Hallberg has to do the arranging for the transitional music between the classical and jazz segments of the programme?" I never got an answer to that question.

STAN AT THE METROPOL

In April, 1960, Stan Getz was one of two main attractions at the Metropol. He was scheduled to play with pianist Janne Johansson, but the rest of the band was to be put together by me. He did have a special request, though, and that was that he wanted the same drummer – Svein Erik "Atom Jørgen" Gaardvik – who had played with him at a jam at my house in 1958. To complete the quartet, I chose Erik Amundsen – one of Norway's leading bassists at the time. Getz was to get a thousand Norwegian kroner for the gig, and it cost only ten kroner at the door to get in. He called me from Sweden and said that he would pick up Janne on the way, they would drive all night and arrive early on Thursday morning in Stan's new Alfa Romeo. I had taken time off from work so as to be home when they arrived, since both were going to be staying at my place.

Stan Getz, Janne Johansson and, on drums, Svein Erik Gaardvik at the Metropol, 1960

When they did arrive, it was obvious that Stan was exhausted and in a terrible mood. He refused to play at all, but I thought I would be able to convince him. Janne said that we might as well cancel the job, considering Stan's state of mind. He didn't think they would be playing at all. Gerhard Aspheim from the Big Chief called and asked what had happened to the musicians – he was expecting them at the rehearsal with the Norwegian musicians at his piano warehouse. I covered by saying that they had decided to drop rehearsal and would be coming directly to the job at Metropol. I was still optimistic, but I

Stan and Janne unloading the Alfa Romeo at Gartnerveien, 1960

knew I would have to goad Stan somehow to get him to play.

"I don't think you're in any shape to play," I said. "Putte Wickman will do a better job than you."

"Are you comparing me to Putte Wickman?" said Stan, irritatedly.

"Yes. Putte only got paid 150 kroner to play at the Metropol and people were crazy about him, but you – for 1,000 kroner – won't even pick up the horn. Janne can play the gig alone on piano – it'll be just as good. Plus it'll save the club a lot of money."

"Gimme the saxophone!" snapped Stan, getting more and more riled. But there was something wrong with one of the keys. "I haven't even touched the horn in eleven days," he admitted.

"No, you don't need to rehearse anything just to play little old Metropol, right?" I said sarcastically.

He played a few phrases, and then suddenly he asked me to order a taxi. Janne was ready, but still a little sceptical.

"Get a hold of that girl who sang at the Grand and ask her to come down. I need support," said Stan. And that young girl was Magni Wentzel, now fifteen years old.

When we arrived at the Metropol Stan was still angry but he was determined to show me that he could play! Kjell Karlsen's band was playing when we arrived, and without any announcement, Stan walked right up on stage, pitched the sax case into my arms and started playing with Karlsen's band. Later on, Magni showed up, and of course I got blamed by the other musicians for "pushing" her on Stan. None of them knew that he had specially asked for her. Harald Bergersen also played during a good portion of the evening, and he acquitted himself very well.

The next day, Stan was in much better form and asked me very nicely to forgive him. He was normally very sweet to me.

JANNE AND REINHOLD

While Janne was in town with Stan, the blind Swedish pianist Reinhold Svensson was playing with Hasse Kahn's band at the Grand Hotel. Reinhold always attracted a large public with his fat, round sound and rightly he had top billing. Obviously Reinhold hadn't had a chance to hear Stan's concert the night before, so we put together a jam at Gartnerveien instead, featuring Reinhold and Janne playing four-handed piano.

Janne was a man of few words – he could be glib on occasion, but that was very seldom. But he did enjoy the meeting with Reinhold, and his mood came out in the music. They played for each other, and one of Reinhold's tunes that made a big impression was 'Kors I Taket', written by Östen Hedenbratt, himself once a guest in Gartnerveien, when we had a grand piano. Tor had since sold the grand and bought a smaller piano, which he took with him when he moved out. A few days later, I bought a new Schimmel piano from Gerhard Aspheim on an installment plan with only 100 kroner downpayment. Fortunately he understood how important it was for me to have a decent instrument in the house, since I was always getting visits from such fine pianists.

Reinhold liked the piano and often used to play for me when he had a day off. Once when he was visiting, another pianist – Øystein Ringstad – was in the house. Reinhold had heard that he was the one who made up the local musicians' jargon. When Øystein – or "Tinka",

Janne and Reinhold playing four-handed piano at Gartnerveien, 1960

as he was called – sat down at the piano, Reinhold blurted out, "Aren't you going to take off your gloves when you play?" at which Tinka got really angry. After the jam, someone offered to drive Reinhold to the hotel, but then he was asked if he would like to go to a little party first.

"What do you have to drink?" asked Reinhold.

"Homebrew. Moonshine."

"No, thanks. I'm already blind."

When I visited Stockholm in 1965, I had dinner with Reinhold and his wife Eva. Reinhold and I listened to some old recordings and were both so carried away by 'Cigarette Stomp' – a tune recorded during the war – that Eva got upset because the dinner was getting cold. When we apologetically sat down to eat, however, even Eva started humming the song. Like her husband, Eva was also blind, but I didn't realise this until we sat down at the coffee table. "Tell me when the cup is full," she instructed, but by the time she told me that, it was already too late.

That was my last meeting with Reinhold. He did send me "letters" on cassette – both his voice and his sense of humour reminded me of Martin Ljung.

One of the last times Janne Johansson was in Oslo must have been in 1965, but I did meet him later in other countries and I remember especially how well he played with Rune Gustafsson during the Prague Jazz Festival in 1966. He also won third prize in the composition contest at the same festival, and he was given so much Czech money that he bought an alto saxophone for Arne Domnerus, plus a lot of art books. Janne and I went sightseeing in Prague, and he borrowed my movie camera. Karin Krog, Jan Garbarek and I posed for him – Janne was known for being a good photographer.

The last time I met him was in Tallin, Estonia, at the first international jazz festival there, in 1967. Janne had been in Tallin before, and was not only familiar with the city, but he had good musician friends all over town. When he died in a tragic auto accident in 1968, Soviet TV broadcast a memorial programme for him in the Tallin local network and a famous composer wrote a special composition for Janne. When I heard about the accident, I couldn't believe it was true and I had to call Reinhold just to have it confirmed for me.

"Yes, Swedish jazz has just died," Reinhold said.

I mentioned I was happy that we still had Reinhold, but he too died of a stroke only a fortnight after Janne's death. Two personalities in Swedish jazz who were not only great pianists, but who also succeeded in creating a broader audience for Swedish folk music, were gone.

WIVI-ANN THE DANCER

Both my daughters have been very interested in jazz, Christina playing jazz piano when she was only ten, and the older, Wivi-Ann, suddenly deciding to dance jazz ballet. She was twelve the first time she came home from school and asked if she could dance a little bit for me. But did I have any "sweet music"? She had gone to ballet school when she was six, but had soon given up. Now quite unexpectedly she was ready.

It was a revelation to see Wivi-Ann express herself through dance. She took out one record after the other and improvised. She sang along, too – together with the jazz singers on the records. I only regret that we had no one to help her, to accompany her.

It became a tradition that Wivi-Ann would dance for visitors. She

131

loved an audience, and when I sent her to some ballet teachers, she got free lessons from three separate places just because she was so talented. But even though she loved dancing, she disliked instruction – and she seldom liked the type of jazz used at the dance schools. Her dancing began to become more and more confined to the living room at home, and often late at night.

When she heard that I had visitors, she would always ask if she could come down and dance, and soon she had performed for Barney Bigard, Louis Armstrong's clarinettist, and other greats like Bud Powell and Dexter Gordon. I remember one particular episode with saxophonist Leo Wright who was clearly fascinated, but he thought Wivi-Ann had rehearsed what she performed. Even when I asked him to select some records himself (I had upwards of five thousand LPs) he remained sceptical.

"You can't improvise like that," he said. "She must have heard the records before. I'll come back tomorrow with my own."

But the next day Leo had to admit defeat. He played a lot of afro jazz, and Wivi-Ann just danced and improvised as normal. "These are great, Mamma!" she exclaimed.

Once Wivi-Ann danced for the entire Mingus band, too. And at the same time Mingus was in town, two Swedish TV producers who were visiting offered her a programme on Swedish television. She can improvise as much as she wants, and she can choose the music herself, they said. Nathan Davis, the American saxophonist, wanted to write original music for her and when trumpeter Idrees Sulieman saw Wivi-Ann, he immediately recognised her talent.

"Don't let her have any teacher," he said. "She's like Charlie Parker when he improvised; nobody can teach her."

Wivi-Ann soon earned an engagement at the Norwegian Theatre in the play *Blues For Mr Charlie*, in which she danced with the black dancer Conrad Pringle. It went off well, because she had a feel for the music, there was only minimal instruction and she and Pringle thought alike. The most important element for Wivi-Ann was the joy she felt while dancing. But once she became an adult, her interest in dancing disappeared just as suddenly as it had begun. Her talent is not forgotten, however, nor are the many fine performances she gave us. Today Wivi-Ann's daughter Miranda has taken over, but she studies classical ballet.

With Quincy Jones, Antibes 1962

MY FIRST FESTIVAL – AND OTHERS

"Since you're so interested in jazz, why don't you go along with Syver to a festival?" said Veronica, *Aftenposten*'s notorious columnist. "They've got a lot of great jazz in France."

It was Veronica's suggestion that fired my insatiable appetites for festivals. We were talking at the Big Chief Jazzband's tenth anniversary party, where she was standing with her husband, jazz writer Syver Reff.

"Write and ask for a press card," she said. The letter had to be written in French, so I got a French colleague of mine – Suzanne Braaten – to say that I was a jazz writer for *Filmjournalen* and *Dagbladet*.

Just before I was to leave, the answer came back. It looked lovely, with all those French expressions of politesse. Armed with this letter, my suitcase, a portable typewriter and my camera equipment, I boarded the train that would bring me, one-and-a-half days later, to the French Riviera.

At the festival headquarters, the woman looked at me wide-eyed after reading the letter I had handed her.

"Do you understand French?" she asked.

"Not too much," I replied.

"It says here that your presence is not desired at the festival!"

I could only laugh. In the end I asked to speak with the boss, Jacques Souplet, who had written the letter. How we became such good friends has been a mystery to me even to this day, because basically he knew no English, but I somehow got my press card.

This was in 1961, my first festival in Juan-les-Pins. The programme listed among the attractions: Count Basie and the vocal group Lambert, Hendricks and Ross, and Ray Charles, plus singer Beryl Bryden, with whom I was to share a room at Les Pergolas, the little, inexpensive hotel that I have stayed at ever since. The festival week made a strong impression on me and I soon fitted in. One day I organised a jam session with Annie Ross and pianist Les McCann out on the street; another evening I was privileged to watch McCann play drums out on the Mediterranean. I went sightseeing with Dave Lambert in a rented car, and horseback riding with Sonny Payne. And Basie let me use his bathroom to develop film. I had a marvellous time and sent mental messages of gratitude to Veronica. Syver was at the festival, and we ran into one another on occasion, but I was always in a rush to go off in some other direction, carrying my camera and my first festival book – an album in which the musicians wrote greetings. John Hendricks, known for his lyrics, wrote a whole page in rhyme, and I also got a poem from Budd Johnsen, Basie's saxophonist, with the following opening: "Hope is but breath of air by another name/But it is to life as fuel is to flame."

"Someday I'll write music to that poem," Budd said. I met him many years later in Molde, but now he has passed on.

I became an annual visitor to Juan-les-Pins. The year after, I experienced Gillespie's recording sessions, *Dizzy At The French Riviera* – with Quincy Jones as producer-director – and I met Mimi Perrin, leader of the vocal group Les Double Six, to whom Hendricks had introduced me the year before. In 1963 I met Miles Davis and Sarah Vaughan – fleetingly – but my friendship with South African pianist Dollar Brand was more lasting. I also managed to take pictures of Brigitte Bardot for *Dagbladet* – she was at the festival in the company of Claude Bolling, who was leading a Dixieland band.

KARIN KROG'S BIG BREAK

After Karin Krog released her record *By Myself* in 1964, she wanted to perform in Juan-les-Pins with the same musicians she had recorded with – pianist Egil Kapstad, bassist Per Løberg, and drummer Jon Christensen – so could I arrange it? Suzanne was enlisted to help with the French again, and letters flew back and forth between Souplet and me for several months on the question of whether Karin could be included in the festival programme.

Karin, Egil Kapstad, Per Løberg and Jon Christensen had their international break in Antibes, 1964

Everything worked out, and we even got inexpensive lodging at Les Pergolas. Karin and the band were to have the honour of opening the festival, which they did with great success. She also established a lot of new contacts, and both she and her talented rhythm section got rave reviews.

That year I had taken along Wivi-Ann who had just turned fifteen. Guitarist George Benson, who was playing with Jack McDuff, was interested in going out with her, but she politely refused, saying she was too young. I reminded him of that in Nice a quarter of a century later – and he noted that he had been pretty young himself at the time.Today he's a superstar and a multi-millionaire.

The Blue Notes from South Africa were also at the festival that

Horace Silver quintet: Carmell Jones, Joe Henderson, Roger Humphries, Silver and Teddy Smith, Antibes 1964

Herbie Hancock, Antibes 1963   Georgie Fame and Wivi-Ann, Oslo 1968

Brigitte Bardot visiting the Antibes Jazz Festival because of her close friend Claude Bolling, 1964

Ella Fitzgerald and Beryl Bryden in Antibes, 1964

With Willis Conover and Leonard Feather, Berlin 1972

year, featuring seventeen-year-old bassist Johnny Dyani, who I thought was exceptionally promising. When I mentioned this to him, he asked if I could help him get into Berklee College of Music in Boston. Dave Brubeck helped me and even got Dyani a scholarship admission. I wrote proudly with these glad tidings to The Blue Notes' manager in London, where the group had located, but she never passed on the news. It wasn't until many years later, when Dyani came to Norway, that he heard about it. By then it was too late.

Today, Antibes – or Juan-les-Pins – is not what it once was. The festival is still held in the same park, but the atmosphere is a lot more starchy. The Nice Festival was more enjoyable. There it was easier to attend more concerts, as well as wander around in the park, meet and talk to friends, eat New Orleans-style food and listen to great jazz played from three different stages at the same time. The choice is yours. Musicians move around from stage to stage, so if one can't attend a particular concert one day, there's always a chance of catching it the next day. In Nice, I've actually heard Miles Davis give an hour-and-a-half concert, and then, on the same day, I've caught the Basie band and Dizzy Gillespie's big band. I've heard saxophone greats like Dexter Gordon and Stan Getz play at the same concert, and I've witnessed concoctions so rare as Benny Carter playing with guitarist Larry Coryell. And during the daytime, you can relax on the beach. Since JVC – with George Wein and Simone Ginibre as leaders – no longer has anything to do with the festival programme, Nice is also no longer what it once was. Another minus, of course, is that we have lost so many of our jazz legends, but this is something that has affected the majority of festivals.

AT WORK AND AT HOME

Many famous musicians have popped into my office at work just to say hello, and some of them have been recognised by colleagues of mine who know something about jazz. I remember fondly the time Dollar Brand came too early and waited by the reception desk, flute in hand, as the flow of workers passed by on their way out the door. And the time Tubby Hayes, England's most famous saxophone player, came from Fornebu and I asked him to wait in the cab outside Norsk Hydro, where I was then a secretary. Tubby, who was in a bit of a haze – and thirsty – sent the taxi off, came into the reception foyer, and ordered a bottle of champagne. The boss I worked for was standing nearby, unfortunately, at exactly that moment, and he told me that there was a strange English-speaking guy down in the reception area: "He's undoubtedly here to see you, Mrs Hultin."

NOT ONLY JAZZ ARTISTS

We haven't entertained only instrumentalists at Gartnerveien, there have often been vocal groups, too. The visits of The Deep River Boys and The Delta Rhythm Boys were especially memorable. The latter group was under the leadership of Lee Gaines, who had written lyrics for Duke Ellington. He always cooked when he was at my house, and he was quite a chef. I'm always happy when a guest can cook, because I don't consider it one of my talents. In my guest books, one often reads: "Randi, you are a wonderful cook, thank you for the spaghetti." The frequency of the compliment reveals my culinary limitations.

Stevie Winwood from my guest book

Pop and rock artists have also visited the house from time to time, both Norwegians and foreigners, but mainly because all of us have had a common interest in jazz. I remember fondly when Georgie Fame was in Oslo to sing 'Bonnie And Clyde' on Norwegian TV. The British saxophonist Dick Morrissey had told me that Fame really wanted to sing jazz, so I wasn't surprised when Wivi-Ann and Georgie sang a duet to the accompaniment of a Mose Allison record. Allison was a pianist and singer well liked by both of them. Fame, of course, has since sung jazz several times in Norway

Eric Burdon from my guest book, 1965

– both on recordings and in concerts.

Once I was supposed to meet The Spencer Davis Group at a press conference, although I went mainly because of Stevie Winwood, whom I felt had strong inclinations for jazz. He didn't appear, so I called the hotel and invited him and the head of Island Records to my home. Stevie was soon sitting at the piano playing good jazz, telling me that he was going to start the group Traffic, which was why he didn't attend the press conference. I was ready and willing to print something about Traffic in the newspaper I worked for, but in England this was still a well-kept secret.

Another personality who knew a lot of jazz artists was Eric Burdon of The Animals. We had common acquaintances and played jazz all night long after the Oslo concert.

The evening I spent with The Rolling Stones in Oslo had very little to do with jazz, however. We were all invited to a late night supper – *suppé* – at a restaurant where Thor Dynna's orchestra was playing chamber jazz. This was midsummer's night, featuring the restaurant's regular menu. Keith Richards ordered soup, and the waiter answered that, yes, today was *suppé* day.

"I want soup," repeated Keith.

Yes, sir, answered the waiter, you will be served *suppé*. But when the waiter arrived with beef steak, Keith became so outraged that he threw the plate of meat onto the floor. The Stones wanted to go somewhere else, and since it was midsummer's night, with bonfires burning along Oslo fjord, I decided that Ingierstrand Bad, always a popular place in summer, would be a suitable place to go. But when we got there, it was full.

"Yes, but I've got The Rolling Stones with me," I said.

"So what," scowled the doorman.

And so we spent the rest of the evening in traffic driving back to the hotel, where fans stood in crowds outside, waving posters: "We love you, and want to get stoned like you." I might have invited them for soup at Gartnerveien, but I went home alone.

CECIL TAYLOR'S TRIO

Pianist Cecil Taylor made his European debut in Oslo on 8 October, 1962, at the Metropol. He was sceptical of the audience because his music was so avant-garde, which makes the fact that he and I hit it off immediately even more bewildering. It could not have been the food that made him come to my house almost daily during his week at the Metropol. The club was jam-packed the first evening. Many of these were curiosity seekers, but I think the only two who really understood the music, hearing it for the first time, were Johs Bergh from Norwegian Broadcasting and Arild Wikstrøm. The rest of us didn't comprehend much of it.

It had been decided that Erik Amundsen would substitute on bass for Cecil's regular bassist who had had to stay in America. But when Erik heard the band, he turned around and walked out of the club. Jimmy Lyons played sax, and on drums was the very eccentric Sunny Murray. So far out was the jazz Cecil presented, that Norwegian Broadcasting aired a special talk show about him, discussing the question of whether his music was a hoax or an art form, and whether it was worth listening to. Unfortunately, this programme, like so many others, can no longer be found in NRK's archives. I did establish a personal rapport with the musicians, but their music was actually very strange. It was like a modernistic painting, requiring time to appreciate the details. Today, in retrospect, I find the music easy to appreciate.

Sunny Murray came to my home alone one day and wanted to be given a tour of the house.

"Do you have a cellar?" he asked. I sent him down to see the cellar, and he came up again, pleased. "I'll be back in two months to marry you."

I laughed.

"Why are you laughing? Don't you think I'm serious?"

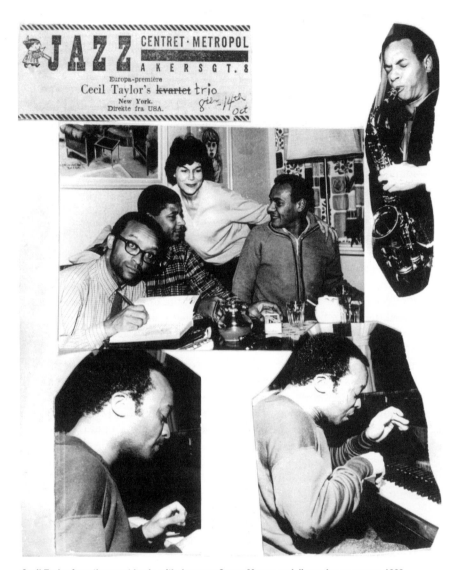

Cecil Taylor from the guest book, with drummer Sunny Murray and Jimmy Lyons on sax, 1962

"I like you," I replied, "but I have no plans to marry you."

"Do you think my hair's too long? I can do something about that.".

I must admit that I hadn't actually noticed his hair, short and curly as it was. When Christina came into the living room, he listened intently to her voice – she talks as much and as rapidly as her mother.

"Interesting," said Murray, and he scratched down several symbols on a piece of paper. "I'm gonna write down what her voice sounds like for Cecil. He can use it in his music."

For the trio's last night at the Metropol, the club had hired a second band as well because people wanted to dance and they definitely couldn't do it to Cecil's music. Consequently the restaurant was filled with people "out on the town", mindless of whatever music they had to hear. We were to have a farewell party afterwards, and I was at home getting things ready, when Karin Krog suddenly called and announced that the party would have to be cancelled.

"Cecil is in a terrible mood, and his musicians say it's up to him," she said.

I hadn't heard anything from Cecil, so I was sure that he would show up for the party. And he did. At two am, there was a knock on the veranda door. Cecil flew around the dining table and slammed his fist into it at regular intervals to vent his anger and frustration.

"Do you know that they hired another band in addition to mine? We didn't get to play everything we wanted! And somebody must have stolen Jimmy's music. He missed a whole set. And do you know that when we were supposed to be on TV, Sunny had to wear a hat – he shaved most of his hair off because of you!"

I asked Cecil to calm down. "Who would steal Lyons' music? Nobody even understands what you guys are playing..." I put on some jazz to listen to, and it helped. But there was no party afterwards.

Despite that evening, Cecil kept in touch with me by letter for several years. He wrote interesting, intellectual letters, full of thoughts.

COLEMAN HAWKINS

In February, 1963, the world's first significant jazz saxophonist – Coleman Hawkins – came to visit and I wish I'd had a tape recorder, because he had loads of stories to tell. He had a room at the Grand,

5th febr, 1963

All best wishes
from
Yours truly
Coleman Hawkins,

but he found it immensely cumbersome to have to find his way to the liquor store each day in order to get his special brand of whisky, especially when he heard the stores close at one o'clock on Saturdays.

"I don't get up that early," he moaned.

"But you can get the hotel to do your shopping for you."

"That'll probably be real expensive," said Hawkins, who was known for being tight-fisted when it came to money.

"One crown will cover it," I informed him, and he realised how silly he'd been for not using the hotel service before.

Coleman Hawkins had been in Oslo before, I learned as I interviewed him. He had played at the Bristol Hotel for two weeks in 1935 with Willy Johansen's band, which had Robert Levin on piano.

"I remember he had to teach me how to play 'Little White Gardenia', Hawkins told me. Aside from that, he remembered very little about the band, only that it was easy to get girls up to his room. From thirty years old, Coleman travelled around Europe for five years on his own, working with different groups of different styles: the worst job he ever had was with a band in St Moritz that only played waltzes, while one of his happier engagements was with a 100-man orchestra in France, where everything was arranged specially for him.

When Coleman played the Metropol, he was fifty-eight years old, but his playing was as youthful as ever. Accompanied by "Pastor'n" Iversen on the piano, Jarle Krogstad, bass, and Ole Jacob Hansen, drums – who all impressed the great man – the session was filmed for TV.

Even though Hawkins had played sax since he was nine, and even though he was the first to gain acceptance for it as a jazz solo instrument, he also had his favourites.

"Coltrane is one of my best friends," he said. "Both he and Sonny Rollins call and ask for advice when they have a question about the saxophone."

Hawkins liked to think of himself as young, and often became incensed when people expressed adulation for him as an institution. Like the time a seventy-five-year-old fan came up to Hawkins and said, "Mr Hawkins, you have been my favourite ever since I was a boy."

Tubby Hayes with Ron Carter and Toody Heath, 1966

"I felt like I was 100 years old," said Hawkins.

TUBBY HAYES

When Tubby Hayes played at the Metropol in March, 1963, along with his lifelong trumpeter Jimmy Duchar and Allan Ganley on the drums, I had no idea that I would one day have a son-in-law who would take over the drumsticks in Tubby's quartet

Visiting Tubby in London before his first heart operation

and big band. Happiness followed Tubby everywhere. He was far from being reserved, and when he played, it was always with energy – whether on the tenor, the vibes or the flute.

The first time he was at Gartnerveien, we had a great party, and he came back many times after that. I also met him in Antibes at the festival there, and in London under sadder circumstances because he was in hospital and about to undergo the first of his heart operations. He had lived a strenuous life, and everyone was apprehensive, but not long afterwards, he was back at work, fulfilling recording dates with the Norwegian Radio Big Band – his first job after the operation. He stayed at my home for that engagement, and told me that he was having nosebleeds during the night, because directing the big band was sapping his strength. He also told me about his Finnish lady friend, Liz, who was very supportive: "She's very kind, I couldn't manage without her." Liz Greenlund later became godmother to my two grandchildren in England. She was with Tubby until the end. He died in June, 1973, during yet another coronary operation, only thirty-eight years old. In my opinion, he is one of the greatest musicians England has produced, besides being an adorable jester and a true friend.

Cat Anderson with my cats, April 1963

"WHERE'S THE BED?"

Many musicians have stayed at my house, and as a rule, these visits have been pleasant. On occasion, however, if musicians were invited spontaneously for the purpose of interviews, it did happen that they misunderstood my intentions, after all, I was divorced and probably didn't look like a prude.

One of the men who became very irritated because I really meant business about an interview with him, was Ellington's high note trumpeter, Cat Anderson, who played at the Metropol at Easter, 1963. I had my children at home, and a babysitter, but I also had my little cat family in mind when I invited him. I could already see in my mind's eye the picture I would take of them with Cat. The first thing I did when we came in the door was to set up the picture, with the cats wriggling in his arms. They were crawling all over, both the kittens and the mother, and he got a little vexed.

When the photo session was over, and I had made some tea for us, I took out a pad and pencil.

"Tell me something, you didn't actually mean that about an interview, did you?" said Cat. "Where's the bedroom? Let's have some fun."

The visit lasted only ten minutes. I called for a cab and sent him out of the house. I did get my interview though, later that week, when Cat almost grovelled at my feet when we met by chance at Marine House – another place where there were jam sessions, inhabited by people from the American embassy. He slinked around me cautiously for a time, and finally said that I could have an interview with him. I wouldn't even have to ask any questions – just take shorthand, he said. He was well prepared. I learned, for example, how he became a high note artist:

"I played with another trumpet player who played a lot better than me and who got all the girls. I finally got so mad that I played high C and D as loud as I could, and that's when I started to play in the upper register."

WHISPERING STUFF

Stuff Smith came to Oslo in 1965 to play at the Metropol. He had been the world's leading violinist for years – nobody could swing like he could – but before he arrived, I remembered with consternation his

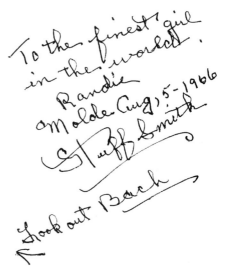

Private lessons

Stuff gave me the violin with no warning
and the automatic camera did the rest

raucous behaviour in my living room eight years earlier.

When I saw him, he could only whisper into the microphone – his voice had disappeared as result of a bad cold. We called him "Whispering Stuff" in the club, but even though he was a little out of his usual form, he still wanted to come to my house on the first evening. I wasn't thinking of hosting a jam session, but I did want to interview him and play a little music.

Stuff told me that he had played the fiddle since he was seven years old and that the fiddle he now used – a Guarnerius – had been in his possession for thirty years. His real name was Hezekiah Leroy Gordon Smith, but aged fifteen a band leader began to call him "Stuff", because he thought it sounded better. Armstrong had inspired Stuff to play jazz, because, as he put it, "Armstrong was the first jazz musician." Stuff also told me that he had met Svend Asmussen both in America and in Copenhagen; Svend and guitarist Jørgen Ingemann had been playing onboard a ship and visited him in California in 1955.

While Stuff was visiting, I played a record of Jean-Luc Ponty – the French violinist I had heard the year before in Antibes – and he was really impressed. He was equally impressed when he heard Robert Normann's guitar virtuosity – not to mention *Focus*, an LP of Stan Getz with strings: "I have a dream about making a record with background like that," said Stuff.

In Oslo, he recorded for radio with Thorleif Østereng's big band before continuing on his tour, and at my home he made an historic tape recording. He wanted badly to record something for me, but since I couldn't accompany him, I took out a *Music Minus One* record that Wivi-Ann used to sing along to. I was unfamiliar with it, and so was Stuff – he didn't even ask what melody I was going to put on. The record was an EP with four tunes on it, and what I didn't know was that it was to be played at thirty-three – not forty-five RPM. In the beginning of each melody, they play an A, for tuning, but of course, since the record was on the wrong speed, the tuning note was much higher. Stuff began playing anyway, and he didn't stop – not even during 'Crazy Rhythm', which played at an insane tempo – he still made it swing. When he was finished, he asked who it was playing so fast on the record.

"Well, one of them is Milt Hinton, on bass," I replied.

"I'm gonna tell him about this when I get home," said Stuff.

But he never returned to the States. Much later, however, in 1990, I sent a copy of this recording of Stuff Smith in double time to Milt Hinton. I also had bassist Eddie Jones and pianist Nat Pierce as guests, and I played it to them. Nat had a good laugh.

"Randi, do you know that that's me playing piano on that record?"

I didn't know.

The morning after Stuff's visit, Wivi-Ann asked how the violinist had played at the club. She was too young to go to the Metropol, so I said, "You can hear a recording he made yourself. He was here last night."

"But, Mamma, that's the wrong speed," said Wivi-Ann immediately.

Honestly, Stuff and I were both tired, and the recording was made about five in the morning. Hopefully those factors will excuse the oversight on the speed.

"I wish everyone understood music like you. Keep listening," wrote Stuff in my guest book – a little ironic, since I didn't hear that the record was playing at the wrong speed. But I have listened, again and again – and the recording is one of a kind.

EXHAUSTING ROUTINES

A couple of days later, I arranged a meeting between our own great jazz violinist, Frank Ottersen, and Stuff – an event that changed Frank's life. Stuff was one of the main reasons that Frank moved to Copenhagen, and Stuff relinquished voluntarily the only jobs he had there. He was supposed to go to Stockholm after the Metropol gigs, and since it was Easter, I had also planned a trip to Stockholm to visit Jamila and Idrees Sulieman. I was going to take the train, but Stuff had a plane ticket and suggested we exchange, so I wouldn't have to sit on the train. Fortunately, I didn't take him up on his suggestion. First, I had Christina with me, and besides, I wanted Stuff to travel as comfortably as possible. He would also be able to sleep later in the morning. Stuff suggested instead that we meet at the station in Stockholm.

When I arrived, however, there was no Stuff to be seen anywhere, and I became uneasy. After enquiring at the club where he was supposed to play, I learned that he was ill. Before he left for the airport that morning, he had come down with something like whooping cough – he had difficulty breathing and had to be rushed to the hospital. Thank goodness he wasn't sitting on the train when he had this attack! Instead, he lay in the hospital in Oslo for several days, quickly becoming a favourite with the nurses there with his high spirits. Later that same year, on my way to Antibes I went via Paris where Stuff had once again been admitted to the hospital. This time it was his stomach. In June, 1966, he came back to Oslo, to perform both at the Manhattan and Downtown key clubs. It was tremendously difficult for him, but he still found the energy to come to my home and watch the moon landing on television, although he was so tired that he fell asleep. "Wake me before they land," he said.

To play two places every evening was far too much, because he wasn't healthy enough to easily whip up the audience, although he always opened with 'When You're Smiling'. Worst of all, he had to pack and unpack his own sound equipment twice a night and carry it from place to place. I helped him a few times, but I always felt that the establishments who hired him should have provided porters. Stuff was very popular, but the strain sometimes caused him to fall asleep over his glass of beer during an intermission. Even though he was totally exhausted, he never complained. A job was a job. Stuff was also in Molde that year, the same year that trumpeter Art Farmer and sax player Don Byas were at the festival. Both Byas and Stuff were a little under the weather, and Byas was sometimes a bit rude, especially to women. During the festival, I got a call from Oslo from another "character" – tenor master Ben Webster

"I hear you got Don and Stuff there how come I wasn't hired?"

"That's all we need," I said. These three together would have been perfect. "What are you doing in Oslo, anyway?"

"I'm making movie music," he laughed. "I've never done that before."

"Where are you staying?"

"For the time being, I'm at your house. Wivi-Ann just made some

Phil Woods with Asmund Björken on accordion at the Molde Festival

great food for me." Both my daughters had lots of practice taking care of musicians, and they were better cooks than their mother.

PHIL WOODS

Phil Woods has been the world's leading alto saxophonist for as long as I can remember. He was everybody's favourite in the fifties and sixties, and he is no less a star today. One of his biggest fans in Norway was saxophonist and clarinetist Erik Andresen who, when he heard that Phil Woods was coming to Molde in 1968, packed his bags and went to the first jazz festival of his life. Phil arrived with Chan – Charlie Parker's widow, who later became Phil's wife – and performed with his own quartet to tremendous response. When the time came for the first jam session to be kicked off in the Alexandra Cellar, Phil was ready with his whole band – he was always ready to play – but he never got the chance to play, because avant-garde musician Manfred Schoof hogged the stage.

"We'll go up to the Vardestua," I suggested. "There'll be a jam there, too, and you can take the stage first."

The result was a musical battle between Germany and the USA – where America, once again, was victorious. The Germans finally had to content themselves with dancing to Phil and his band's music, because he never relinquished the bandstand. Several Norwegian musicians played, too – Asmund Bjørken and Erik Andresen, to name only two.

Earlier in the day we had been out to visit Hjertøya – an island, where we could swim and enjoy a meal of fresh fish, as is the fine tradition that the festival has maintained over the years. When we got to the island, we were met by an accordionist who sat on the edge of the pier and welcomed us with a swinging waltz. I had asked Phil to notice this accordionist, because he was also a big fan of Phil. Asmund Bjørken was his name – a very talented alto saxophonist as well, besides being a veteran exponent of Norwegian folk dances on the accordion. That same night, Woods and Bjørken would jam together. Per Borthen and his boys performed at Varden also, which Phil enjoyed a lot.

Some time later, it was to be "Student Week" in Oslo. Simone Ginibre, who was Phil's manager in Paris, called me and asked if I could arrange things for Phil – preferably give him lodging, too, because that way the clubs would be better able to afford to hire him.

Phil stayed a whole week and played at the Student Centre at Sogn and at Club 7 with Terje Bjørklund, Arild Andersen and Jon Christensen. Phil was always obsessed with teaching. As he put it – it was a shame that several of the world's leading jazz musicians sat around idly in Europe without anyone taking advantage of their vast knowledge.

"Just look at Don Byas and Ben Webster hanging around Amsterdam without anything to do. Abandoned and forgotten. It's a shame when you know what those two have meant for jazz."

'RANDI'

While Phil was at my house, he got the urge to jam, so I called around to several musicians, but nobody had the time or the desire – some had relatives visiting them, others were "tired" – and we had to give up. It wasn't like in the old days. Nowadays I was starting to feel as if musicians wanted to be paid to come to a jam. But when Phil heard that the Borthen band had a job at the Down Town, we rushed down there and Phil blew his horn hard that night.

Phil has been a guest in my home many times. This time, though, as he was about to leave, he told me that he had written a composition to me as "payment" for his stay: "I know you won't take any money anyway," Phil said, "so I've written a ballad that I hope will make you famous – and me rich!" The song, called 'Randi – The Princess Of Jazz', is today one of the most played pieces in American college band repertoires, or so I heard some years ago from an American professor I met in Warsaw. It was recorded during the Wichita festival in America, by Clark Terry's big band, with Phil Woods himself as alto soloist. In Oslo, it has been recorded by Appaloosa Mainstream Ensemble, who boasted in its ranks players like Erik Andresen and Einar "Pastor'n" Iversen. The tune is played by big bands all over Scandinavia, and is featured in Jimmy Heath's and Clark Terry's big band repertoires. In 1992, it was recorded by Claude Tissendier's Saxomania in Paris, with five saxes plus Phil as soloist on the CD *Out Of The Woods*. The first one, however, who told me that he had performed it was Art Farmer, who had played it with Erich Kleinschuster's big band on Vienna Radio. 'Randi' was Phil Woods' first big band arrangement. When he was composing it in my house, I taped him singing his own lyrics and playing the piano. I am very fond of the

composition and it has been performed for me on many occasions.

Each time Phil phones me in Oslo, he whistles "my" melody, as he did again during his 1991 visit, when he was one of the main attractions at the Oslo Jazz Festival. He was accompanied by his wife, Jill, whom he met in 1973, not long after he had moved back to the States from France. It was Jill who suggested her brother, Bill Goodwin, as the new drummer in Phil's American group, where Bill has been a member since 1974. He and bassist Steve Gillmore have been loyal backers of Phil for many years.

When Jill and Phil decided to get married in 1985, things happened that they will never forget. Only a few days before the wedding, their house burned to the ground, and Jill was hospitalised with severe burns. Phil did not want to postpone the wedding, and so they were married at the hospital. Today they live in a new house built on the same plot in Delaware Water Gap, Pennsylvania, and Phil has managed to restore most of his music archives with the help of a computer.

CLARK TERRY AND RICHARD NIXON

Three whole big bands visited my house in the seventies, and one of them was Clark Terry's. Terry is one of the world's leading trumpeters and has had his own big band for several years. I met him for the first time at the Vardestua in Molde, and it was Dexter Gordon who introduced us. When Clark heard my name, he asked if I was the Randi that Phil Woods had written a ballad for: "I've played that tune with the big band for a long time."

The next time he came to Molde, in 1973, I heard 'Randi' played by the big band. Clark stayed at my house for a week and when he was ready to leave he called me at work and

My toilet and Clark Terry's decoration, 1973

thanked me: "I've done something in your house that I've always wanted to do. I hope you won't be mad," snickered Clark.

I imagined that he had done drawings on the walls, but no murals were to be found as I entered the house.

"You'll find it soon enough," said Christina, who knew that Clark had glued a portrait of President Nixon to the inside of the toilet lid. It is still there to this day. When Terry later came home to my house with his whole big band, he had just finished a concert at the Chateau Neuf in Oslo. Phil Woods' 'Randi' is always third on the programme, and when it had been played, Terry announced to the audience that the whole band was planning to go to my house after the show. I knew nothing about this beforehand, and I was naturally very surprised. We barely manoeuvred the huge band bus up along narrow Manglerud Road, between cars parked on both sides, and when we finally arrived, trombonist Quentin Jackson asked for the bathroom. When he came downstairs, he was smiling from ear to ear:

"This place is okay," he exclaimed, "because Nixon's on the toilet lid!"

Clark Terry was amazed that the picture was still there, and he sent his band members up the stairs, one by one, on a pilgrimage to admire his work, which even bears his signature.

By now, Clark knows that I have built an extension to the house, with an extra toilet, which means that his decoration in the old one, is forever preserved. I call it my "jazz toilet", since Louis Armstrong also plays a certain role when it comes to the decoration.

JAZZ WEDDING IN TEXAS

In February 1992 I was invited to Texas, where Clark Terry was to marry his sweet Gwen Paris. Jazz pastor John Gensel took care of the ceremony. Milt Hinton, Plas Johnson and Red Holloway were playing, there were plenty of singers and musicians – young and old – and lots of family. Besides me, Clark had also invited Bengt-Arne Wallin, Hans Fridlund and Olle Swensson from the Nordic countries. I'll never forget the wedding night, when Gwen surprised everybody by singing 'Misty', soon followed by her husband on flugelhorn. Beautiful, very romantic, and what a jam session! Al Grey and other musicians were lined up to join the newly married couple and it became a real jazz wedding.

CHAPTER 8

John Coltrane – "Trane"

My first encounter with John Coltrane in 1963 made a big impression on me. Both his name and his music evoked awesome respect. He was an innovator whose tenor sax playing was nothing less than sensational. He was a trailblazer who left his own indelible traces on the history of jazz in the same way Louis Armstrong, Charlie Parker and Lester Young had done before him. In Oslo, there was excited anticipation awaiting Coltrane's quartet – McCoy Tyner on piano, Elvin Jones on drums and Jimmy Garrison on bass – on 23 October. The concert was to be given at Njårdhallen, and the musicians were booked in at the Continental.

Jan Erik Vold was a critic for *Dagbladet* at that time, and I also planned to do an interview. Coltrane was a little sceptical at first when I phoned and asked if I could come over as soon as I had finished my day at work. He said he was tired and needed to rest. I asked him when they were planning to rehearse, and in the midst of the conversation, he suddenly changed his mind and said that I could come over any time. I don't know what caused this sudden change of heart – perhaps he felt somehow I had a rapport with jazz musicians. When I got to the hotel, it didn't take long before we were in deep conversation. He was very personable, but he had an aura that inspired great respect at the same time, somewhat serious mannered – and shy, in a way. It is always fascinating to meet the person behind the music and Coltrane seemed so much gentler than his output, but that of course only belied a deeper personality. He became lost in conversation and practically forgot the time.

"Music can't be easy to understand – you have to come to the music yourself, gradually. You can't accept everything with open arms."

"One can hear that you are inspired by Indian music."

"That's right. I've been interested in Ravi Shankar a long time, and I hope that I'll meet him one day. There's another musician I admire a lot – harpist Carlos Selcedo. He plays Spanish music, but he's really a universal musician. I like strings, but the tenor is my living."

"Which saxophonist did you admire first?"

"First Johnny Hodges, but Lester Young has always had a big place in my heart. Later, it was Dexter Gordon. I really hope to meet Dexter while I'm in Copenhagen."

"How were the years with Miles Davis?"

"I played with Miles for five years, and that was a very inspiring period. It was the first time I changed my style, but I've changed again since then."

"Do you ever play at jam sessions?"

"No, preferably not."

"What about outdoor concerts?"

"If the weather is nice, it's all right. I get really inspired if I can find a deserted stretch of shoreline to play on. When there's no wind, the horn sounds good, and I can practise for hours. I like silence – there's nothing like driving long stretches of country road. I always travel by car when I'm on tour at home."

WELCOME

When I asked Coltrane if he liked pop music, he answered that some of it is all right, "but they don't write any great melodies anymore. Not like Rodgers and Hart – that was great music. Everything recorded today is ruined by those aggravating pop rhythms and guitar amplifiers. I take notice right away when a good melody is produced, and I think it will happen again soon. In America, everybody's got to have pop music on radio and TV. Even kids two and three years old can dance the twist. Pop music will last a while – it's up to the individual just how long lasting it will be.

With Coltrane at Antibes, 1965

Impresario A.s

NJÅRDHALLEN
ONSDAG 23. OKTOBER 1963 KL. 20

The John Coltrane Quartet

FELT A
5 rad nr. 5

Kr. 10,—
Billettsalg i Dagblad-sentralen

Maybe it will lead to an interest in jazz – who knows?"

What he didn't know then was that The Beatles would appear a short time afterwards with new, lasting melodies.

Coltrane had just released his record *Impressions* when he was in Oslo, as well as an album with singer Johnny Hartman. "Don't ask me how Hartman sings," he said. "I can't explain it. He's a baritone. You don't have to explain music."

"It's too bad you couldn't play at the Metropol, because then we could have listened to you for a whole week, like we did with Cecil Taylor."

"I would love to be here a whole week. The way we travel, we never feel like we are in touch with the people at each place. We live in a hotel, and outside of that, we only see the concert hall. We don't even know if people like our music."

Since I had turned the subject to Cecil Taylor, I mentioned that I had just received a letter from this modernistic pianist who had been the object of so much attention in Europe. "You can read it. It's personal, while at the same time it could have been written to anyone. It's been a year since he was in Oslo – his first meeting with Scandinavia. His language is difficult to understand, and it's written in the third person."

Cecil had ruled off the letter's pages in squares, four per page, sixteen in all. Coltrane read intently.

"You're right. These are interesting thoughts, and this is a very intellectual letter. I'm glad you showed it to me – it tells me a lot about Cecil. I always feel refreshed when I hear him in concert, but I have never talked to him. I like his music."

Coltrane talked eagerly, but I found it best to end our conversation so that he could get some rest before the concert.

"Do you promise to come to the dressing room during intermission?" he asked.

"Of course. And if all of you want to come home with me afterwards, you're welcome to."

NO DRUMS

The Njårdhallen concert hall was filled to capacity and the excitement was almost tangible. But when the musicians walked onstage they found that Elvin's drums hadn't arrived yet. Eventually they were brought up, and Elvin had to unpack and set up his kit, not only in front of the audience – but with Coltrane looking on as well. He leaned relaxedly against the grand piano and waited patiently while Elvin set up. Not a word was spoken.

The acoustics were peculiar. I sat on one side of the hall at first, and the drums drowned out everything else. After the intermission, I chose to sit directly in front of Elvin, deciding to concentrate on the drumming which seemed like a band in itself. During the intermission, I went downstairs and took a picture of each of the musicians. The pictures were all good – another lucky break – and all four of them were later reproduced on a page of the Coltrane biography *Chasin' The Trane*. Before I left Coltrane during intermission, he asked if my earlier invitation still stood. McCoy preferred to go off on his own, and Jimmy and Elvin were going out on the town but Coltrane wanted to go with me.

"Can I take along a record?" he asked. "In Stockholm I got a record by Albert Ayler that I want to listen to."

I set out goat cheese and frozen fish when we came home, and asked if John wanted a beer. He declined.

"It's been ten years since I last tasted alcohol. I prefer tea."

He wanted to hear Norwegian folk music and Norwegian jazz, and the hours went by quickly. In the end we forgot to play Albert Ayler. At that time, I had no idea who Ayler was and, in retrospect, it would have been interesting to hear Coltrane's opinion of his music. Ayler was very controversial, and I must admit that when I listened to the record later, I found it to be the longest LP I'd ever heard in my life.

I spent some fine hours with Coltrane. He opened up, he showed a warm sense of humour, and he seemed to enjoy himself.

When I asked him to sign my guest book, he leafed through and glanced at what others had written.

"Would you write a few bars of your favourite composition?" I asked.

"Okay," he said, and he notated the first bars of 'Naima', the tune he had written to his first wife.

When he was about to leave, Coltrane gallantly kissed my hand and asked if he could give my regards to Cecil Taylor. "Then I'll have an excuse to talk to him," he said. The thought of John Coltrane needing the pretext of bringing greetings from Norway just to talk to Cecil Taylor bemused me, but Cecil told me later that Coltrane actually had greeted him from me when the two men met in New York. Even stranger, I learned later that Taylor and Coltrane had made a record together *before* John visited me in Oslo. But, according to Cecil, they hadn't said a word to each other during the entire recording session. Coltrane had never mentioned any of this to me when we talked about Taylor.

ENCOUNTER IN ANTIBES

In 1965, I was again in Juan-les-Pins, and I was looking forward to seeing Coltrane. At his hotel I was stopped at the reception desk, but when they called his room and announced "Randi from Norway", they got the green light. When I entered his room, there were two gentlemen sitting on the floor, awaiting an interview, one of them Mike Hennessey, an excellent jazz journalist. Coltrane was standing with his back towards them, practising and recording everything he played on a tape recorder. "I want to check my pitch," he said.

"Would you like something to eat?" he asked me politely. I declined, and decided to write some postcards while we were waiting for him to finish playing. The other two were just sitting there, waiting patiently. Finally, Hennessey asked if he could start the interview. "Go ahead," Trane said. He was then asked about his plans for the future. Did he have any special musician in mind that he wanted to use? While Coltrane was pondering the answer, I remarked that the next time he was making a record, it ought to be with an accordion player. A dead silence followed until John suddenly started laughing. He alone had understood that I was trying to break the tension.

After finishing the interview, we had dinner in his hotel room. What a scrumptious meal – and what service! That evening, I went with John to the concert. Elvin had arrived at the last minute in the company of a blonde lady, and even though Coltrane didn't utter a word, he had been very nervous. I asked John if Elvin's friend was French. "I have no idea," he said. "The musicians never tell me anything."

The atmosphere when Coltrane and his band walked on stage was similar to that at a Beatles concert, he was so tremendously popular. For forty-eight minutes, he played a version of 'A Love Supreme', intensely and aggressively, and without a break. It was very demanding, but the audience cheered and everybody acknowledged his genius. His playing was obviously influenced by Indian music, but at times it would sound like the lowing of cattle, or the barking of angry dogs. Whatever its inspiration, the musicians in the audience were chuckling with exhilaration, and not just with Trane. McCoy, too, played a marvellous solo, having obviously developed a great deal rhythmically since the last time I had heard him, and Garrison played a ten-minute bass solo that was anything but dull.

After the concert, I invited John over to my hotel. As usual I was staying at Les Pergolas, where I had a refrigerator, kitchen, bathroom and bedroom. We walked from the festival grounds in the park named La Pinède, to my hotel, located just a few yards away from the Grand. Four or five fans were walking on each side of Coltrane, asking him the strangest questions. One of them said, "Mr Coltrane, do you have a record player with you? I would love to hear some of your records..."

"Randi, what is he saying?" The fellow was speaking English, but I'm sure that John thought, like I did, that he must not have heard right.

Just before we reached Les Pergolas, I observed some Swedish musicians at the street corner. Later they told me that when they saw Coltrane coming down the street, they nearly collapsed. They wanted to meet him, but the two of us had suddenly disappeared up

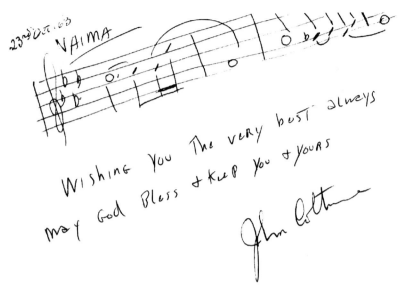

23rd Oct. '63
NAIMA

Wishing you the very best always
May God Bless & keep you & yours

John Coltrane

Europe was Just Grand. I Really enjoyed this Tour - Thanks to you! So Glad that you were There. Let's hope that these fond memories will take form in the Realm of Sound Through music - Could be Beautiful — Do you agree?

Randi, please do not measure my affections with the brevity of my letter. I assure you that they are quite opposed, it is Just that I am a poor, poor writer & the longer I write the more inconsistent it all becomes, perhaps with practice this can be overcome. I hope so, anyway.

Stay Beautiful - work hard (not too hard tho') Pray - meditate - keep Loving & you will be happy. God has surely blest you & we know he always will—

with you.
With Love -
John

From the guest book – including a few bars of 'Naima' and my painting of Trane

164

a flight of stairs – at the time, I didn't know who these Swedes were.

I was boiling an egg, and I asked Trane how he wanted it. "Five minutes," he said, so I timed it very carefully, but it still turned almost green. "This egg must have been pretty hot already when it came out of that French chicken," I observed. We relaxed and talked. I think Coltrane appreciated getting away from the big hotel, where the journalists – especially the photographers – would be lurking in the bushes. At the time, I did not consider myself in either of those professional categories. I was merely a friend.

We talked about everything, including our families. He had recently split up with Naima. It happened that we even talked about a new French lighter named "Cricket" for about a quarter of an hour. It is strange to be remembering such details, but I'll never forget how we examined this lighter which had just come out on the market. I also remember how John would all of a sudden start singing 'O Sole Mio' – only the first bars. I don't know if he was even aware of it.

DISSATISFIED

Naturally, we talked about music. John asked me what I thought about the concert. I told him what I felt to be true – that to me, it sounded "too coarse". "You played so angrily it sounded like you were irritated at something."

"I sure was! I can get pretty irritated with Elvin sometimes. At the same time, I worry that I won't be able to keep the quartet together, and without them I wouldn't have the guts to come back to Europe. I'm really afraid of losing Elvin, he's really special. It always takes some time before he gets going, but when that happens, there's nobody like him. I wasn't too pleased with the concert myself – it didn't take off the way I wanted it to. It isn't always that easy. I'm constantly trying to move one step further."

"Are you playing a lot of concerts in America?"

"Mostly clubs. I also have a contract to make three records every year, which isn't easy either. The company always expects me to come up with something new."

"Have you thought about the responsibility you have? If you mixed your music with, say, Finnish jenka, a whole lot of saxophone players all over the world would try to do the same thing."

"I never thought of myself in that way."

"When you made that record with Johnny Hartman, was that to prove that you could play beautiful ballads if you wanted to?"

"Sometimes I get the urge to play something more commercial. He's a fine singer, and I wanted him to make a comeback. A recording like that is also relaxing for my musicians. I'm not always up to presenting something new. I want to give everything I've got, and I want it to be good."

I understood John when it came to self expectations. I explained to him my own feelings about modern art. If I were to paint in a modernist style, I would have to learn more about life – perhaps attend more schools. It was easier to paint nice portraits.

"Strange you should be saying that. That's exactly the way I feel. I would like to go back to school to learn more. Not necessarily about music, but about things in general...that way, I could express it all in my music. Actually, though, I think I'm too lazy for that. I really had planned to practise four hours a day. I need to do that, but I'm always skipping it. I've gained a little too much weight lately, and that dulls your will and your physique. A musician has to be in shape in order to perform at his best."

"What do you think about the Albert Ayler record? A lot of people say he doesn't even know his horn."

"I don't agree, I have a lot of faith in Ayler. He's developing all the time, and he does know his horn."

"What about the concert tomorrow – couldn't you play a few more melodies, so that people can have a few breathers? A few ballads, perhaps? What about that beautiful 'Naima'? – it's very popular in France. Les Double Six have arranged that one in their own way. And what about 'Blue Valse' or 'My Favourite Things'."

"We'll see," John said. The next day, he played 'Naima', followed by 'Blue Valse', before going directly into 'My Favourite Things'. It was beautiful and lyrical, and I felt very proud and happy. As a matter of fact, he got even more applause than the previous night. A record was released in France from that first concert, with 'Love Supreme' on it, and many years later, a double album came out including 'Impressions', 'Naima' and 'Blue Valse', Part I and II. A bit stunned, I

Coltrane in Paris, 1965

read in the liner notes that Randi Hultin from Norway had persuaded him to play those particular melodies. The last day in Juan-Les-Pins, John actually did rent a record player, because I had brought a couple of Norwegian records along on the trip. Karin Krog wanted me to let Coltrane hear her version of 'My Favourite Things' from the Metropol record, because in it she had written a lyric about Coltrane. I had also procured some authentic Norwegian folk music, with mouth harp, harding fiddle and stev.

"That's an interesting vocalist," John said, "she's into the right thing when it comes to improvising." Aside from the vocalising, he was particularly intrigued by the mouth harp.

WITH TRANE IN PARIS

I caught an earlier plane to Paris than John, and I took advantage of the opportunity to work in flight, writing captions for frames of the film I had developed at the hotel, and putting the finishing touches on my article. Coltrane had told me where he would be staying in Paris, but when I contacted the hotel, I was told the musicians had been moved elsewhere. I called Salle Pleyel, where they were supposed to play, and learned that they were staying at the Mac Mahou. Coltrane was pleased when I phoned.

"Can you buy some hamburgers, eggs and milk? They don't have any food at all here!"

I got hold of Nathan Davis, the saxophonist who lived in Paris at that time, and he went along with me to shop for eggs and milk. We could buy hamburgers and French fries at a local kiosk. I asked Nathan if he was planning on going to the concert that night, but he said he couldn't afford the price of the ticket. "Ask for me," I said, "and I'll let you know."

The first person I met at the old hotel was McCoy – as aloof as always, but polite – who told me where I could find John. McCoy and I eventually became good friends, but it always takes time before he accepts new acquaintances. Coltrane was famished, but he wanted first to check with his manager that his airline tickets were in order, as well as check on Elvin. Elvin was flat out on his back in bed, obviously dead to the world for the time being. In front of the bed stood the manager, who never had a sober moment after noon each day. It was late afternoon now. No one knew where the plane tickets were, and Elvin was sleeping.

"Let's get out of here," John said to me, "let's go eat."

We sat on the edge of the bed and had our simple meal on a pile of newspapers. The food tasted good. After that, we were driven to Salle Pleyel. Even Elvin got there on time. In the dressing room, a gypsy lady appeared, offering bulls with red ribbons tied around their necks – only ten francs. Coltrane bought one. Elvin then barged into the room.

"Mister, you buy a bull?" the gypsy supplicated. "Louis Armstrong buy one from me, you use it as a piggy bank."

Elvin grinned broadly: "Bullshit. No, no."

Coltrane was wearing new shoes, and they were hurting his feet. He slipped out of them for a second and wiggled his toes.

"Put the shoes in water, Mister, it helps," advised the gypsy woman.

In the middle of the concert, Elvin got mad at the drum pedal and walked off the stage, leaving Jimmy Garrison standing there alone. Elvin went out and picked up a whole bag of drum equipment, which he then dumped unceremoniously all over the stage, nuts, screws and bolts clattering onto the floor. Coltrane stood in the wings, calm as usual.

When the drums were repaired, Elvin began to play with Jimmy, but after a short while, the audience began to clammer for Coltrane: "We want Trane, we want Trane."

"You'd better go on," I said, "you'll cause a riot."

"These people are impolite. They can listen to the people who are already playing."

John and McCoy did eventually go on again, and when the concert was over, the audience shouted and clapped for an encore. Coltrane said, however, that we were leaving.

"The last time I played here, they threw tomatoes at me. I don't have much respect for French audiences."

After we had left the stage, the manager opened a side stage door and yelled in to the audience, "He's not going to play any more for you, so you can just go home!"

IN JAZZLAND

When the young Frenchman who had driven us to Salle Pleyel came to pick us up, I tried to explain to him that we were going out to see some of the Paris jazz clubs. Coltrane had promised to keep me company until my flight to Molde early the next morning, when I would have the honour of Donald Byrd's company on the plane. Byrd also lived in Paris.

I asked the young French driver to take Coltrane's tenor and soprano saxophones and drop them off at his hotel. "Take them there directly," I said, trying to sound authoritative. What I was thinking of mainly, was that John wouldn't have to drag around the instruments.

Before we went to the clubs, we ate at a Japanese restaurant where Japanese music was played and Oriental ladies tiptoed daintily about. The place positively oozed with authentic Japanese atmosphere – and we ordered two plain omelettes. We had to laugh, because we definitely showed no deference to the Japanese decor and traditional cuisine. But we had a pleasant meal there.

Afterwards, we went to Jazzland, where Art Taylor and Johnny Griffin were playing. They were very surprised to see us. Griffin even accompanied us, to show us the way to Le Chat Qui Pêche. On the way to the club, we met Elvin – big, stocky Elvin, who got so excited when he saw Griffin that he lifted him high over his head and grinned his pearly-toothed smile. He was in high spirits, and meandered on his way.

Inside Le Chat Qui Pêche, Don Cherry was playing with his international quintet. I had heard the group before I went to Antibes. Don had invited me to a musicians' party, but I didn't have the cab fare and told him that I would return after Antibes. When Coltrane and I came through the club, each of us carrying a stool that we plopped down three feet in front of the bandstand, Don was astounded.

"I told you I'd be back," I said.

Coltrane was very interested in the music and said that it sounded exactly as I had described it when we talked about Don back in Antibes. As the night dragged into the wee small hours, it was soon time to pick up my luggage from Coltrane's hotel. As we got out of the taxi, he rushed into the reception area ahead of me.

Elvin enjoyed the snow at Gartnerveien

Elvin and football trainer Åge Hareide in Molde, 1984

"Did you get my instruments?" he enquired.

Poor John. He had sat thinking about his horns all evening. I regret that he didn't simply stop me from sending them back to the hotel. None of us knew the Frenchman who had driven us – and I am almost naively trusting. But yes, they had received the saxophones.

Suddenly there was a phone call for Coltrane at the reception desk. Elvin had fallen asleep in a club – what should they do?

"He'll have to handle it himself," said Coltrane. Shortly afterwards, John stood on the front steps of the hotel, waving goodbye to me as I left for the airport. That was the last time I saw John Coltrane, but I did receive several greetings, and some wonderful letters. When I came to Juan-les-Pins in the summer of 1967 and stood outside the press office before opening hour, I filled time idly chatting with a critic named Maurice Cullaz about Eric Dolphy. I mentioned that he had been a very close friend of Coltrane.

"What did he die of?" Cullaz asked.

"Diabetes."

"No, I mean Coltrane," said Cullaz.

And that's how I heard the news that my friend John Coltrane had died – 17 July, 1967, only forty-one years old. His death was attributed to cirrhosis, the condition that is often linked with alcohol abuse. But Coltrane hadn't had a drop in ten years when I met him for the first time. He lived a very healthy life. I left Cullaz standing there and returned to Les Pergolas to be alone. Both Eric and John were gone now.

ELVIN JONES

Elvin Jones has been one of the world's leading drummers for many years, and his stint with John Coltrane has gone down in jazz history. When I met him at the Berlin festival in 1972, it was like meeting a new person. We talked about John, who was dear to both of us in different ways. We had both lost a friend. Elvin was polite and quiet and we didn't say much at all, but our brief meeting was a sign that something had changed in our lives. He gave a fine concert with his own band in Berlin. As an extra added attraction, we were treated to a rare drum duel between Elvin and Art Blakey towards the end of the festival.

"I'd already met Keiko then," Elvin remembered, when we reminisced about Berlin several years later. We were sitting in my living room, taping an interview that was to be broadcast on Norwegian television. Elvin was full of laughter, but somehow serious at the same time. In the kitchen was his sweetheart Keiko, preparing food, while Elvin's musicians were upstairs looking at videos. Our relationship hadn't been this idyllic the first time we met after the Berlin festival, in September, 1974, at Club 7 after the

Keiko and Elvin

173

concert with Coltrane.

This was Elvin's first visit to Norway on his own. He arrived at the club during another concert, in the company of his Japanese wife Keiko. The rest of the band were still in London and it was impossible to find a hotel room in Oslo, so Arne Dahl, who was responsible for the engagement, asked me if I could possibly put them up for a few days. If looks could kill, then I probably would have keeled over at the club, otherwise definitely when we came home and I showed them the bedroom on the second floor. Keiko was unbelievably broody and suspicious, and she couldn't get used to the idea of living in the house of another woman – especially a woman that Elvin knew from earlier. But I used my diplomatic skills, and eventually we became friends.

Keiko is tough, and Elvin needs her. She administers his whole life. She even sets up his drums for him – efficiently, quickly and with finesse. Keiko books his jobs around the world, and in New York, no one gets to talk on the phone with Elvin as long as she is in the house. Keiko takes care of anything and everything. Even the shopping is delivered to the apartment, so that Elvin doesn't even have to go out of doors.

But in Oslo, Keiko, Elvin and I went shopping at the supermarket in Vika, and later Elvin and his wife were observed on their own at the Manglerud Shopping Mall. They are easy to spot – him large, stocky and athletic, her tiny and Oriental. Keiko is a bit strict, but she can also display a radiant, sunshiny smile. I prefer the smiling side of her. Keiko is also good at choosing clothing for herself and Elvin. They are always elegantly dressed, often in matching colours.

Each time Elvin has played Oslo, there has always been a host of drummers up front, "ringside". He is a popular, dynamic drummer, as well as an innovator. His polyrhythmic play is a pleasure to the ear. I can listen to Elvin soloing on drums indefinitely, without it becoming boring, his playing is so thoroughly musical.

"Elvin is the best drummer I know," said Jan Garbarek once when Elvin was playing at Club 7, and both Jon Christensen and Arild Andersen had similar evaluations.

We had many a fine time when we finally got to know one another, Keiko and I. We had lots of fun. Elvin and I always had a good rapport with one another, and Keiko soon found out that I was not a rival. Elvin is charming and intelligent, and he is interested in many things. He has strong opinions, and he is concerned about the human race. During his first visit, he asked if I had met his son. I didn't even know that he had a son, at least not one that I should know. "He plays drums with Charles Tolliver," said Elvin. "Alvin Queen." He smiled warmly when he talked about his son.

Elvin and Keiko had known one another for seven years at this time. "I heard him play in Japan with Coltrane," said Keiko, "a short time before Trane died. For me, Elvin was a genius, and he'll always be one. I was happy when I was able to take him around sightseeing. When I came to America later to study American showbusiness, I was met by Elvin at the airport. I was shocked when I found out he was unemployed, and I felt like it was my destiny to take care of this drummer genius. When I heard him in Japan, I was sure he had a big house with servants."

It didn't take long for Keiko to become Elvin's second wife, manager and composer. His everything. Keiko has composed much of the Japanese-inspired jazz he plays.

"She doesn't talk much about her music," Elvin said, "but she's actually very good."

ELVIN AND COLTRANE

Elvin and I talked often about Coltrane. Playing with Trane had been the most significant factor in his development as a drummer, but the way in which Coltrane played was not only inspiring, it was highly challenging.

"I got to develop in a new way, and the time with John is the most satisfying time I've ever experienced in my life. He was a great inspiration, and we had a strong common musical identity. Everything was so natural. We never rehearsed. When John came in with a new composition, I just played what I thought he wanted to hear."

"Do you think anyone can fill the void that Coltrane left?"

"No, not in our time. Coltrane was like a preacher: he took music seriously and thanked God humbly for his ability to play."

"Why did you leave the quartet before Coltrane died?"

"It was because he wanted to have two drummers, and I couldn't take that. It was a bad feeling. I wanted to play alone."

"So you took the job with Duke Ellington's orchestra?"

"I had always dreamed of playing with Duke, and when I got an offer to do it in 1966, I quit the band with Trane. But my new job also only lasted a couple weeks, because for some reason, Duke also wanted two drummers. A misunderstanding. We played completely different styles, and the soloists kept on following my beat. It ended up like a drum battle, and I didn't like that."

"Was it your brothers who inspired you to play drums? There was already a pianist and a trumpet player in the house..."

"I never had to leave the house, anyway. We had an old portable record player, and Hank had some seventy-eight records of Art Tatum and Duke Ellington. I had always been interested in the drums, and I joined the school band when I was thirteen. The first drummer who inspired me was Chick Webb. I wasn't so interested in jazz in the beginning, but I did want to learn everything there was to know about the drums – to be as professional as possible – play the timpani in a symphony orchestra.

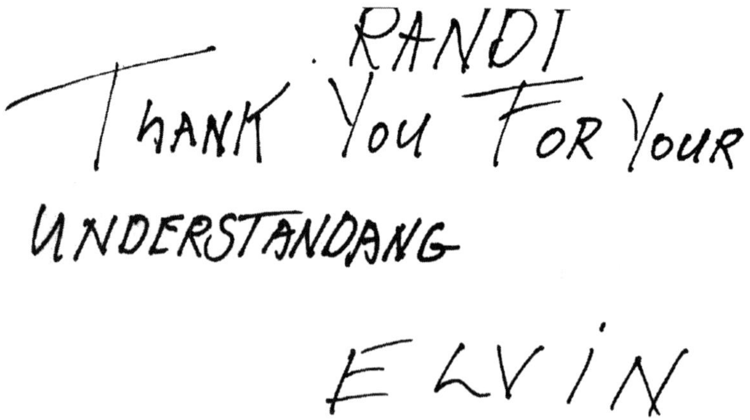

RANDI
Thank You For Your
UNDERSTANDING

Elvin

Elvin's thanks, from my guest book

176

"I got my chance when I was in the Air Force, and it was at that time that I heard a record with Charlie Parker for the first time, where Max Roach was the drummer. I was really excited. This was a new form of rhythm, it was like a revolution to discover how well the drums fit that type of music. It became a big challenge for me and I wanted to do something like that in a group.

"My first encounter with Coltrane was a turning point in my life. I had sort of half accepted an offer from Dizzy Gillespie when I heard that Coltrane was hunting for me. He showed up a couple of days later by plane from California and knocked on my door."

"THANK YOU FOR YOUR UNDERSTANDING"

Elvin has played several times at Club 7, in Kongsberg, Molde, Vossa-Jazz Festival and in Bergen. Once Keiko called from America and asked if they could spend their winter vacation with me. Usually they went to Japan, but his time they didn't want any gigs – just a nice relaxing vacation, and I was always happy to have them. The next time they came, Elvin was to play with Norwegian musicians at Jazz Alive, as well as instruct a drum clinic, eventually staying at my house for a week and a half.

They arrived directly from Copenhagen, where Elvin's brother, trumpeter Thad, lay on his deathbed with cancer. Keiko can be extraordinarily charming, but woe to the person who treads on her toes. To this day I don't know what went wrong during their visit – could it be jealousy because of the special relationship Elvin and I had after his brother died? Something, at any rate, caused her to become increasingly furious. Keiko had never had much to do with Elvin's brothers. Thad had said to me that he loved his little brother, and he used to ask me to send him his regards. He was sorry he never got in touch with Elvin more often, but it wasn't through lack of trying. "Every time I call him in New York, I get the answering service," said Thad, "and Elvin doesn't call back."

Elvin and Keiko had been my guests a week's time when the announcement of Thad's death came from Copenhagen.

"Are you going to the funeral?" I asked them.

"No, he's dead. What can we do?" answered Keiko. Elvin was very depressed, and I sensed that he wanted to talk about Thad. He liked to hear that Thad had talked so warmly about him, although they had seen very little of one another in the last years.

Thad had a son who plays drums and who of course idolises his uncle Elvin. He wasn't more than two years old when he played the first time with his father at the Kongsberg festival. Elvin laughed when I told him about that little boy, and he was somewhat cheered up when I told him that the boy's favourite video was a programme about Elvin. Keiko seemed to get more and more bitter as the days went on, and I felt sorry. Elvin felt that way, too, because when they left, he wrote a quick note that read: "Thank you for your understanding."

CHAPTER 9

Mingus – The Great

One date which has been etched indelibly in Norwegian jazz history is 12 April, 1964. On that afternoon Oslo University's auditorium was full to capacity, and on the stage stood Charles Mingus, the world famous bassist and composer, with arguably his best ever entourage: Eric Dolphy on alto sax, flute and bass clarinet, Clifford Jordan, tenor sax, John Coles, trumpet, Jaki Byard, piano, and Dannie Richmond, drums. Looking around, we saw that the cream of Norway's promising young talent was present In the audience.

The evening before, the musicians had arrived at the Hotel Continental, accompanied by two well-known Swedish television producers. The Swedes were in Oslo to plan an upcoming television programme in Stockholm and one of them, Lasse Sarri, worked with jazz productions.

This was to be a matinée concert in the auditorium. I went in a bit before it started in order to give John Coltrane's regards to Eric Dolphy, as I had promised John I would. I invited Dolphy home after the concert, and Mingus asked if he could come along as well. "Everybody is welcome," I said.

It was a fantastic concert. Even today, more than thirty years later, Mingus's music sounds contemporary. It was very modern then, but with solid jazz roots, and the concert was very well received by the audience. His arrangements were unique and it was fascinating to

Mingus and Dannie Richmond in Kongsberg, 1975

observe how he controlled the music by use of dynamics from his bass. The intervals, the dynamics, the beauty, the tension – it all remains clear in my memory.

I had taken a stage seat to the left of the band, and right in the middle of the concert, I noticed Jaki Byard motioning desperately for water. I had already surmised the situation, because Richmond was obviously about to doze off at the drums. He was in rather poor shape, and he needed water quickly. So I turned the concert into a happening. I descended into the dressing room and returned to the stage, tiptoeing across to the drummer with a glass of water. How many noticed the reason for this incident, I'll never know. Some in the audience certainly thought to themselves, "There she goes again!"

SWINGIN' COFFEE

After the sensational concert, people filed numbly out of the hall and remembered those heavenly sounds all night long. As for me, I went home in the company of Eric Dolphy. He had his saxophone with him, because he wanted to try some new reeds – a whole box of them. After a half hour, Mingus himself arrived, along with George Wein – manager, pianist, and director of the Newport festival. Another member of the entourage was Mingus's secretary, Tony – young, elegant, sporting a briefcase held under his arm. The first thing he asked for was a typewriter. While Eric continued to try out reeds, Mingus began to dictate letters, and Wein seated himself at the piano.

After a while, Mingus asked where the girls were: "I want a Chinese girl, and an Indian, and a Norwegian...and that's just for me!"

"I can't help you with that on a Sunday, Mingus. If you'd given me advance notice, I would have contacted the embassies," I replied. The answer seemed to humour him, but after a while Mingus got very irritated with Eric.

"Stop practising," he instructed. "Play with George instead."

Eric took no commands from Mingus. He was planning to quit the band in a couple of months anyway and get married in Paris, and because so he more or less didn't care what Mingus said. Meanwhile

181

Mingus affixing a plaster, 1964   **With Clifford, Coles and Byard, 1964**

George continued to play his sweet melodies on the piano, and Mingus continued yelling at Eric: "Why don't you stop tryin' reeds? You'll never play in tune on that sax anyway. The guy who had it before you could really play it." At this point Mingus dropped a name, but it was unfamiliar to me.

"He never played on this saxophone," said Eric.

"Randi, call my wife collect," said Mingus. "I'm gonna get this straight."

I called, and when his wife answered, Mingus took the phone and began chatting away about the family. His wife was expecting. He asked her to contact the saxophonist in question and call him back. He talked for twenty minutes, but his wife never called back.

Eventually other musicians started to show up. I had told them that Jamila Sulieman was going to be singing at the Gamlebyen jazz club, so most of them had gone there. Jamila stayed with me, and she had prepared a lamb roast for the party that evening. Before all the guests had arrived, Mingus had taken possession of the roast. He sat and gnawed on it for an hour-and-a-half, never giving a thought to the other guests, washing down each mouthful with coffee mixed with his own sweetener. "This is really swingin' coffee you got," he said. It was of course this episode which Jaki Byard reminded everyone of in New York decades later.

Clockwise from top left: John Coles in my kitchen; Clifford Jordan fixing a drink; and Mingus, all 1964

12-4-64

Randi

Thanks for a warm and wonderful time. Keep your nice and strong interest in music. We need people like you everywhere.

Eric Dolphy

Or: From greetings
Mingus Charlie
(with a mirror)

**Eric Dolphy and Mingus
(backwards) from my guest book**

Charlie Mingus

184

THE JAM CONTINUES

After a while, Jaki Byard and Clifford Jordan arrived together with Jamila, and a little later Coles came, along with several Norwegian musicians. I played some of my private tape recordings. Mingus turned out to be a great blues fan. When I put on Oscar Dennard, the blind pianist who left behind practically no recordings of his music, Mingus asked me to turn it off. "I want to hear the blues singer. Why should we listen to Dennard? Is he so good just because he's dead?"

Mingus was still setting the tone of this party and finally Eric decided he wanted to leave. I was both sorry and upset: "If someone has to go, it better be Mingus – he just causes trouble." But Eric asked me to call a cab, and he went out through the veranda door. He wasn't feeling well, either, and he asked if I could come down to the hotel the next morning, before they left on the next leg of their tour. Mingus came running over to the veranda door: "Just go on! You are hereby fired. I've found somebody to take over from you."

Eric just disappeared, and after a time, Mingus also left with Wein and young Tony. The party could then begin now that Mingus's cloudy presence had left the house. First Byard sat down at the piano and demonstrated some Art Tatum stuff just for fun. On either side of the piano stood Arild Wikstrøm and Egil Kapstad, both of them all ears. Clifford borrowed the bass and pretended to be Mingus, and Byard moaned a sort of song while he played.

"I know I'm just groaning, but if I stop singing, then I stop playing, too. It's just a sign that I'm having a good time," he said. The ambience was improving, and things got even livelier when Byard grabbed an alto sax. He loved it. Jamila surprised the Mingus musicians with her voice, especially on 'You're My Everything', with which she commanded a spontaneously silent room.

"She sounds like Lady Day," Byard conceded.

ERIC DOLPHY

The next day, I went down to the hotel to see Eric Dolphy and he offered me tea, with honey. "It's healthy," he said. We talked about the Molde Festival. He wanted so much to return to Norway, and he talked about his plan to settle in Paris. I called Johs Bergh to check out the possibility of a Molde gig. He was very positive, and all that was needed was the go-ahead from the festival committee. I later got the contract and sent it to Eric's address in Paris, the apartment of his fiancée Joyce.

Eric played his last Paris club job in St Germain, before leaving for Berlin, and among the band was the Norwegian drummer Ole Jacob Hansen. A couple of months after the Mingus jam at my home, Eric Dolphy died of diabetes, only thirty-six years old, in the middle of a concert in Berlin. He had been sick and was unaware of it when he collapsed on stage. As fate would have it, he lay there too long before something was done for him. It was tragic. I wrote a letter to Eric's parents in Los Angeles and sent them a picture I had taken of him – perhaps the last portrait photo. Saeda and Eric Snr kept in touch with me for the rest of their lives. They also were privileged to witness the great outpouring of memorial records and concerts for Eric, their only son.

I heard later from trumpet player Donald Byrd that the baby Mingus's wife had been expecting was a boy, and that he was named after Eric Dolphy. Deep down Mingus was very sorry – especially since Eric had planned on quitting his band.

LAST WISH

In Stockholm, however, where the Mingus band had a television recording date the day after they were in Oslo, Mingus was back to his old self. As usual, Lasse Sarri was using his flute to call attention to himself but this time Mingus went berserk. Quite sensibly most of the band walked out and fled downtown.

The only one who remained behind was Jaki Byard. "I get fired five times a week, but I don't worry about that," he said later. Jaki stayed with me for two weeks eight years later, along with his wife, son and daughter. This was right after one of the Molde Festivals – a gig he had gotten through me during the previous Oslo concert with Mingus. We had several visits from Mingus, both at Njårdhallen and at Club 7. But when I was asked by the Molde organisers to approach Byard about playing alone at the upcoming festival, it was as if

Mingus in Berlin, 1972

Mingus had a sixth sense that something was going on and it became practically impossible to speak to Byard alone.

Mingus even wanted to come up to the room, so I grabbed the opportunity to get an interview with him on a little hand held recorder. Amazingly, when there appeared to be no sound on side two, Mingus just said we could simply record it over again. I'd never seen him that patient. It transpired that, on advice, he was taking pills to stay calm, so that this European tour would not be as agitated as the previous one. But the pills made his speech slurred and difficult to understand. Mingus later died on 5 January, 1979, and his cremated remains were strewn over the River Ganges. His new wife, Sue, hand-carried his ashes in a box to India, and said that she and Mingus's son swam out into the river to fulfil her husband's last wish.

Clifford Jordan has also left us. He died in March, 1993, sixty-one years old. In the autumn of 1991, he was told that he had lung cancer, but he continued to play each week with his own successful big band in New York. His health became increasingly worse, and in January 1993 he was taken to the hospital and put on a respirator. He could not speak, but his wife Sandy gave him greetings from all of us in Norway. He had many Norwegian jazz friends. When musicians showed up in New York, he was always ready to take them around town. I experienced this myself many times.

Clifford was a very pleasant person, and along with Byard, he was a true friend of mine ever since his first visit on the Mingus tour. Clifford visited Norway very often, playing clubs and festivals. He was one of the greatest tenor players in the world, while remaining nice and genuinely human. His passing was a big loss for jazz.

CHAPTER 10

Bud Powell – Quiet Genius

Bud Powell came to the Metropol in September 1962 from Copenhagen. He was living there while he played in Scandinavia, but Paris was the real European base for him, Buttercup and his son Johnny. We were reverent when he sat down at the piano, and the musicians who were to play with him were slightly nervous. The drums were shared between Ole Jacob Hansen and Jon Christensen, and Bjørn Pedersen was playing bass. There were great expectations – and then came the familiar pulsations, the authentic harmonies, the swinging music. Real bebop – the music we had been awed by when we heard the records. We drank in every note of it. There was humour in the solos, even though Powell was deadpan. He said nothing – not even to the musicians – and simply concentrated on the keyboard, lost in his own world.

The fans flocked around the bandstand but I stood behind him, camera in hand, not wanting to wreck the atmosphere with flashes; it was so enjoyable just to listen. Suddenly, as if he had eyes in the back of his head, he turned around.

"Aren't you going to take a picture of me?"

I was surprised and smiled. Just as I took the first picture, he pulled a wristwatch from his pocket and pretended to check the time. He repeated this antic several times, taking out the watch with his left hand while he continued to play with the right. This went on repeatedly until he saw it was time to take a break. It was then that he

Bud, Johnny and Buttercup at Gartnerveien, 1962

would be allowed a beer – Buttercup had promised. The watch was his son's – Johnny, who was at the Standard Hotel. All the musicians who played the Metropol stayed there.

Bud closed the keyboard cover, and suddenly grasped my hand. "Will you sit at our table?" he asked. On the way to the table, he stuck his head in through the kitchen door and asked to have his beer.

Buttercup was waiting at the table. She was friendly and full of laughter – a big stocky woman with a pretty face. "I love Bud," she said, but as I got better acquainted with her, I began to have my doubts. I got the impression she considered Bud as inferior. As soon as he said something, she would interrupt him: "Bud, leave this to me." Bud had had some emotional problems several times in his life, being admitted and released from the hospital on and off. Someone said that he had hit his head as a child; others maintained he was schizophrenic.

As far as I was concerned, he was a genius – not only because he played fantastically, but also because he often read my thoughts. He was definitely a very special person, and I felt a growing relationship with him. Sometimes I wanted to be able to read his mind – but often he revealed what he had been thinking. He looked at me with his gentle eyes and gripped my hand.

Several people came to our table to meet him. I remember one person in particular who came to shake hands with Bud. He thanked him for the great music. Bud looked up at him, shaking his hand and staring into his face all the time while the young man talked and talked. He proudly told him about all the Bud Powell recordings he owned, going on to name compositions and personnel. All the while, Bud looked like he was listening.

"But I miss Charlie Parker here this evening," the young man lamented. It was at this point that Powell withdrew his hand, abruptly, and then said, "Can you buy me some beer?" I've often thought after this incident that this was a brilliant method of handling overbearing people – just close one's eyes and pretend that you're listening, while thinking of something totally unrelated. Bud was thinking about beer. But he only got light beer. Buttercup had decided that.

SANDWICH AT THE STANDARD

When the evening was over, we stood out on the street for a while. I invited Bud and Buttercup home, but Buttercup declined.

"Some other time."

Bud protested: "Can't you hear? She's inviting us."

"She can come along to the hotel instead," Buttercup said.

They had one room at the Standard Hotel, where Johnny had already gone to bed. Bud immediately went over and handed the boy's wristwatch back to him. Buttercup ordered three sandwiches while we sat around and talked and then Bud wanted another sandwich, he was still hungry.

"No," Buttercup snapped, "we can't afford it."

"But I'm hungry," Bud said. "I'm not asking for a beer."

"No, you are going to bed soon." I offered Bud my sandwich.

"No, I want her to buy some more food. I'm making the money. I know she's calling Henri in Paris all the time, and that's costing me a lot of money."

191

Bud Powell at the Blue Note, 1964

Henri was a pudgy French bass player who stayed with Buttercup at the Hôtel de Seine in Paris. Buttercup protested when I said he could have my sandwich.

"He can have mine," she said, then spat on the remaining sandwich and handed it to Bud. She slapped her thighs and laughed. I thought it all quite depressing, even if she had intended it to be funny.

That night I couldn't sleep. I was thinking about Bud all the time. What a life – and to think of all the joy he gave everyone through his music. He was absolutely right, too, about being the one who made the money.

BUD'S BIRTHDAY

Bud was playing at the Metropol for four days, but he stayed in that same hotel room for two weeks. During his Metropol run, he was going to do some recording for radio. Buttercup wanted me to come along to the studio. Maybe she was afraid that he would become difficult.

In the studio, Ole Jacob Hansen sat waiting behind his drum set while Erik Amundsen leaned against the grand piano with his bass. They had been waiting for some time when Bud sat down without removing his overcoat – still gripping my hand. All the time, he was examining me.

"How come you've got calluses on your palms?" he asked.

"Because I always carry so much stuff around," I said.

"Buttercup, we have to buy some gloves for Randi," said Bud.

"Won't you take your coat off and start playing now, Bud?"

Bud just kept staring at me: "Are we going to go over to your house afterwards? Do you have any beer around? Do you want me to write in your guest book?" I was very surprised by this last remark. My guest books have always been somewhat special, and I don't think Bud was accustomed to writing in guest books generally. How could he have known that I had a thing like that? This was his first visit. "What do you want me to play?" he asked.

"Play something you like, I'd love anything you played."

Finally he took his coat off and joined the waiting musicians. Buttercup had been staying in the background all this time. She was probably happy as long as he was doing his job.

On 28 September, Bud had his thirty-eighth birthday and there was to be a celebration at the Metropol. The champagne was on the house, and on such an occasion Buttercup was more relaxed about Bud's alcohol consumption. This was going to be a party! Afterwards, the couple and some other musicians went to my house and Bud was getting happier by the minute. He couldn't believe that he was allowed to drink as much as he wanted to, but then Buttercup wasn't paying much attention to him – she was too busy flirting with someone else.

Suddenly, Bud grasped the edge of the coffee table. I'll never forget it – he was in great spirits: "Could somebody please hold this table?" He must have had the feeling it was moving. He was incredibly funny and it wasn't long afterwards that he slipped happily out of his chair and landed flat on the floor.

"IS THIS YOUR DAUGHTER?"

Another time Bud was at my home, Wivi-Ann, who was fourteen years old at the time, wanted to dance for him. I took out a record featuring Bud, Wivi-Ann danced and Bud watched intently. Wivi-Ann improvised down to the minute details of the music, and when she had finished, Bud asked, "Is this your daughter, Randi?"

"Yes, she's my daughter, Bud."

"Is this your daughter?"

"Yes, Bud, this is my daughter..."

"What's her name?"

"Her name is Wivi-Ann."

"Wivi-Ann," said Bud, "can you come and kiss me on the cheek?"

He was visibly moved and asked Wivi-Ann to continue to dance. Bud never played when he was at my house, and I asked Buttercup if they had a piano in Copenhagen – it would have been normal, since they lived there for months on end.

"No, we don't have a piano, but every time we're in Switzerland, I let him play."

Bud was not so often in my home during the course of the fourteen days they were in Oslo, but I dropped by his hotel almost daily, because I felt that he appreciated the visits. Still, it was Buttercup who dominated the conversation.

Friendship

With Bud in Paris, 1964

I kept in touch after the Metropol gigs were over. One day I took along a pile of pictures of well-known jazz musicians to the hotel to entertain Bud. All the pictures were of musicians with whom he was acquainted. I handed him the snapshots, but Buttercup intercepted them and tore them from his hands.

"He doesn't know anything about this."

"I like to look at pictures, too," Bud protested, but he had to wait his turn. When he came to a picture of Count Basie, he asked, "Who do you like best – Basie or me?"

"Do you mean as a pianist?" I asked. But Bud seldom answered questions. "I think I prefer you, Bud. You are gentlemanly, and you would never dare to think of me as a journalist, would you?"

"Did you hear that, Buttercup? Randi is a journalist. Did you know that?"

It wasn't long before Bud fell asleep, because Buttercup had given

195

him sleeping pills, so that she could then slip out alone in the evenings. She reminisced about New York, and about the time she went to visit Bud in the hospital to tell him that he had become a father. "Here's your son," she said, rocking the infant in her arms. A short time afterward, she began planning the trip to Europe.

She also told how angry she had been at Oscar Goodstein, the manager of Birdland in New York. "He owes Bud money. I went down to Birdland with Johnny on my arm to pick up the money while Bud was playing there, but I was chased out again. 'Get out of here with that stray child of yours,' Goodstein said." While we talked, Bud suddenly awoke and began singing scat:

"What's the name of this tune, Buttercup?"

"Be quiet," Buttercup retorted. "Why are you asking about that?"

"I was dreaming that I was playing that with Basie," Bud answered.

"Crazy," said Buttercup. "Basie plays piano himself."

"I was playing drums," Bud said.

Another day, Bud, Buttercup, Johnny and I were invited to Don Fitzpatrick's house. Don was employed at the American embassy and used to frequent the Metropol. His apartment had a little utility kitchen where he kept a bottle of whiskey so handy that Bud had no trouble locating it. He had plopped down on a chair nearby and kept taking trips to the kitchen. He returned happier and happier each time. Don also had a full set of drums rigged up in the apartment. Johnny sat down, took a pair of drumsticks and tried to play along to a Miles Davis record. Buttercup was totally engrossed in talking with young Fitzpatrick, while I was bemused by Bud's increasing state of inebriation.

Suddenly Bud focused on Johnny's drumming and excitedly approached Buttercup: "Listen to Johnny, Buttercup! Do you want him to be a musician?"

"Don't bother me. You can see I'm busy," said Buttercup.

"Well anyway, I want him to be a drummer," Bud replied.

Instantly, Buttercup became aware of what was going on, and she got up and went over to Johnny to show him how he was supposed to hold his drumsticks.

"No, Mamma, I want Daddy to show me," Johnny answered.

It was truly strange to witness this show of respect, because Johnny was more or less brought up to believe his father was less than capable.

Photo: Francis Paudras

Bud in Normandy

"Yeah, I'm gonna help you, Johnny," Bud said. "I started as a drummer, so I know what I'm doing."

INEZ CAVANAUGH

The singer Inez Cavanaugh was to take over the Metropol stage after Bud, and she had several other jobs in Oslo, with various musicians. I went down to the Standard Hotel to join Bud and Buttercup for Inez's concert.

Outside the hotel, Bud sat begging money from passers-by: "Give me one crown and fifteen øre, please." He knew exactly how much a half light beer cost. I asked him to come up to the room with me.

"We're going to listen to Inez tonight," I said. In the elevator, he asked if I could spare a few øre. "But hurry up before Buttercup hears me," he said urgently. He never got any spending money of his own.

"No way is he going with us!" boomed Buttercup when we got upstairs. "Go to bed!" I found this embarrassing to listen to, but I couldn't intervene, because then Buttercup would simply have severed all contact with me, and I wouldn't have been able to meet Bud anymore.

"I'm tired of eating pills. I don't want to go to bed, I want to go out and listen to some music," Bud said.

Buttercup went to the telephone and pretended she was making a call: "I'm calling the hospital to get you admitted."

"Okay, okay." Bud went over to the bed and started to get undressed. He dutifully hung his suit on a clothes hanger, looking so sad. I felt so sorry for him, and I thought about him all evening long.

The following day, Inez, Buttercup and I were to go shopping for a dress for Inez. I'll never forget how I helped Inez get into a dress and accidentally pulled off her wig. She was not amused. Bud was alone at the Standard, where he had met some sailors – there were almost exclusively sailors and jazz players at that hotel. They invited him for a drink, and Bud of course couldn't refuse. There was quite an uproar when the ladies returned to the hotel and the bird had flown the coop.

BUD IN JAIL

In the meantime I had gone home and then returned with Christina in order to introduce her to Johnny. When we came to the hotel, Johnny was alone.

"Yippee! Daddy's in jail, Daddy's in jail!" Johnny sang. He was proud, because his mother had managed to get the police to pick up Bud. I was confused and curious at the same time, but I sat down to keep the children company while we waited for Buttercup who, Johnny told us, had become angry when she found Bud with the sailors.

"But Daddy was mad, too," said Johnny. "He was holding a chair up over his head, and Mamma thought he was going to throw it at her, so she called the police."

We waited and played Ludo, but Johnny thought we cheated and had a tantrum. He was a bright seven-year-old, but easily angered.

In the evening, Buttercup came to my house together with some musicians, among others, "Pastor'n". She told me that Bud was at the police station: "Ha, ha! now it's his problem! Now he'll have to find his way back to the hotel alone." She giggled spitefully, while the rest of us felt sorry for Bud, poor man. Buttercup asked if we could get hold of Bud's bassist, Bjørn Pedersen. "He's handsome," she said. I don't know if Bjørn ever found out that she was one of his admirers.

My sister, who at the time worked in the police department, told me that she had had a strange couple down at headquarters – both coloured, and the woman was large and stocky. She wanted her companion put in jail, and the two of them weren't even married. "Do you know this person?" Eva had asked.

We all had to suffer a lot of abuse from Buttercup just to keep in touch with Bud. If I hadn't dropped by their hotel every day, he would have been drugged to sleep all through his stay in Oslo. Just the same, I did stay away from the hotel for a couple of days because of Johnny's disposition, but I did want to see them off the day they were to leave. When I came to the hotel, Bud was visibly pleased.

"Where have you been, Randi? I haven't seen you for two whole days." Not many people would have thought Bud was capable of distinguishing one day from the next in the state he was in.

I helped them carry the baggage and took the elevator with Bud and Johnny. Bud accidentally stepped on Johnny's toes, triggering a fit of rage which was vented by Johnny stomping pitilessly on Bud's feet.

"What's the matter with this son of mine? He's not like other boys,"

Bud said. I mentioned that it was Johnny's behaviour that had made me stay away from the hotel a couple of days.

When we arrived at the East railroad station, Bud took a trolley and began to wheel the luggage to the train. He was actually jogging along with the trolley, because I had promised him a beer when he was finished loading the luggage. When we boarded the train, we ran into Buttercup.

"Did you know that Johnny misbehaved in front of Randi and her daughter?" said Bud.

"He's just like his daddy," Buttercup answered, suggestively tapping her temple with an index finger.

When Bud and I were alone for a few seconds, he asked if I would miss him. "Are you sure you're gonna think about me?" he asked.

"I'm coming to visit you in Paris," I answered.

TO PARIS

The following year I did have a layover in Paris on the way to the jazz festival in Juan-les-Pins. This was in July, 1963. I checked into the Hôtel St Andrés des Arts, right across from Le Caméléon jazz club and went to visit Buttercup at the Hôtel de Seine, where she and Bud rented a couple of rooms when they were in Paris – a hotel where she could cook meals herself. In the evening, I met Bud at the Blue Note. He seemed musically inspired, there was humour in his playing, but he was frail and did not look well.

"Yes, I remember you," he said when he sat down next to me during an intermission, but he didn't say much more than that, although he did take my hand and sort of chuckled strangely to himself. This was only a short time before he was admitted to Bouffemont, a hospital outside Paris. By then he had become friends with one of his biggest admirers, designer Francis Paudras, who visited Bud daily at the hospital. Johnny Griffin and Kenny Drew also played at the Blue Note, and they listened reverently to Bud's playing.

BUD AND FRANCIS

Rumours reached me via other musicians to the effect that Bud Powell no longer lived with Buttercup and that Francis Paudras

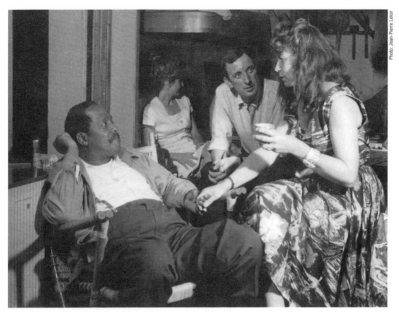

With Bud and Alan Bates after recording in Paris, 1964

looked after him now. Since I was again in Paris the next year, on my way to the Antibes festival, I decided to find out for myself what had actually happened. Unfortunately I was obliged to visit Buttercup at Hôtel de Seine in order to get Bud's new address. She acted like nothing had changed.

"If you sit down here, he'll show up," she promised. We sat at a table outside the Café de Seine and, sure enough, Bud came along in the company of Francis, and I could see instantly that Bud had changed tremendously. He sat down next to me, took my hand in his, and stared at me, grinning all the while.

"I know we're close friends," he said suddenly, breaking a ten-minute hand-holding silence. "Your name is Randi, isn't it? You'll have to excuse me, because everything that happened in Scandinavia is all black for me." After a short while, he suddenly blurted out: "Is your daughter still dancing? Did you tell her what I told you? – that she had to keep on dancing?"

Bud had a remarkable memory. One of the stories that circulated about him concerned the time he met Baron Rosenkrantz outside Birdland, and Rosenkrantz asked what time it was. Bud didn't answer, but just stared straight ahead. But a couple of years later, he met the baron again at exactly the same spot, and Bud said spontaneously, "A quarter to four."

Buttercup began to talk about the Chicken Shack, the club she had started in Paris together with her friend Henri. "I didn't use Bud's money to finance the club. That's a big lie," she said, referring to when Bud had been hospitalised for pneumonia, and there had been a collection for him.

"Did you know I was sick?" Bud asked.

"Of course, the whole world knew."

Buttercup continued to talk about money, and Bud abruptly announced to Francis that he wanted to leave. "Francis takes care of my money now, Buttercup."

"May I have your address, Bud?"

"I'll give it to you," Buttercup cut in.

"I can write it down myself," Bud said. "Do you have a pen, Randi?"

He wrote the address neatly in my address book, and he inquired whether I would be coming by the Blue Note that evening. His address was Rue de Clichy where he lived in the same house as Art Taylor and Johnny Griffin – two friends who were close to Bud, but who didn't especially like Buttercup. Buttercup was kind towards me and towards many musicians who visited her, but it was difficult to fathom her relationship with Bud. Francis, on the other hand, loved Bud in a special way: he sacrificed both his job and, I think, his first marriage because of his love for Bud.

That evening, I joined Art Taylor at the Blue Note, where Bud alternated with Ted Curson's band. Bud was very happy to see me when I showed up.

"Did you come to hear me, or the other band? They play too modern for me," he said.

"I mainly came to hear you."

He took my hand once again and held it all the time until he had to play. "You want to come up on stage with me?" he asked. Bud played so fantastically that I was overwhelmed. After the trio had played three melodies, he turned and asked what he could play for me. He was accompanied by Art Taylor on drums and Michel Gaudry on bass.

"I have heard about a new melody you wrote called 'In The Mood For A Classic' – can you play that for me?"

"Yeah, that's good. We need to practise that one. We're gonna record that one," Bud said. Then he turned to Art and Michel and explained how he wanted the song to go.

The melody was fresh and typically Bud Powell. When he finished the set, he took my hand again: "How did you like the new melody. Did you find anything classic in it?"

"I think you mean it's going to be a new Powell classic – that's what it sounds like. Are you satisfied with my answer?" Bud only smiled. When we returned to the table where Francis was sitting, Bud said that he wanted to dedicate the song to me. He also wrote down the names of the other songs that he was planning to record.

'UNA NOCHE CON FRANCIS'

"Wait a minute, Bud! It's supposed to be 'One Night With Francis'," said Paudras.

"No, the tune sounds Spanish, so the name has to be Spanish," Bud replied.

"Maybe you should call the other one 'In The Mood For A Classic With Randi'?" Francis quipped.

"No, it'll just say 'Dedicated to Randi'."

I asked Bud to write that in my festival book, because I didn't trust the record producer to include it in the title. And I was right: the dedication was never mentioned in the liner notes. But Bud wrote it himself, on July 31, 1964: "To Randi, one of my sweethearts, I dedicate 'In The Mood For A Classic' to you." He wrote this two years to the day before he died.

AT A RESTAURANT

Bud was unusually talkative, and he seemed so happy. I even got an interview with him at the club – something that would have been

unimaginable at the time he was in Oslo. When he had finished for the evening, he invited me out to a restaurant. "Come on, let's get out of here, I'm so tired of this club," he said. At a little place nearby, obviously frequented by him many times before, he ordered red wine for both of us. Art Taylor had asked, as we were leaving the club, if he could join us later.

I began to draw Bud's portrait, and when I was about to begin a second sketch, he protested: "People are staring at us." It was strange to hear Bud talk like that – strange even to hear him talk so much.

"You are like a bear coming out of hibernation," I said.

"How long does a bear stay in hibernation?" said Bud.

"Don't you ever go out and listen to your American musical colleagues when they play in Paris, Bud?"

"Can you see me at a concert?"

Bud always answered a question with a question. I had gotten used to that. Suddenly, though, he launched into a soliloquy about a concert with the Basie band: "The trumpet player played so pretty on 'Stella By Starlight'." He was talking about Sonny Cohn. "Do you know Dave Brubeck, Randi?"

"I've been along on a little tour with him in Sweden."

"Have you heard him play 'Some Day My Prince Will Come'?"

"I've heard it, yes."

"You're lucky," said Bud, and he began to sing the melody.

"He changes key like this," he continued, and sang the key change. I was very impressed. Bud Powell – a Brubeck fan! This was news. But he told me many times later of his admiration for Dave Brubeck and his music. Then he asked, "Randi, have you ever met Monk?"

"No."

"Would you like to meet him?"

"Yes, can you arrange that, Bud?"

Buttercup, Francis, Bud and Wivi-Ann, 1964

"No."

This was one of the rare occasions on which he gave a direct answer to a question. I knew of his great admiration for his pianist colleague Thelonious Monk – another jazz legend – and I understood how his mind was working. Suddenly into the restaurant walked Art Taylor in the company of two English ladies. They joined us at the table. Art teased Bud, asking to borrow ten francs for a beer.

"No," said Bud. "I have to save my money now that I'm going back to New York. I can't afford to." Just the sight of Bud with money of his own was new and unusual.

"Just for one beer, Bud?"

"No," said Bud, and put his hand over the change tray. He changed the subject by striking up a conversation with the two ladies who had come with Art, asking where they came from and how they liked Paris.

A couple of years earlier, no one would ever have suspected that he was capable of being so sociable.

"Do you remember who gave you your first job on drums?" Bud asked.

"Sure, it was you," said Art, "but after that you started playing with greats like Max Roach."

"Max Roach was too weird for me," said Bud, and we had a good laugh – the thought that someone could be weirder than Bud was really funny.

When Art and his ladies had left, Bud asked if I wanted another glass of wine.

"Okay, but I'm paying this time," I replied.

"No way. We'll spend this," said Bud, indicating the change tray. "Francis lets me have as much money as I want. Look at this!" He brandished a wallet fat with bills. "But Buttercup took my passport. Do you think that's right? What do you think about Buttercup?" he asked suddenly.

"She's never done me any harm, if you understand what I mean…" And I think he did understand.

Bud told me that he both dreaded and looked forward to going back to New York. "New York is dangerous for me, but I want to see my friends."

It was Bud who suggested that we leave, because he had to get up at seven am when he was going to get a new passport. As we were getting up, a rather foggy-eyed individual tottered over to our table and asked if Bud was a musician. "I think I recognise you by your cap," he said.

"Are you a taxi driver?" Bud asked. "I could use one right now."

BUD POWELL SAYS "HELLO"

I rode home with Bud to Francis' place in Rue de Clichy, and I mentioned to Francis and his wife Nicole how fantastic it was to experience the "new" Bud and how he had changed. "He even asked me one day if I needed money for food," said Nicole.

"Randi, why don't you tell Francis a little bit about Buttercup?" Bud asked. "I don't remember much. I just know she wasn't good to me."

I related the incident with the sandwich at the hotel in Oslo, and told how ghastly I thought it was that she spat on it before offering it to Bud.

"Randi, did I eat that sandwich?" he asked. Truly, I couldn't remember.

"I'm so fond of Bud," Francis said. "I think it must be God who sent him to me.

Before I left them, I promised to come back after the festival in Antibes, so that I could be present at Bud's recording session. Bud asked me to greet the musicians at the festival for him. "Tell them Bud Powell says hello," he said.

Buttercup was also in Antibes, but without Johnny. She told everyone how well Bud was, without mentioning that they were no longer together. I personally gave Bud's regards to Roy Eldridge, Lionel Hampton, and several others – but not to Ella Fitzgerald. I found Ella together with my good friend Beryl Bryden and asked if I could take a picture of the two of them. Beryl naturally agreed, but not Ella. "You're always flying around with a camera," she said.

"It happens to be my job, and I need a picture of you." I didn't find the time appropriate to convey Bud's regards to her. When I came back to Paris, I was unfortunately a couple of hours too late to be in on the recording session, but I did ring home to Francis to tell him I had arrived. This resulted in an instant invitation to the record celebration. Francis asked Bud to come to the phone.

"Shall I pick you up, Randi?"

"No, Bud dear, I can find my way, thank you."

Bud stood downstairs in the stairwell when I arrived, and he was happy to see me. When we entered the apartment, he asked Francis to put on some Brubeck for him.

"You and your Brubeck," said Francis, laughing. "Bud's always asking for that."

Bud said that he had seen film coverage of the festival on television. "Is that where you were, Randi? Did you give them my regards? What did Hamp say? What about Roy?" I brought return regards from everyone I could think of but deliberately left out Ella. We changed the subject and got talking about something else. Suddenly Bud asked, "Did Ella put you down, Randi?" Bud never ceased to amaze me. A couple of seconds later, he blurted out: "Do you still like Count Basie?" He was probably thinking about the picture he had seen in Oslo two years earlier.

All the time, while we were talking, Bud was chuckling to himself, and I finally asked him what he was laughing at. "It's awful when I don't know why you are laughing," I said. But he offered no answer. A half hour later, he asked curtly, "Did you give Art any pussy?" I laughed.

"Is that what you have been thinking all this time? – about whether or not Art and I had an affair? Why? Because he went to the Blue Note with me? No, Bud, we're just good friends." The party was in full swing, with some of Bud's closest friends present, and of course Alan Bates, the record producer, as well as photographer Jean-Pierre Leloir, who was everywhere. Bud held my hand all the time, and this was also captured on film. I received the picture later, through Francis.

INTERRUPTED RECORDINGS

Francis told me that the recording session had not gone smoothly, because in the middle of the session, Buttercup had burst in, demanding a guarantee that she would be given a share of the money. Bud became ill and had to go out to vomit. Buttercup remained adamant and refused to leave the studio. When Alan Bates finally threatened to call the police, she called his bluff: "Okay, let 'em come." Bates made the call. At the police station, Buttercup was asked to produce her passport, which upon examination revealed that she was in fact not married to Bud Powell. This fact was enough to allow the police to sanction Bates' exclusion of Buttercup from the studio.

Powell - Paris 22.7.64

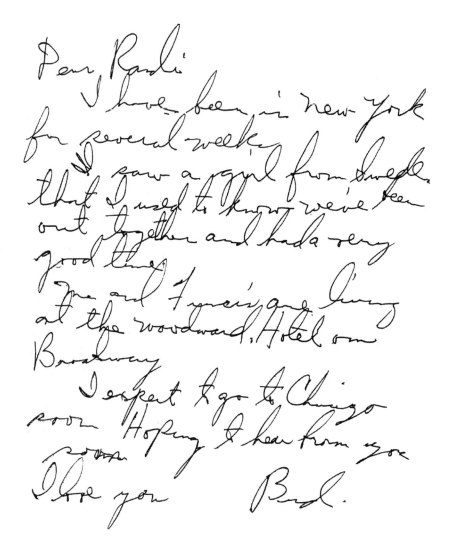

Letter from Bud, 1964

LETTERS AND CARDS

"Write down Randi's address, Francis. I'm going to write to her," said Bud.

"*You* are going to write?" asked Francis in disbelief.

"Yeah, I've got two girlfriends now, Margareta and Randi," Bud announced with a smile.

I received both cards and letters from Bud, first from Normandy, where he stopped before continuing on to New York, and then from the city itself – big flashy New York postcards telling me how much he missed me and how busy he was with all his interviews. "Hello Randi, I'm in New York having a ball – Kisses – I love you." And another: "We're very busy because of the interviews. But anyway, I think of you." Just before Bud passed away in Harlem, I got a long letter, in which he told me that he was going out with a Swedish lady he had met. This was Margareta, with whom he was already acquainted. "Francis and I are going to Chicago," he wrote, but he never got there.

THELONIOUS MONK

According to Francis, one of the first things he and Bud did when they got to New York was to visit Thelonious Monk. They rang the doorbell. Instead of showing surprise and shouting for joy at the reunion, Monk simply said: "Do you want to hear an airplane?"

Monk's big concert grand piano stood with its long end sticking out into the kitchen, offering Monk's wife Nellie a convenient shelf on which to place salt and pepper shakers and other spices. Monk dragged Bud inside the door, went over to the piano and slammed both forearms down onto the keys: "Here's an airplane!"

The spice tins rattled and vibrated, and Monk seemed pleased with the sound. What Bud thought is unknown, but Francis couldn't believe his own eyes and ears. This was truly a strange reunion of friends who hadn't seen one another for years.

Bud opened at Birdland the same evening as pianist Horace Silver, on 25 August, 1964. One of the guests that night was sixteen-year-old Celia, Bud's daughter with Fran. He had never seen Celia before and was very happy. He played especially for her all evening – actually for four evenings in a row. "It was a fantastic experience," Francis said later. He was proud of the fact that the audience was now hearing an emotionally balanced Bud Powell. I only wish I could have been there myself. I hadn't yet been to the United States. Time was not yet ripe.

Francis had to give up his hope of taking Bud back to Paris with him. The first few weeks went well, but the pushers were on Bud's heels all the time. New York turned out to be quite a bit different from what Paudras had imagined. After Bud had met Celia, and later her mother, Fran, they used to have get-togethers at the home of the baroness, Nica. Bud said that he wanted to stay in New York. Francis's wife in Paris was expecting a baby, and he decided to head home. Bud declined the offer to return to Europe, and that was the beginning of the end. Bud would certainly have lived a better life if he had gone along with Francis. When Francis arrived in Paris, there were thirty people waiting to welcome them. They were all greatly disappointed when Bud didn't get off the plane with Francis.

Francis Paudras died in sad circumstances in November, 1997. Another really good friend gone.

MONK IN OSLO

In Oslo, I had the pleasure of meeting Thelonious Monk, and under strange circumstances. Monk was supposed to play a concert in the university auditorium, featuring, among others, saxophonist Charles Rouse. This was 15 April, 1966, three months before Bud died. I was standing with Rouse in the lobby of the Hotel Continental, when Monk approached us as he was exiting the elevator. He came straight up to me and asked point blank: "Do you want to meet Nellie?"

"Of course," I said, and went along with him up to his room. Nellie was sitting on the sofa, and I was asked to have a seat. Monk washed out a glass for me and talked a blue streak. I told him what Bud had said the time he asked me if I would like to meet Monk. But Monk didn't laugh: "Bud is beautiful. But he's not doing so well in America, he's sleeping in the gutter," he said.

"Why don't you help him?" I asked. "You live there. You're one of his friends? I've never even been to America myself..."

Monk gave no reply to this, but rather continued chattering away,

Thelonious Monk and his aura, April 1966

talking openly, as if we had known one another for a long time.

When we got to the auditorium, he asked me to come down to the dressing room during the intermission. He had a weird way of entertaining his fellow musicians.

"It's interesting being in an insane asylum," he said. "The most fun is studying the doctors."

I asked him if I could take a picture of him.

"Go ahead."

I took only one picture, and it turned out bad. Still it is special in its aberration, because it captures, in a way, Monk and his aura.

When the concert was over, Jo Vogt came leaping up on stage and placed a Peer Gynt-style hat atop Monk's fur cap. She had come to the concert wearing green stockings, I remember – and had brought her husband and child. She was married to the president of the university, Hans Vogt. Jo herself was a ceramist and had designed one of the jazz federation's award statuettes (the "Buddy"). She was a near and dear friend of jazz. I would later be able to tell Jo that Monk had put the cap on Nellie's head when we got back to the hotel. Monk had worn his own cap during the concert, but not in the hotel room.

After staying a time with him and Nellie, I said I wanted to go down to the other musicians. They were in the bar, and I had invited them home to my house. "I'll be down in the bar," said Monk. When I mentioned this to Monk's musicians, they didn't believe me: "Monk will never come down to the bar!" But he did.

"How's it goin'?" he asked. "Is everything okay? Are you being taken care of?"

When I replied that everything was fine, he turned and disappeared again.

The next time I met Monk was at the airport. He smiled sadly, because he knew that both of us were thinking about Bud and his untimely death. Bud died on 31 July, 1966.

Monk himself died on 17 February, 1982. At that time I was staying with Eubie Blake for his ninety-ninth birthday. I was riding in a taxi when I heard on the radio that Monk had died – just as we were passing the Apollo Theatre in Harlem. A few days later, I was having dinner with singer Sheila Jordan, when she got a phone call with the request that she sing at the funeral. The world of jazz is singularly small.

CHAPTER 11

Long Tall Dexter

I n November 1962, Dexter Gordon came to the Metropol Jazz House. This was our first meeting with the tall, lanky, incredibly charming saxophonist – and actor. Even before I met him, I knew that he had played the lead in *The Connection* in California – the story of a narcotics addict. I knew also that Dexter himself had served time for narcotics abuse – but mainly, I thought of him as the distinguished musician he was. Both Sonny Rollins and John Coltrane, two other saxophonists who are equally as well-known, said that Dexter was one of their sources of inspiration. On some of the older records, we can actually hear the similarity. Dexter took his time when he played – he was never in a hurry, and that was the first impression one got from him, a lasting trait he left with people.

On opening night at the Metropol, there was something wrong with his instrument, and a Norwegian saxophonist, Totti Bergh, helped him out. In the meantime, Dexter stood at the microphone and talked about anything and everything for a half hour, full of humour and with a broad smile on his face. Dexter's smile was pervasive, I recall, always there, even in hard times. He was always a bit boyish, and the odd thing was his ability to spellbind men as well as women in his audiences. He exuded charm and was fascinating to watch. We saw him in down times, as well, very tired and exhausted. He never gave up playing until the end.

Dexter became a great friend of Norway, guesting at our clubs several times during the sixties and seventies. He was enormously popular at the Molde Festival, and it was also a memorable occasion the year he played at Vossa. Once he came to Oslo, especially to make a record with Karin Krog – a recording born in extraordinary circumstances. He was actually under restriction at the time and not allowed to leave Denmark, but *Some Other Spring* turned out to be a very fine record. Dexter's personal playing style shines through – virile, warm, comforting – and the way in which he gets the accompaniment to coalesce around his soloing makes this record extra fascinating.

There is much to tell about Dexter – and most of the story centres on happiness and friendship. I do, however, remember clearly an experience that has a nightmare dimension: it occurred during one of the first days he was at the Metropol.

"BE THERE IN A MINUTE"

Dexter had built up a sizeable group of fans before he came to the club, through his records and appearances in the USA. I don't know how many were aware of what was going on behind the calm, engaging musical facade that was his trademark, but I knew, and when asked to drop by and pick him up at his hotel, I accepted right away. The idea was to see that nothing interfered with his showing up on time. I was attending a modelling course in the neighbourhood, anyway, so it was on my way.

He didn't come down promptly at all. When we called up to the room from the reception desk, he answered that he would be right down. I sat and waited and waited, talking with the receptionist for one-and-a-half hours before Dexter finally arrived after a series of calls to his room. He came out of the elevator grinning, saxophone in hand, his tall frame slightly swaying, with that characteristic unsteadiness at the knees. I had trouble returning his smile at that point, since he had repeated "Be down in a minute" every time I had called his room. I did realise what he had been up to, however.

At the Metropol I was assailed by the staff: "What did you do? – talk a hole in his head!" I only wish that they could have experienced what it was like to get Dexter to come out of his hotel room. Dexter was Dexter.

Greetings from Dexter

JAZZ CENTRET · METROPOL
AKERSGT. 8
Den berømte saxofonisten
DEXTER GORDON
KUN DENNE UKE

1/7 November 1962

Dexter digs in

TENOR SAXOPHONE
Dexter Gordon
Roland Kirk 26
Archie Shepp 14
Stanley Turrentine 13

Dexter's first visit, 1962

He played gorgeously, of course, and he charmed the audience with his small talk. During the last intermission, I asked him if he would like to come home for an interview. I preferred to sit at home rather than in a noisy club. Absolutely – Dexter gladly agreed to come along, but he would have to drop by the hotel first, he said. "Just give me your address."

As time plodded by and I waited at home, I kept calling the Standard Hotel and the answer was always: "I'll be there in a minute." Minutes became hours and finally, I called the Standard to ask them to inform Dexter that he could forget the whole thing. I was expected in the office early in the morning and was beginning to get tired.

At five am Dexter showed up at my door. By then I had fallen asleep on the couch, having given up hope of interviewing him.

"Put on the coffee," he said. You're going to get an interview like you've never had before!" Whereupon, he paced about in the living room, talking about his dream quartet. Humour shone from his face. I melted, became wide awake, took notes and laughed.

"I'm gonna have Oscar Peterson, Ray Brown and Art Blakey, and if they aren't interested, then I'm gonna have Kenny Drew, Kenny Clarke – or maybe Max Roach. As press secretary I'll have Charles Mingus, as personal manager Darrel Zanuck, and Ava Gardner will be my official hostess. As male vocalist, I'll have Frank Sinatra, and as female vocalist Marion Anderson. AT&T will take care of my financial interests and pay for six months' rehearsal in Acapulco, Mexico, because down there there's a beautiful white beach and blue ocean. We'll have two stage outfits, two sets of instruments per man, and a band bus – it has to be a Cadillac, though. And I want the Russian Bolshoi Ballet to dance on special occasions, and Bobby Kennedy will be my lawyer."

Quite a setup. Dexter was in great spirits and said that this form of interview was new and something he'd never tried before. "Let me have a copy of it in the newspaper." It was published in *Dagbladet* eventually.

By now it was seven-thirty am, and I had to go in to work. I offered to let Dexter share my cab back to his hotel, but no – he would rather lie down here at the house, if I had a room. He didn't feel like going back to the hotel. I was unable to convince him otherwise, and since the maid's room was vacant, he was given that. I wrote down the number of the taxi station and my own telephone number, and then I went to work. I knew I had a hard day ahead of me – secretarial work at Norsk Hydro, and then later a photo session in church. Trulte Heide Steen was marrying trombonist

Andreas Skjold. Kristian Bergheim and Anita Thallaug were to be best man and maid of honour.

The pictures were taken, and I went home to develop the film. Wivi-Ann would have made dinner – she was always so helpful – and everything would be ready when I got home, I thought.

"Mamma, how long is that guy going to be here. We've only seen his arm so far. He stuck his arm out of the door and asked us to buy some cigarettes."

I was surprised. Hadn't he gone yet? I had so much to do. When I knocked on his door, he said he'd "be out in a minute". But I knew his minutes were lengthy, and it did take one hour-and-a-half before he came down to dinner. He was in a great mood – smiling and passing the food around, conversing and asking questions about the government and other things he was interested in; some of the questions were too difficult even for me to answer. Caramel pudding was his favourite dessert, and Wivi-Ann had made that – purely coincidentally.

Dexter with his sax, Molde 1965

"YOU NEED A PLUMBER"

While we were having coffee, Wivi-Ann danced jazz ballet for Dexter. I asked if I should call for a taxi, but no – he was going back upstairs to "make myself together". Of course I wasn't going to deny him a trip to the toilet, but instead he went into the bathroom – and stayed there.

I actually pulled out the telephone wire when I saw that it was getting late. I refused to take the blame over the phone for his being late. I implored him to come out, to think of his public at the

Metropol. "People are waiting for you," I insisted. He remained locked inside the bath – me outside the door.

"Metropol, my darling," sang Dexter, but I didn't see the humour in this situation. The children, who by now had gone to bed, began asking what was the matter with this man. "Is he drunk?"

"Try to go to sleep," I replied. "We'll talk about it later." I was quite worried it was already time for him to be at the Metropol.

"Your faucet leaks," said Dexter.

"Yes, I need a man around the house."

"No, you need a plumber," Dexter replied.

I scolded and pleaded. Suddenly it became very quiet in the bathroom – deathly still – and the feeling was awful. I knew what he was doing, but I couldn't forcibly drag him out.

A couple of hours later he came down the stairs: "Call a taxi, will you? I'm gonna blow them away in the second set."

I called for a cab, and I asked Dexter at least to phone down to the Metropol right away and inform them that he was on his way. "But for God's sake, please don't tell them where you are! I don't want the blame for this."

While Dexter stood swaying at the knees, with the telephone in one hand, the doorbell rang. I opened, thinking it was the cab driver, but it was not. It was someone from the Metropol.

Dexter with Karin Krog, Molde 1965

"I'm really sorry," I said. "This is not my fault. Dexter is talking to the Metropol right now," I explained.

"Shut up!" he shouted, pushing me to one side. He crossed the room and grabbed the telephone from Dexter's hand, shouting into it, "I've found him, drunk on his ass at Randi's." This was then relayed by public announcement at the Metropol to the waiting audience, people who were there confirmed this for me later.

I wanted to shrivel up and die on the spot. It was little

consolation when Dexter passed me on his way out of the door, kissed me on the cheek, and said loud and clear, "Randi, thanks for a wonderful night!"

IN COPENHAGEN

I was sick for two days – sick with despair and bedridden. Dexter called to ask why I wasn't coming down to listen to him. He also wanted to know how the interview was coming along. "It was a lot of fun," he added.

But it didn't take a long time before I forgave Dexter. He came to my home several times, and on those occasions he was beyond reproach. Always in a great mood, he became a good friend, warm and pleasant, and also very thoughtful. I got letters, and he always sent a Christmas card. His Christmas cards were specially made for him in Denmark.

We met one another afterwards – in Molde, in Voss, in Copenhagen, Nice and Warsaw, and elsewhere – and we became better and better acquainted. I can remember specially one year I was obliged to stay over in Copenhagen on my way to Juan-les-Pins. There was a strike at the airport in Paris, and I was put up at a hotel in Copenhagen. When I saw that Dexter was playing at Montmartre, I just had to go there, although I really should have gotten some sleep. I was overworked and exhausted, having spent the entire preceding day and night preparing for the trip.

At Montmartre, we had a happy reunion. Dexter introduced me to his lady friend Lotte, his companion at the time. When he had finished playing, I should have gone directly back to the hotel, but I was enticed to hear the Danish band that was to follow Dexter.

Suddenly I felt like the whole room began to spin. It was midsummer and very warm, and I had to be escorted out of the club. There stood Dexter with his arm around Lotte, but I honestly don't remember anything else, until I regained consciousness in the middle of the street. I awoke in the arms of Dexter, having fainted for the first time in my life, just as I was getting into a taxi. "Please take care of yourself. We need you," Dexter said. I'll never forget those words.

'FAIRWEATHER'

Two trumpet players who were to become important to both Bud Powell and Dexter Gordon, were Kenny Dorham and Chet Baker – later I can also add Don Sickler, trumpet player and publisher. Life's coincidences have never ceased to amaze me.

Kenny Dorham was playing at the Metropol one week in January 1964, and on several occasions he would come to my home before the concert in order to play piano and sing, which he loved. I recorded him, normally erasing whatever he said in between songs in order to save tape. For that reason, I cannot remember that he mentioned any name when he played the beautiful melody that always comes to mind from those days – a tune that I myself titled "Fairweather".

"Listen good to this one, Randi, it's Bud Powell's lyrics and music! Listen to the lyric! Bud wrote it while he was together with Fran – Celia's mother..." And so Kenny sang: "How can a house be built on angel wings...Fairweather...together."

It is a beautiful lyric, and Kenny was especially fond of it. The version he sang on tape has since been played for many musicians, and one who was particularly surprised was drummer Max Roach.

"This is a rare event. You should let Francis Paudras hear that, Randi. Francis is right now putting together a film script about Bud Powell, and this might be used in the film. They're going to make it in Paris."

Not long afterward, I got a call from Paudras – Bud's close friend in Paris – who had asked me to send a cassette to Chan Parker, Charlie Parker's widow, whom I knew already. She lives just outside of Paris and was asked to assist in writing down the lyrics and music from the cassette. When she had finished, I got a copy of the sheet music – but she had changed the title to "Brothers".

"Why'd you do that?" I asked. "I've always called it 'Fairweather'."

"Okay," said Chan, "I just wanted it to have a name."

ROUND MIDNIGHT

After I met Bud in Paris, I had been in regular touch with Francis Paudras. I had also helped him with details of Bud's stay in Norway which he needed for his book – a monumental work published in

Dexter with Bertrand Tavernier, filming in 1985

French. He also used the stories about Bud and Buttercup in the well-known film *Round Midnight*, where the main character is named Dale Turner and his wife Buttercup. Buttercup was played by actress Sandra Phillips.

In the film, Dale is a saxophonist, but of course the story is based on Bud Powell's life. As most people know, it was Dexter Gordon who played Dale Turner, a role for which he was nominated for an Academy Award for Best Actor. Turner's young fan is based on Francis in real life, and that role was played by a French actor.

The melody Bud wrote was to be used in the film, and it was decided that Chet Baker would sing the lyric. Herbie Hancock, who was responsible for the film's music, arranged the melody and rehearsed an entire day with Chet. Baker both sings and plays trumpet, and the result sounds marvellous. I have later received recordings of the rehearsals, because on the day they were rehearsing, I was at Chan's home. It was Chet who asked Francis to record the rehearsals.

Dexter during the filming of *Round Midnight*, 1985

Dexter and Wivi-Ann during filming, 1985

I was also privileged to be present during the actual filming, which was done in Studio Eclair outside of Paris. Jan Horne from Norwegian television was also invited, and I had brought along Wivi-Ann. Dexter was thrilled to see us again, and he thought it was extra pleasant to see Wivi-Ann. She was only fourteen years old when she had made him caramel pudding in Gartnerveien – some twenty-three years earlier.

"She looks like you did at that age," Dexter said.

Dexter loved to act, but he found it fatiguing.

"I'm not used to getting up so early. But tomorrow morning I'm going to get to slap Buttercup, so then it won't be so hard to get up!" he said. Buttercup had not been very popular among Bud's musician friends.

We were on the set two days and met the renowned director Bertrand Tavernier, who was very satisfied with Dexter's performance. It was fun to see Dexter in action as an actor. Saxophonist Wayne Shorter was proud because he got some lines, and so was Bobby Hutcherson, the well known vibes player. I met several old friends, and one of them, drummer Billy Higgins, was in Dexter's movie band. Guitarist John McLaughlin was also there. I had just seen him at the Kongsberg Festival in Norway and now he had a role in the film – but he was more proficient as a guitarist. Chan Parker and daughter Kim were extras. Dexter's wife Maxine, who had been his manager earlier, was very supportive of him during the shooting of the film. He was busy from early morning to late evening, and in the evening, we previewed the scenes that were completed. It was an enjoyable experience – and exciting to hear Dexter's comments from the row behind us:

"Please! No more closeups, okay?"

BUD POWELL'S MELODY?

When I entered the film studio, I was met by a hearty embrace from Herbie Hancock.

"Thanks a lot for 'Fairweather'! Hope you like the arrangement."

I had known Herbie since he played piano with Miles for the first time in Antibes in 1963. We had made the rounds of jazz clubs in Paris afterwards – Herbie, Nathan Davis and I. In the film studio I also met Celia Powell for the first time – Bud's daughter with Fran, who had stayed with Bud during the forties.

I asked Bud once if he could remember 'Fairweather' – the melody he composed at the time he was together with Fran, Celia's mother. As usual, I got no answer to my question, but he did pose his own surprised question: "Randi, what do you know about Fran?" Regardless of his non-answer, when the film came to Oslo, I was very surprised to see in the credits that 'Fairweather' was composed by Kenny Dorham. I mentioned it to Hancock the same year in Warsaw, when he asked me what I thought about *Round Midnight*. I said I was surprised to read that Dorham was listed as composer.

"But, Randi, it sounds like Dorham," Hancock replied.

When I was in New York in 1988, I got a phone call from Don Sickler, trumpet player and the gentleman who deals with Dorham's

Kenny Dorham's lyric and composition for 'Fairweather', written out by Chan Parker from my 1964 recording of Kenny, 1985

music and copyrights. He protested against my statement, saying he himself had proof. 'Fairweather' is registered in Dorham's name in 1959, he said. This was an interesting coincidence, because I had called the tune "Fairweather", since Dorham didn't say any name, but he sings about fair weather. In 1997 I got a copy of the registration from Second Floor Music, and Don said he took over the worldwide copyright in 1987 from the US Copyright Office, where the tune was registered on 9 July, 1959, under the registration number eu584516, and under the name "Fairweather" (like Brothers – Clearwater).

As far as the dispute over the author of 'Fairweather' is concerned, Max Roach said to me

Chan Parker with Charlie's saxes

in New York in 1988 that Dorham used to stay a lot with Bud Powell in the old days, just as Fats Navarro did – everyone loved Bud's mother. "Kenny learned a lot from Bud while he lived there. Of course, I must be wrong. Dorham could have meant another song being composed by Bud. He sang and played a lot at my house. Dorham was certainly a fine composer. Listen to 'Una Mas' – and now 'Fairweather'.

Don Sickler told me that Dorham never recorded it – not before I taped him in 1964. And I am glad he did. In this way – through film, record and now my included CD – the beautiful tune and lyric by Kenny Dorham has been spread all over the world. I also thank both Kenny Dorham's widow Rubina, and Don Sickler, the third trumpet player who became involved with 'Fairweather'. Also Art Farmer, who has recorded the song with singer Magni Wentzel.

When I met Chet Baker after the film opened, he told me that he

Kenny Dorham from my guest book, 1964

Page 1

FORM E

Application for Registration of a Claim to Copyright
in a musical composition the author of which is a citizen or domiciliary of the United
States of America or which was first published in the United States of America

CLASS	REGISTRATION NO.
E	Eu 584516
	DO NOT WRITE HERE

Instructions: Read the information provided on page 4 before completing the form. Fill in applicable items on all pages. Follow the instructions which accompany each item. In the case of published works the application should give the facts which existed at the date of publication. Pages 1 and 2 should be typewritten or printed with pen and ink. Pages 3 and 4 may be carbon copies. Mail all pages to the Register of Copy-

rights, Library of Congress, Washington 25, D. C., together with:
(a) If unpublished, one copy of the composition and the registration fee of $4.
(b) If published, two copies of the composition and the registration fee of $4.
Make your remittance payable to the Register of Copyrights.

1. Copyright Claimant(s) and Address(es): Give the name(s) and address(es) of the copyright owner(s). In the case of published works the name should ordinarily be the same as in the notice of copyright on the copies of the work deposited.

Name _____ Kenny Dorham

Address _____ 1499 President St Brooklyn 13, N.Y.

Name _____ Same

Address _____ Same

2. Title: Give the title of the musical composition as it appears on the copies. _____
" Fairweather " (like Brothers — clearweather)

3. Authors: The citizenship of the author and information concerning domicile must be given. If an organization is the author and was formed under the laws of the United States or one of the States, citizenship may be stated as U. S. A. The term authors includes authors of music, words, arrangement, and any other copyrightable part of the work. In the case of a work

made for hire the employer is the author. If the claim is based on new matter (see item 5) give information about the author of the new matter. If the author's pseudonym appears on the copies rather than his legal name, the pseudonym should be given in the application, and the legal name may be included if desired; e. g., John Doe, pseudonym of Richard Roe.

Name _____ Kenny Dorham _____ W _____ Citizenship _____ U.S.A.
(Name of country)

Domiciled in U. S. A. Yes ☐ No ☐ Address _____ 1499 President St Bklyn, NY _____ Author of _____ words + music
(State which: words, music, arrangement, etc.)

Name _____ Same _____ Citizenship _____ Same
(Name of country)

Domiciled in U. S. A. Yes ☐ No ☐ Address _____ Same _____ Author of _____ Same
(State which: words, music, arrangement, etc.)

Name _____ Same _____ Citizenship _____ Same
(Name of country)

Domiciled in U. S. A. Yes ☐ No ☐ Address _____ Same _____ Author of _____ Same
(State which: words, music, arrangement, etc.)

4. Date and Place of Publication (for published works only):
(a) Give the date (month, day, and year) when copies were first placed on sale, sold, or publicly distributed.

(b) Give the name of the country in which the work was first published.

5. Previous Registration or Publication:
If a claim to copyright in any part of the work was previously registered, or if part of the work was previously published, check the appropriate space in (check both if applicable):
☐ previous registration
☐ previous publication
and give a brief general statement of the nature of the new matter in this version:

Kenny Dorham's copyright registration for 'Fairweather', 1959

The last time I saw Dexter was at the Nice Festival in 1988. He died two years later

had been disappointed with *Round Midnight* – he disliked especially the manner in which his song was handled: "I can barely hear myself," he complained. And the criticism is valid. The soundtrack from the film contains beautiful and fascinating song and trumpet takes by Chet, but in the film itself, when Dexter puts a tune on the turntable, "Buttercup" bursts in and turns off the record.

CHAPTER 12

Portrait Of My Pals

In November, 1964, Lars "Lasse" Gullin came to the Metropol to take over Dexter Gordon's engagement. Dexter was detained in Denmark, and his replacement was Sweden's great baritone sax player. Gullin was born in Gotland, where he started as a pianist – a concert pianist.

He arrived in Oslo with his baritone, some music paper, and his dear Mailis; they were happy to be able to stay at my home. In Stockholm, they didn't have an apartment or anything else, only music, each other and a lot of worries. They were often given a place to sleep on people's floors, and their address was The Golden Circle.

Everybody expected to be treated to four straight nights of top jazz at the Metropol as Lasse was accompanied by Tore Sandnæs on piano, Bjørn Pedersen on bass, and Ole Jacob Hansen on drums. We weren't disappointed and Lasse's vulnerable, warm tone, often melodically influenced by Swedish folk music, left a lasting impression. And of course he was rated among critics as one of the world's best: *Down Beat*'s critics' poll, he had been among the top players since the fifties, several times. He had made records with Zoot Sims, Stan Getz, Chet Baker, Clifford Brown and Quincy Jones. His records abound, not the least of which feature his own compositions. He was a great composer with a personal touch.

Lasse had had a serious operation when he was very young, and when he was released from the hospital, it was said that he had so much morphine in his body that it would take some time to get it out

Lasse Gullin, Pouline and Mailis and music composed in Oslo, November 1964

of his system. The situation was not made better by the fact that he was a promising young musician who went on the road in Sweden with Chet Baker and Stan Getz. When he came to Norway, he was a legalised, card-carrying user. The Swedish government was quite understanding when it came to supporting outstanding artists in need, though, and a short time after his visit to Oslo, he was awarded a house and guaranteed a stipend so that he could compose.

When Lasse and Mailis were in my home, however, the situation was not so good. Mailis was pregnant. "But don't say anything to Lasse," she begged. "He has enough worries already."

They stayed a week, and they wrote in my guest book: "The nourishment was marvellous, both physically and spiritually".

LASSE GULLIN'S "GOLDEN RECORD"

The joy was mine, as well. Every day, Lasse played piano, often all night long. He hadn't touched a piano in fifteen years, but for hours on end, he resurrected his repertoire of Mozart, Debussy, Beethoven, Rachmaninov – with emotional introductions and impressive keyboard technique. Some of what he played was as good as any piano recital, the piece lasting up to twenty minutes' playing time.

"It's strange I can remember all this," he said. "I wrote this piece for the Gotland Concert Society when I was seventeen years old, and I was the soloist for the premier performance. But I've forgotten a great deal otherwise. Originally I was supposed to become a concert pianist."

"Did you start as a pianist?"

"No, actually as an accordionist," he laughed, "but then I was only three. I took up the clarinet when I was thirteen and learned to read music in the army band. When I was fourteen, I started to practise piano on my own, and by the time I was seventeen, I had my piano concert finished. I called it 'Andante Scherzo'."

"What about jazz?"

"I started playing in a Dixieland band when I was fourteen. I moved to Stockholm when I was nineteen and started taking harmony and piano lessons. Later on, I studied baritone sax with Seymour Österwall, almost by accident. I happened to hear a record by Miles Davis's nine-man band, and Mulligan's baritone playing made a big impression on me."

"Were you inspired by Stan Getz, too?"

"Of course. We worked together a lot both when he came to Sweden and later, after he moved to Copenhagen. I was a frequent guest at his home in those days, because I also lived in Denmark a couple of years."

While Lasse and Mailis stayed with me, he also played baritone sax, even making trick recordings with himself on piano accompaniment. He also started writing his work 'May Day' from *Jazzamour*. This was later performed by a large string and wind orchestra for Swedish television.

I remember the time Lasse borrowed 100 kroner from me, promising that I would be repaid. He was expecting some money from Stockholm. I'll never forget the day he received the letter from Sweden. He came to me immediately with the money, and then he went to town to buy food for the household – happy and proud. It was a touching gesture.

He also recorded for radio in Oslo. His interpretations of 'Joy Spring' and 'I've Seen', which was his own composition, are unforgettable. At Gartnerveien, he recorded a number of his own compositions on my reel-to-reel, hoping that I might one day write lyrics to them. At this time, his record *Portrait Of My Pals* was ready to be released – a beautiful recording with strings which was later awarded the gold record prize in Sweden.

At the piano in Oslo, 1964

When Lasse and Mailis got back to Stockholm, they found a place to live, and I visited them there while Lasse was working at the Golden Circle with drummer Bosse Skoglund and pianist Lasse Sjösten. We also kept in touch via letters and cards. I got a sketch version of 'May Day', written for my youngest daughter Christina. She played the piano well, and Lasse hoped that the streamlined version would be suitable for her.

Lasse and Mailis had a daughter, Pouline, whom I saw for the first time during the Molde Festival in 1965. She was an infant then, and I had the pleasure of taking the first pictures of her cradled in the bell of Lasse's baritone sax. "This makes three sons and three daughters," Lasse announced proudly, as he held Pouline in his arms. One of his sons – Peter – has followed in his father's footsteps as both baritone saxophonist and composer.

The next time I met Pouline, she was a ten-year-old sitting on the stage at the Kongsberg Jazz Festival, experimenting at the piano. That was also the last time I saw Lasse. He died 17 May, 1976, only forty-eight years old. I'm sure, however, that he enjoyed some fine years, especially after he moved into his own home in Trångsund.

ART FARMER AND "BIRD"

Art Farmer plays the way he looks – like a gentleman of jazz, composed and intelligent. When I think of him, I always remember the beautiful tone of his flugelhorn. Few play as lyrically and sensitively as he does.

I met him for the first time in 1963, at the Antibes Festival. He was rather depressed at the time, having recently lost his twin brother Addison, a bass player.

"It's like losing a part of myself," Art told me.

A couple of years later, Art came to Oslo, where he played several of our clubs. He has also guested at Molde, and over the years he has become like a member of the family. Both of my daughters have had the pleasure of his company after they moved abroad – Wivi-Ann to London, and Christina during the time she lived in Paris. Wivi-Ann's husband, drummer Spike Wells, was one of Art's favourite rhythm accompanists when he played in England. It is unbelievable how our friendship has grown, when I think back on our first chance meeting in Antibes.

Today Art lives in Vienna – where he plays frequently with Austrian musicians – and the United States. As one of very few great lyrical players on his instrument, he is in demand. The first time he was in Norway, early in the fifties, he played with Lionel Hampton's band, and later collaborated both with saxophonist Benny Golson and guitarist Jim Hall. In recent years, he has again toured Europe with Golson.

Art Farmer, Stuff Smith and Don Byas in Molde, 1966

I asked Art once if he had met Charlie Parker.

"I was a close friend of Parker's during the time I lived in California and went to high school – this was in the forties, just after he left Dizzy Gillespie. Addison and I had rented a big room to practise in, and Charlie Parker used to come there often – sometimes to get away from people, and other times because he didn't have anything else to do. We used to go to the movies together, but nobody had any money, so we waited until the film was almost over. They used to let us in free.

"Charlie was a very nice guy, even though many people thought he was just the opposite. I remember especially one evening I heard him play with a pianist I thought was terrible – when you're sixteen, you have strong opinions. This was an after-hours place where people could come in and play. Parker suddenly got out his horn and started playing with this piano player. 'Why'd you play with him?' I asked Parker on the way back to our room.

"'If people want to try to play, then they have to be able to do it,' Parker answered. 'It's the only way they're gonna learn.' That was an important lesson for me.

"We became close friends. Parker was the type who just played when he felt like it, and if he didn't feel like it, he was known to just stay away from the job. I remember one time I was playing with Lionel Hampton at a place right near Birdland, where Parker had a gig. But instead of playing there, Parker came over and played with us. You can imagine how mad they got at Birdland, where people had paid money to come in and listen to the great 'Bird'! It happened a lot that he didn't show up for a gig, but then he would come in a few days later and play for free. That's how he was – an eccentric genius."

Art Farmer is open and well-mannered, with a warm sense of humour and we have had many memorable conversations over the years. He is also among the most dependable letter writers. He answered immediately when I asked him if he would be interested in making a record with Norwegian guitarist Thorgeir Stubø, and later with Magni Wentzel. Thorgeir was thrilled to meet Art in the studio. Tragically, Stubø died even before the record came out, but the recording session with Art was one of his finest experiences before his early passing.

RAHSAAN ROLAND KIRK

In October 1964 I had the pleasure of hearing Rahsaan Roland Kirk for the first time. A fantastic multi-instrumentalist, the blind Kirk played saxophones and flute – sometimes two or three instruments at a time. He played at the Johanneshov Ice Stadium in Stockholm, at the big "Newport In Europe" festival. Most of Europe was covered in a heavy fog at the time, and musicians were stranded at various airports far and wide. While we waited for late arrivals, George Wein sat and played swing piano for an hour-and-a-half in order to fill time. Later, Miles Davis played for over an hour. The concert lasted more than eight hours altogether, because of delays.

L-r: Stein Thue, Carmell Jones, Per Borthen and Kirk in Kongsberg, 1967

One by one, musicians arrived in Stockholm – George Russell, Coleman Hawkins, Dave Brubeck – only the *crème de la crème* among jazz players. We were treated to the music of blind pianist Tete Montoliu, and finally Roland Kirk. I had heard of Kirk some years earlier, and I had refused to believe that it was possible to play several saxophones at one time and still make the music swing. He was an accomplished musician, with a wealth of ideas and musical personality.

When the concert was over, close to three in the morning, Kirk asked if there wasn't somewhere we could go to hear even more music. He was in fine spirits. I was staying with Idrees and Jamila Sulieman, who invited all of us, with Kirk and a group of other musicians, to a

Dec 4, 1968

Dear Randi
    Its been so nice being
here again. I feel like I'm
at home in your house thanks
to your hospitality plus the
special way it is here in Oslo.
Many Many thanks for having
me as your guest. I've enjoyed
every moment of it.
May all blessings be yours.

Love
Art Farmer

Pictured with Jimmy Heath, Art Farmer's message in my guest book, 1968

party. Later that morning, everyone was to return to the hotel, because the tour was moving on to the next location in only a few hours. My suitcase was full of cameras, and as we were to split up with Kirk and Edith, his wife at the time, the Suliemans and I took our own cab in the opposite direction.

Suddenly I discovered that my cameras had been loaded into Kirk's taxi. We drove after them like the wind. I would have to get my photo equipment before it was loaded onto the tour bus. Just outside the hotel we saw a pile of luggage that was being packed into the bus. My suitcase was not in sight, however. Ironically, it was Kirk – who was blind – who got my luggage back for me. He ordered the driver to take out all of the luggage and, of course, right in the middle was my suitcase.

I took down Kirk's address when we met, just in case someone in Norway was interested in having him play, and it turned out that the organisers of the Kongsberg Festival did hire him. I wrote to Kirk and asked if he might be willing to come and if he could lower his fees – Kongsberg didn't have a very large budget. Kirk willingly agreed. When he came for the soundcheck, he recognised my voice on the stage, and

Art Farmer, Wynton Marsalis and Red Rodney in Nice, 1981

Kirk with his wife Dorthaan from my guest book, Oslo 1973

A mysterious shot of Kirk in Molde – the result of over-warm chemicals used to develop it before hanging

that impressed me. It had been almost three years since we had first met.

After the concert, he asked where the jam would be, and I offered to take him to a place where the Per Borthen Swing Department band was playing. I should add that I am the world's worst guide, because I have absolutely no sense of direction. Even in a small town like Kongsberg, I have managed to get lost several times. This of course happened again as I was leading Roland Kirk around town.

"I thought you said it was right nearby?" Kirk said. When we finally found the place, the Borthen band asked me where we had been.

"Sightseeing," I said. Kirk liked that. Then he surprised the band thoroughly by producing a clarinet from his jacket and joining in, playing swing era music with them. To the Borthen musicians, Kirk was a typical modernist, but he proved to have an appreciation for swing music, and he was truly enjoying himself in the company of the Norwegian musicians. He played Totti Bergh's tenor saxophone, too. A little later, he asked where

Karin Krog was singing, because now he felt like accompanying her. Eventually, we came to the Grand, and Kirk went straight up onto the stage, joining in and changing style with the greatest of ease – despite the music being more contemporary.

That same year, Kirk played the Molde Festival and experienced for the first time flying in a light plane. "I've been filming you with the Romsdal mountains in the background beneath us," I said. "It's a shame you'll never see the footage."

"This won't be any trip to remember anyway," Kirk moaned.

Roland sent me cassette tape letters. He was the first one who told me about Miles Davis' new record *Bitches Brew*, which represented a revolutionary style innovation for Miles. Kirk played excerpts from the record in his cassette letter, with the background noises of television and his son Stritch running around the apartment. Stritch was named after one of Roland's musical instruments. Roland was capable of listening to more than one music source at the same time, while keeping them separate. He actually enjoyed a lot of sound.

In Molde, Kirk played with his own quartet, performing on clarinet, stritch, flute and tenor saxophone. It was a memorable concert. He also sang with great feeling. Later, in 1970, he had a concert in the Oslo University auditorium, and an engagement for Club 7. In 1973, after Roland had played with The Vibration Society at Club 7, he came to my house together with his new wife Dorthaan. She was very nice, really, and I felt that Roland enjoyed her company. The next and last time I saw him, he had suffered a stroke in 1975, and I felt a little sad. I knew it was difficult for him to play, but that didn't stop him. Despite being incapacitated in one arm, he still managed to give the audience at Club 7 a memorable evening.

Dorthaan has kept in touch all the time ever since I first met her. Our next meeting – in 1988 – was to be a big surprise. I was invited to do a radio programme in Newark at WBGO-FM, in connection with my TV shows in Manhattan, and who else but Dorthaan was wishing me welcome. As WBGO's Music Coordinator, she was responsible for all the musical events, arranging interviews with musicians, and taking care of the ticket giveaways. It was great to meet her again, and since then, we at least keep in contact at Christmas.

With Ben Webster, 1965

BEN WEBSTER

Ben Webster first came to the Metropol in February, 1965, already regarded as "master of the ballads" thanks to his sense of the lyrical and his personal style. He was a member of many famous bands, but his stints with Duke Ellington were the most significant, and it was the latter he talked most about privately.

He arrived in Oslo aboard the Danish ferry with his fiancée, Grethe Kemp Pitts – Ben never travelled by plane. The ferry trip had taken its toll – or perhaps it was Ben's weakness for the Danish "Elephant" beer on board – because he was unable to play the first engagement,

246

scheduled for the evening he arrived. He tried, but soon discovered he was suffering from "sea legs".

"I still have these sea legs," he explained a couple of days later. When he eventually did get back into shape and played at the Metropol, we were treated to a glorious musical feast. No tenor player has since been able to match his tone. When he played, it was as if the notes remained suspended in the room long afterwards – like musical smoke rings. It was a treat to hear him play in Norway.

"I've never flown," Ben said, "that's why I haven't been in Europe with the Jazz at the Philharmonic tours or with Duke Ellington. But I like it here and I wouldn't mind living in Scandinavia. People are so lovable, and I've met so many fine people – not the least of them being Grethe," he added, smiling. He was head over heels in love with his "Grethe fix", as he usually referred to her. Grethe was a jazz singer, but Ben had never heard her sing.

Ben had spent a lot of time in London and had become a good friend of Ronnie Scott, as well as a frequent attraction at the Londoner's jazz club. On one occasion when I was visiting Ronnie Scott's, Ben had not yet arrived, and when he did, he appeared a little under the weather. He spent a lot of time getting ready to play, and when he spotted me in the crowd, he began to make a long speech, talking

Kenny Drew, Freddie Hubbard and Ben Webster in Molde, 1967

about me for at least ten minutes as both friend and critic. I was embarrassed and felt in a way responsible for delaying his performance even longer. When the band began to play, he deliberately gave away all the solos to the other band members – "Play, piano man. Play, bass man" – and eventually he had to be escorted off the stage. This was a Tuesday night. I promised Ben I would come back on Friday.

"I'll be gone by then," Ben spat, angry because Ronnie Scott had asked him to leave the stage. Friday, however, he was back again, and sober. He gave us a fantastic evening.

Ben Webster always came to visit me when he was in Oslo, although it was only the first time that he brought Grethe with him. Once we met in Molde, where he performed brilliantly. He had come by train, and he was pleased to learn that I would also be taking the train back to Oslo.

"We have to have escorts, Randi and me – you have to take care of us, Trygve," Ben said. Trygve was the drummer whose job it was to take care of Ben during the festival. When I said that I would be escorted by Joachim Berendt, the administrator of the Berlin festival, Ben looked worried. The last time Ben had been in Berlin, he had also had a case of "sea legs", so much so that he never even made it up onto the stage.

Ben and his fiancée Grethe in Oslo, February 1965

"I'll talk with Joachim," I promised. Joachim wasn't phased. In the morning, he and I waited down in the dining room. I saw that Trygve went upstairs to get Ben out of his room, but Trygve probably wanted to have Ben to himself, because they slipped out of the hotel unnoticed, while we sat waiting. Finally, we had to take a cab because we were by now very late. We radioed from the cab that we would be arriving late and asked that the train wait for us. As we approached Åndalsnes, we spotted Trygve in his car coming in the opposite direction. He must have figured something was wrong, since the train was waiting. When we finally arrived on the railroad platform, Ben stuck his head out of a window: "Randi, what took you so long?"

During the entire journey, Ben moved from window to window, filming the beautiful countryside with his home camera. He was a good amateur film maker and left behind a considerable amount of film memories from his life behind the camera.

Joachim also talked at length with Ben, and it was obvious that the old grudge from Berlin was forgotten. The result was that Berendt produced a record with saxophonists Don Byas and Ben Webster in Germany. When the record was released, it said in the liner notes that the recording had come about thanks to Randi Hultin, during the course of a train trip from Åndalsnes to Oslo.

A long time afterwards, Trygve visited me with Ben, and it turned out they had planned a tour with our mutual tenor sax friend. The dark irony of the situation was that Trygve, who had a pilot's licence, had to remain on the ground, driving Ben all over the country because of Ben's incurable fear of flying.

When Ben Webster died in 1973, he was on a playing job in Amsterdam. He was sixty-four years old.

TAYLOR AND GRIFFIN

It is always a relief for me – and most probably for others, too – when the guests at Gartnerveien take over the cooking themselves. Webster's tenor saxophone colleague Johnny Griffin is one of those who has displayed his culinary expertise in my kitchen. He made a delicious chilli when he and drummer Art Taylor visited.

They actually played for three weeks, including a television recording – for only 700 Norwegian kroner (fifty dollars each) – when they were in Oslo to play Club 7 and Down Town. Their first gig was at the Metropol in June 1964 – a job that came about after Taylor had written to me. "We are top musicians who must have top pay," he wrote, and listed the instruments they played.

I had to smile when I read this letter. Of course I knew what they played and who they were. I wrote back:

"Dear Top Musicians. Who gave you my address, since you seem to think it is necessary to introduce yourselves? We will gladly hire you,

L-r: Björn Pedersen, Art Taylor, Kenny Drew and Johnny Griffin at the Metropol, 1965

but you will receive the same pay as anyone else. We only hire top musicians." I signed it "Love – or best regards, Randi." I wasn't quite sure which was correct.

In their next letter, there was a greeting from AT (Art Taylor) and the initials "L O B R". They had gotten a kick out of the way I had closed my letter to them, dubious as it sounded.

In January 1965, Taylor and Griffin came to Oslo with pianist Kenny Drew. This was during a musicians' strike against restaurant owners, under the leadership of the Norwegian Musicians' Union. Suddenly, the union decided that we would have to cancel the planned Metropol concert. I found this insane.

250

Johnny, Kenny and Art all got Norwegian sweaters, 1965

Art Taylor and Johnny Griffin montage from my guest book, 1964

The bird called "Dizzy" like Johnny's playing

The fact that Metropol was defined as a restaurant should have had nothing to do with the dispute, since the musicians were paid by the jazz club organisers, not the owner of the establishment. And of course there would be a lot of striking restaurant musicians who would now be free to come and listen to top jazz performers. What about the American musician who was giving a concert in the University auditorium? Was that any different a situation than this jazz concert we had planned?

But my arguments fell on deaf ears. I was asked to call the government officials who deal with civil disputes, and I did so, all day long, even talking to the top man.

Nothing helped. The answer was no – irrevocably. When I expressed my disappointment, the administrator said: "Are you aware that you have been able to reach a Cabinet Minister during the course of just one day? That is sensational."

"What difference does that make?" I replied. "The answer is still no."

Then I tried the Musicians' Union, going straight to the central office. After a fight, I managed to get Taylor, Griffin and Drew a special dispensation. The American musicians never did understand what had really gone on. Eivind Solberg had honoured them by giving each one a Norwegian sweater because they had been obliged to sit and wait at their hotel, without playing.

In all other restaurants in town, there was only taped music played – even on New Year's Eve. "Great atmosphere, featuring technical music" read the advertisement for the Regnbuen restaurant. At the Bristol, they had rigged up display window mannequins on the bandstands, with tape recorders playing music next to them.

Taylor and Griffin lived for a long while in France and worked regularly for a time at Jazzland. Once when they visited me at

Jean-Luc Ponty and Yusef Lateef, Kongsberg, 1966

Gartnerveien, they talked about how jobs had been so scarce in Paris that Griffin had taken work as a cocktail pianist. He wanted to demonstrate this, and began to accompany Art, who loved to sing – especially Sinatra melodies. I still have a funny tape recording of 'Randi With The Laughing Face', with Art singing and Johnny at the keys.

Griffin moved to Southern France, while Taylor moved to the centre of Harlem in a beautiful apartment. He had enough to do, with his own radio and TV programmes, in addition to drumming. He also had published two fine jazz books before he died of cancer in 1995, sixty-five years old.

JEAN-LUC PONTY

In 1966, the Kongsberg organisers broke the news that they were able to entice Clark Terry and Dexter Gordon over the Atlantic, and I gladly conveyed this information through my newspaper column. With barely a week until the festival was to begin, Per Ottersen and Kjell Gunnar Hoff came from Kongsberg to my house. I was sitting at the dinner table when they told me what had happened. Neither Dexter nor Terry had returned a signed contract to them. The festival

Tommy Flanagan, Ella's pianist, was a regular visitor to my house – from my guest book

officials thought that when they had sent a contract in the mail, it would then be returned, signed and without a problem. This hadn't happened, and now they needed musicians – fast. They had hired saxophonist Yusef Lateef and I got a hold of sax player Bill Barron. I had also heard a young French violinist in Antibes who was unforgettable. His name was Jean-Luc Ponty.

A telegram was sent, and almost without realising it, Jean-Luc Ponty was on his way to Kongsberg – although at first he thought Kongsberg was in Germany. When he landed at Fornebu, he was picked up in a private plane and flown to an airport outside Kongsberg, from which he was driven directly to the cinema stage door. On stage already were bassist Niels-Henning Ørsted Pedersen and drummer Alex Riel. The two Danes were totally unknown to the young Ponty, but after a quick presentation, the concert could begin. It was a howling success.

Ponty, Lateef and Barron later met again at the Knutehytta highlands cabin, where the festival arrangers offered folk music and dancing and gave Ponty the chance to try the Norwegian harding fiddle for the first time in his life. The atmosphere at this festival was one of the most exciting I have ever experienced, and Ponty was grateful to have got the job. That same year, I recommended him to the Prague Festival, replacing Stuff Smith, and that was the beginning of his international career. Later he toured the world with his own stable of top flight musicians. He now lives in the United States.

Annette Peacock has been a popular guest both in Norway and at my house – in fact I'm godmother to her daughter, Avalon

CHAPTER 13

Bill Evans – The Lyrical

T he first time I talked with pianist Bill Evans, he was standing at Fornebu Airport. The year was 1966. He had just given a superb performance at the Edvard Munch museum and was on his way back to Denmark the same evening. I had been at the concert and was still bewitched by his lyrical playing. Eddie Gomez's fine bass solo was also fresh in my mind. The concert had been taped for television, and the audience, which consisted mainly of musicians and jazz aficionados, had been asked not to applaud after each solo. But when Gomez had played, the house came down. We couldn't resist applauding him. Alex Riel, who played drums, had told me that the group would be leaving Oslo that same evening, but it was still coincidental that we should meet at Fornebu. I was there to meet the Charles Lloyd quartet on their way to play a concert in the university auditorium.

It was a warm meeting between the two American bands at the airport. Seldom was Evans so glib and full of laughter. Usually he was solemn and reticent, as aloof in his dreams and thoughts as he was in his music. I felt this very strongly when we met again the next time, during the jazz festival in Kongsberg in 1970. He was there with his manager and friend, Helen Kean, and I actually met them on the street on their way the cinema. In fact, this was the first time I had ever seen someone go to the movies during a festival. Normally, a festival town runs movies only after a concert, and then both the musicians and the

Bill Evans in Oslo, 1975

audience usually head for the jazz clubs. I asked Evans if I could have an interview with him for radio. He answered that I should come to his hotel later that evening. That was inconvenient for me, however. "We'll do it tomorrow then," he said, and I must admit that this suggestion did not sound promising.

SCANDINAVIAN HOSPITALITY

I sat in the reading room of the Hotel Gyldenløve, across from the reception area. There were many musicians here, as well as a lot of South African fans of Dollar Brand. Dollar himself entertained us with a lecture on yoga, while standing on his head: "Yoga is meant to be healthy. It has changed my wife and me a lot," he expounded. "Yoga has made my wife pregnant."

Max, one of Dollar's bachelor friends, declared that he would never dare to try yoga.

While I was there, Bill Evans suddenly appeared at the reception desk to ask for his mail. He was unable to sleep, and he was urgently awaiting an express letter from America, which he needed to get hold of as soon as possible. When he caught sight of me, he waved and said that he would be able to do the interview right then. It wasn't long afterwards that we were sitting in my room with a tape recorder standing on the table between us. It was four in the morning, the birds were chirping, and out on the street, we could hear the last jam session guests making their way home.

If Bill Evans was generally quiet, he was also capable of opening up and giving a frank interview. I felt sympathy for him. I knew about his drug problem, but I felt that what bothered him most was the fact that he was constantly on the move, that he was always under pressure to keep the trio together and take responsibility for them all of the time. "Can you imagine if somebody would give me a scholarship award? I would really be happy to be able just to sit and write music for a year," he said.

Bill was happy to have been able to come to the Kongsberg festival. "This is an excellent audience, and it's weird to think that a little place like Kongsberg can hire musicians from all over the world just because they like jazz here. I admire the enthusiasm of the organisers who do

all of this without earning a penny for it. Every jazz musician should appreciate this. At least I do," he said. "Jazz can't exist without somebody working for it with love. These days here in Kongsberg have really meant something to me. It's a beautiful place, and I've been able to relax."

"You've been most places in Europe, haven't you?"

"Not really. I would like to travel behind the Iron Curtain. We have been invited, but it's never become a reality. We've been in Scandinavia often, though, especially in Copenhagen. Scandinavia has been good to us. We notice great hospitality, and it's always a fine audience. Actually, we should have gone to Japan, too. I've wanted to go to Japan all my life. Hope we can do it. Haven't been in South America either. People who have been down there say that we have a lot of fans there, but I don't know who to contact."

It struck me that Bill Evans was really quite humble. It was strange to be privy to his dreams and wishes.

NEVER SELF-SATISFIED

"In Sweden, you made a really fine record with Monica Zetterlund. Did you live there for a time?"

"No, Monica had recorded my 'Waltz For Debbie' in Swedish, and it was sent to me in New York. I was surprised when I heard it. It was really good. When we met at the Gyllene Cirkeln, it was almost like we had known each other already. We became good friends, and I wanted to make a record with her. Philips set up a record date, but we didn't really have much time together. We were three weeks at the Gyllene Cirkeln, and during the last week, we practised at Monica's house before we met in the studio. The entire recording was done in only four or five hours. A lot of people over here talk about the record, but I really wish it would be released in America."

"You have played with a trio for many years, haven't you?"

"Yes, for one reason or another I've always wanted to play with a trio – because then I'm more in control of the music. Although I thought it was a great experience to play with Miles Davis, I've always had this urge to work as an independent. Still, to be a solo pianist is almost impossible. Art Tatum was one of the few who could do it – and I'm no Tatum. So, I decided that a trio was the closest thing to what I wanted. But it is a big responsibility holding a trio together, and it costs money.

"After the time with Miles, I met bass player Scott LaFaro and drummer Paul Motian, and we all had the same attitude. We decided to work together to make a successful trio. There weren't many jobs, unfortunately, so each of us worked at other things at the same time. But as soon as a job came up, we dropped whatever we were doing. Then we got a record contract, and the records started selling."

"But LaFaro was killed, wasn't he?"

"Yes, tragically – and then Paul left the trio. It's sad that the two

My painting of Bill

who were responsible for helping the trio become well known never got to reap any of the benefits of its later success. What they were doing was not enough to live on during the first years – not before things started to turn around. By then they were gone. That's just how things were. But since 1960, everything has been going fine, and I haven't had any problem holding the group together."

"Do you play a lot when you are at home? I mean – privately?"

"I play a lot privately, but the trio has never had rehearsals. Not since it started. The cohesion happens on the stage or in the studio. The music develops by itself at each concert. There are times when we might need to practise a little more, though. We play in New York about twenty weeks a year – and then we go out to the West Coast and to Europe a couple of times. Including recording, it comes out to about forty work weeks per year. We prefer to be home, but short tours are all right. Sometimes we get a chance to spend a few days in the same place, and that's nice.

"We get to play what we like, even though I am never satisfied with my own music. I always try to go a step further – always have other ambitions. I want to write more music – something more serious, for example, or music for film. New melodies. But I'll probably play until I go to the grave. I'm never happy if I can't play. After a period without a gig, I get depressed. Everything seems so meaningless. A musician can't just stop playing. You might think of quitting sometimes, but it's too difficult to do."

SOURCES OF INSPIRATION

"Are there some musicians who have meant something special to you – not necessarily pianists?"

"Of course. Everybody from Bird to Getz, and many musicians who aren't even known but who people have heard. Bud Powell was a strong influence on me. When I was sixteen or seventeen, I first heard 'Dexter Side' by Bud, and that made a strong impression on me. I listened to many musicians – big bands, Benny Goodman, Duke Ellington, Don Byas, Earl Hines – but as I said, the one who influenced me more than anyone was Bud Powell."

"Hampton Hawes once mentioned that you used to listen to him."

"I met him on the West Coast and I like him very much, but he came a little too late to be a strong influence on me. He gave me a backhanded compliment once. He said that he had heard my record: 'I like it, I don't care what anybody says.' It was very sincere. I appreciated what he said. I also like the way he plays very much. In fact, I did hear a record of Hampton Hawes a long time ago that I thought was very soulful. It was on an old seventy-eight, 'It Must Be You Or No One'. I mentioned to Hampton that it had a lot of soul. That is sort of the same feeling I got from Bud. He had a lot of depth, which seemed to be coming from way down deep. I always liked that.

"There are different kinds of feelings. There are feelings that are very emotional, but they don't come from as deep a level. Then there are some feelings which don't make you emotional. They don't make you cry, they don't make you laugh, they don't make you feel anything but profound, and that's the feeling I got from Bud. It's like the feeling you get from Beethoven, maybe. You know that it's something deep. It's not that it is so beautiful, in the sense that it's pretty or lush like Rachmaninoff – which I love nevertheless – but it's a different kind of thing. That's what I would hear in Bud. When I think about Charlie Parker, Dizzy Gillespie and Bud, I think that Bud is very underrated. People always talk about Bird, Dizzy or Miles, who have become the giants, but Bud comes in there among those names, too, it's just that he has never gotten the attention he deserves. I think he's a bigger source of inspiration than people realise.

"The same is true for other musicians, for instance the drummer. It doesn't take long before those who imitate are told that they sound just like Philly, or Bud, but there's nobody like the original. I remember the first time I heard Bud, I had never heard anything like it. I mentioned this to Dexter Gordon when we met in Copenhagen and he said that probably nobody ever had. And that's the truth. That was the first time I heard a pianist playing a solo that started, grew, and was ended. It was so thorough, and it showed his depth as a musician. I have never heard a jazz solo that has affected me so strongly. What else could you say about Bud, except that it's a shame people aren't aware of what he has meant. Look at the rock music, or today's pop music. Bud has contributed to the origins of those branches, too.

"When we perform now, I notice that people are more and more interested in jazz and what it's all about. Young people between the ages of eighteen and twenty are starting to show interest, while earlier they only wanted to listen to rock."

JAZZ AND POP

"Can't pop music also lead to an interest in jazz?"

"It ought to, because beat and blues are fundamentally the same, but the emotional and intellectual challenge is so low in this music that if one is not searching for something more valuable, one will not find it. It has to come naturally, when a young person is mature enough for it. Then maybe he'll turn to jazz – because it's actually the same beat, but in a more serious manner. There is more music in jazz. I don't mean to be snobbish, but I know for instance what it cost me to learn a little bit about music. I also know how much shorter the trip is for a pop artist to reach the top, or to learn how to play his instrument. There aren't that many geniuses – only a few."

"What kind of music did you begin playing?"

"Classical. I started to take lessons when I was six years old, but as soon as I heard jazz, I became really interested. I had my first gigs when I was only thirteen. Later on, when I became a professional musician, I played everything I could, and classical besides. I have a degree in music, and I still play classical for my own enjoyment."

"Do you have any favourites among classical composers?"

"Bach, of course, but I also like many contemporary composers. Bartok, Stravinsky, Hindermith, Ravel, Debussy – all of it is good music that gives you something – whether it's a good melody, a symphony or a solo. I think, for instance, that melodies like 'Danny Boy' and 'Londonderry Air' are just as good as any other music I hear. Any good melody is a piece of art. I can mention names like Bach, Bartok and others, but they are already great."

This conversation with Bill Evans has become a cherished memory. I'll never forget this strange early morning discussion in Kongsberg. Parts of the interview were used on the radio, and in 1986, his comments about Bud Powell were published as an introduction in Francis Paudras's monumental work about Bud's life.

I met Bill Evans again a couple of times – once when he played a regrettably ill-attended concert at Chat Noir. The room was only half full of guests. The concert was recorded for radio, but the arrangers had forgotten to inform Bill of this fact. He was quite upset – and here again, I was reminded of the problem of having total responsibility himself. Bill had accepted my invitation after the concert, but instead he remained at the Chat Noir theatre to discuss conditions for the use of the recording, while bassist Eddie Gomez came home with me.

The next – and last – time I saw Bill was in Molde in 1980. I met him in the evening when he arrived, and he wanted to get together the next day. But when the concert was over, he was rushed to the airport and put aboard a plane. It turned out he would be spending the night at a hotel in another country, since it would be cheaper that way, according to his manager.

Bill Evans died shortly thereafter, on 15 September, 1980, just fifty-one years old. He was one of jazz's finest innovators, and one of our greatest lyrical players.

TERJE MOSNES

Greetings Molde, 1980 – shortly before he died that year

JAZZ MOLDE

CHAPTER 14

The Pianists Are Coming

In March 1966, I got a phone call from New York. On the other end of the line was George Avakian. First he introduced himself by giving me best regards from trumpet player Donald Byrd, and then he enquired if I might be interested in presenting the Charles Lloyd quartet in Oslo? "Exceptionally fine musicians," he said. I had heard of Lloyd, but the others – Jack DeJohnette on drums, Cecil McBee on bass, and the youngest of all of them, Keith Jarrett, who was supposed to be a fantastic pianist – were unknown to me.

"Okay, send me a letter," I said. "I'll check with the clubs." A number of letters passed back and forth between us. Petter Petterson in Molde was contacted, as well as all of the clubs. There was a possibility of a job at the Edderkoppen, where Club 7 were holding their arrangements at the time. "But you can't expect to be well paid," I wrote. "In Norway, we have to examine the wares, check out the quality of the goods. If the audience likes you, then there may be new jobs in it for you."

The audience loved them. In the course of eight months, the Charles Lloyd quartet gave five concerts in Norway. The first stop in Europe was Stockholm, followed by the Edderkoppen. Rumours reached us from Stockholm that they were sensational and in *Dagbladet* I entitled an article "Lloyd To Club 7?".

"We can't afford them!" said Attila Horvath, who was the man behind all of Club 7's activities at the time. "You can't write things like

L-r: Charles Lloyd, Cecil McBee, Keith Jarrett, George Avakian and Jack DeJohnette having dinner at my house, 1966

that!" Nevertheless two concerts were realised – one in the theatre hall and one in the club itself, plus a radio broadcast. The concert by Lloyd was something entirely new for us – modern, yet completely spellbinding at the same time. Lloyd thrusting around his saxophone was a sight in itself because he had a Coltrane spirit. Keith Jarrett stood as he played the piano, often plucking the strings inside – something completely new to us. We were fascinated. The melodies were special – original compositions of Lloyd and we listened intently, swept along as if the band "lifted off" from the stage when the music reached a climax. What technique they had! Jarrett was amazing, sounding like he had at least twenty fingers and musicians in the audience had the righteous gaze of disciples. This was a fun experience.

When the four musicians came to my home the first evening, they were dead tired but very happy to be served a plateful of newly made spaghetti. I don't know of anyone more appreciative of my spaghetti than the Lloyd Quartet and Keith Jarrett must have eaten more than eight servings at Gartnerveien.

That night, after we had eaten, we sat around the living room coffee table and talked. One of the few people who had come to the house, aside from the quartet, was Christian Killengren from Club 7. It was such a relaxed atmosphere – so relaxed that everyone began to fall asleep. We all awoke suddenly to the crash of a vase that Christian had accidentally knocked over, discovering to our mutual enjoyment that we had all fallen asleep during the after-dinner small talk, in a kind of chain reaction. The memory of this episode has always been for me the ultimate example of a relaxed dinner party. There is no doubt that these guests felt totally at home.

On 8 May, we celebrated Keith's birthday. He sat at the piano the entire evening and only raised his right hand off the keyboard to greet guests who dropped in.

"Take it easy," said Lloyd to Keith, "you've been playing long

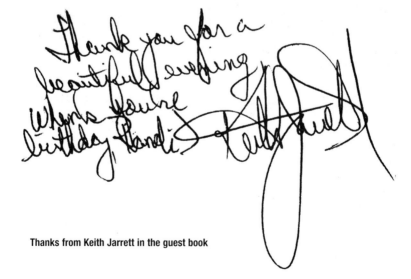

Thanks from Keith Jarrett in the guest book

Keith Jarrett recording his first solo LP while in Oslo to play with Miles Davis, 1971

enough." I, however, didn't agree since it was such a pleasure to hear Keith play the blues, uninterrupted. He even played stride piano like Teddy Wilson at times. When Keith was officially twenty-one years old, all of us joined in 'Happy Birthday' under Lloyd's direction. It was a very advanced, highly harmonious version. Afterwards, I made tape recordings of Keith's impulsive piano improvisations. He was quite spontaneous in his younger years, and his playing was filled with surprises.

LEFT BEHIND IN ÅLESUND

The Lloyd Quartet took the Molde Jazz Festival by storm that same year. At the end of the festival, I was to take the evening flight out of Vigra airport in Ålesund – this was at the time when Molde didn't have an airport of its own. When I arrived at Ålesund, I was met by the smiling faces of the Lloyd musicians.

"Thank God you came, Randi. We were supposed to be in Amsterdam right now, but we didn't get our wake-up calls, so we've been waiting here for the next plane for the last eleven hours. Can we go home with you?"

Of course they could – but I wasn't sure I had anything in the house to feed them. At the Grønland subway station in Oslo, they had recently opened a sundry shop that stayed open until ten-thirty pm, so that when we got to Fornebu airport, I called them, explaining that the famous American jazz quartet had missed their plane, and that it would be a shame if they wouldn't be able to get some food while they were forced to stay overnight in Oslo. I begged them to remain open until we arrived. Getting a hesitant yes, I then read them my shopping list: spaghetti, ground beef, beer...

The shopkeeper did agree to stay open half an hour later than usual, just for us. While the taxi waited, Keith and I rushed in and picked up what I had ordered. I've seen this scene many times since in my mind's eye – Keith Jarrett and me, each with one end of a box of food, laughing, struggling up the subway staircase. The night was saved.

At home, Mrs Lloyd helped me make the meal, and we had an enjoyable dinner. Since this was 9 August, we were also able to make this a celebration of Jack DeJohnette's twenty-fifth birthday.

"WE WANT LLOYD"

The next time the group came to Oslo, in October 1966, they were to give a concert in the university auditorium which was to be recorded for an album. They had a few extra days off, and naturally, they were invited again for more spaghetti at Gartnerveien. One evening I took the quartet to Kongen, the place where Club 7 were holding their arrangements. Keith entertained by playing drums, while Jack played the piano. The audience actually didn't know who was who. Keith played great drums, and Jack had played piano in a cocktail orchestra before he joined Charles Lloyd.

The quartet was also invited to the Bergen Festival of the Arts, and in 1967 we saw one another again in the Soviet Union. Tallin had its first international jazz festival for which Avakian had negotiated for an entire year with the Soviets. However, when the quartet finally were accepted and showed up, they learned that they were not even mentioned in the programme and for their first engagement, they were relegated to an empty television studio. I was present to witness the Soviet festival official's shock when Lloyd refused to play in the studio.

"We came here to play for the Soviet people, not for an empty room with TV cameras," snapped Lloyd, whereupon he demanded to be driven back to the hotel.

The quartet and I stayed in the same hotel, where we rigged our own entertainment each evening. Keith played the melodica and Jack the drums, while George and I performed skits and gags. Outside our hotel room, there was always a big, stocky Russian woman sitting with her arms folded – pouting gloomily. She was definitely not used to jam sessions in the room late at night.

Not before the very last day did Lloyd get to play a concert, and as it turned out, even that was chaotic. The quartet were supposed to play for a quarter of an hour, but that for them was not even sufficient time to warm up. In the end they played for forty-five minutes. People went wild – there was excitement in the air and I filmed the concert without interference from the Soviets. People had come all the way from the Chinese border to listen to this American group – the grape vine had spread the word – and no one was disappointed.

The Lloyd Quartet were due to be followed by an unfortunate Russian trio, but as they entered they were met by five thousand people screaming, "We want Lloyd! We want Lloyd!" Three official-looking men came up onto the stage to calm the crowd – "Comrades! Be silent! Listen to reason..." – but "We want Lloyd!" continued like a rhythmically-determined chant of defiance. Eventually the officials had to leave the stage and sent on instead a Russian symphony orchestra from Tallin with a violin and vibraphone soloist who played 'Laura' in a Hollywood "fluff" style.

LLOYD QUARTET DISSOLVED

Keith Jarrett's next visit to Oslo was not until September, 1969, when he had jobs at Club 7, the Kroa, and in Trondheim. This time he came with his own trio, and he seemed happy to be back in Norway.

"I'm glad to see trees and green nature again. People seem to like us better in Scandinavia. We're more accepted over here. At home, we almost don't get anything to do. People don't go out – they sit and watch TV and think that that's as good as a live concert. Maybe we should do like trick or treat, go around from door to door and ask if we can play for them – whether they like it or not!"

Keith played soprano sax during this visit. He had been playing the instrument for some five or six years, but only when he felt the urge.

"I can't play the soprano as well as I would like to," he said. "Acoustic string instruments are the most beautiful, the most personal. If I had to choose an instrument, I'd choose strings or maybe wooden flute. But guitar is another instrument I like. If I ever get tired of playing the piano, I'd like to play the guitar. Just for myself, not professionally. To me, the guitar is a very personal instrument."

Around this time, Keith was getting little work in America having gone six months without a job after leaving the Lloyd group, and his personal finances suffered. When he came for a visit one day with his wife Margot, I told him about all the cheap charter tours we Norwegians could take with Tjæreborg, a discount travel company started by a minister (we called it Tjæreborg-presten – "priest"). Keith wondered whether he and Margot might qualify for one of these trips, even though they were Americans.

The last time Keith Jarrett visited me was in November, 1971. He had just played a concert in Miles Davis's group, and I was invited backstage to say hello.

"I'm going to make my first solo album for Manfred Eicher while I'm in Oslo," he told me. "Maybe you could come to the studio? And of course you have to invite me to your house for spaghetti!"

On that occasion, he wrote in the guest book: "Wherever I am, I know there is warmth waiting for me at your house. And it is hard for you to stay warm today when the weather of the general Soul grows colder and winds are stronger from the North. You are one of the few people who are able to fan their own fires with the flame of your heart. And there are some of us still left, I hope."

The next time I saw Keith, he was playing the Molde Festival in 1973. He was the youngest piano star, while Eubie Blake, at ninety, was the oldest. As Keith played, I escorted Eubie backstage so that he could hear better. I was also curious as to what Eubie's reaction to this

L-r: Vallace Berry, Miko, Margot, Keith, Gus Nemett and, seated, Magni Wentzel

music might be. Eubie kept looking at his watch during the performance, and I wondered if he thought it was boring. This was very unusual music, and Keith played without ever saying a word to the audience. When he had finished, Eubie said to me, "Forty-eight minutes non-stop, and did you see how he used his hands? Crossed, like this ..."Eubie demonstrated. He had been very observant.

"Randi, could you take me to Mr Jarrett, please? I want to find out what he called this composition," said Eubie.

"I imagine it was a spontaneously improvised piece," I answered, leading Eubie backstage, but since I was covering the concert for the radio I was also interested in being able to give the tune a title.

Keith was visibly pleased that Eubie wanted to meet him, and when I suggested that I needed a name for the composition, he asked me what the date was. I told him, and he replied, "Okay, you can call it 'August The Third'."

When it was Eubie's turn to give his concert, the grand piano had already been played by Sam Rivers and Christian Reim. Keith, hearing that the instrument was out of tune, stopped the concert. "I'm going to tune the piano for him. Eubie deserves to play a newly-tuned grand."

During Eubie's concert, Keith sat on the floor and listened reverently to the music. This was the Keith I knew – but I was beginning to feel that he was becoming aloof from his audiences.

"Don't forget to be yourself," I said.

"Do you mean you think I've changed?" asked Keith.

"Yes, I'm afraid so."

WORLD CLASS KEITH JARRETT

When Keith Jarrett played in Molde with his trio in 1986, I looked forward to meeting him again. Since the time we had met twenty years earlier, he had become a world class star – the best pianist in the world for some people – and was widely held to be a stylistic innovator. He had recorded a considerable number of records since his first one for Manfred, and he is certainly the only person to have released ten records from just one tour in Japan. I had heard that Keith had changed, but I thought I knew him well enough that he would be happy to see me if I met him at the airport. Perhaps he would say a few words for the TV news reporters if I could get him to stop and say hello. I normally don't meet musicians at airports, but this time I wanted to make an exception, just to surprise Keith.

The moving pianist

He arrived in a private jet – and he descended the boarding ramp walking backwards, face away from the cameras. When he approached the little girl dressed in her national costume who was to hand him a welcome bouquet, he snatched the flowers from her hand and hurried to get into a waiting car. I touched him on the shoulder.

"Keith, don't you remember me? It's Randi."

"Yes, I do. Not now," he barked, without turning around to look at me.

I made no further attempts to meet him during the festival. Of course I attended the concert, but I disliked the cold atmosphere and the impersonal nature of the artist that pervaded the hall. After his opening number, he demanded that the piano be moved further upstage. After the next number, the lights were too hot for him. Although he and the other members of the trio delivered first class jazz to the audience, I sorely missed the personal contact with the public. I was disappointed and sat there with a lump in my throat. What in the world had happened to my dear friend Keith? The young, warm, enthusiastic pianist with the twinkle in his eye?

HAMPTON HAWES

Jarrett is not the only pianist who has had a standing invitation at my home. I have fond memories of a couple of the greatest piano players in history who stayed with me for a fortnight. First Hampton Hawes, every Norwegian pianist's idol during the 1950s; and then Jaki Byard, Mingus's piano man for many years. The private recordings I made of these pianists are a continual source of joy.

Hampton Hawes was in Europe in October, 1967, basically because of his wife, Jacqueline, who was a school teacher. She had taken a sabbatical year and was spending it studying how English was taught in European schools. She wrote from Copenhagen and mentioned that she would like to come to Oslo. Her husband was a good pianist whose name was Hampton Hawes, she wrote, and could he maybe get a job playing in Oslo?

I was quite surprised and called Club 7 at the Kongen restaurant. They were very interested. Hampton was hired on the spot. After I wrote an article about him in *Dagbladet*, the phone never stopped ringing. Einar "Pastor'n" Iversen was first on the line, asking if it was really true that Hawes was coming. I told him that Hamp was sitting alive and well at that very moment in my living room and that all Einar had to do was show up at the Kongen later that night to hear him.

Hampton played a series of four engagements with Svein Christiansen and Arild Andersen as his rhythm accompaniment. He also played a lot of good music privately at Gartnerveien, attracting even my piano-playing ex-husband, who came to pay tribute to his

With Hampton and Jacqueline at my house, 1967

Hampton's drawing of an aeroplane, 1967

idol. They alternated, playing for each other, as well as together four-handed.

Hampton was a quiet and patient person, always cheerful. I knew about his past as an addict, plus his desertion from the Korean war, but he didn't look any worse for wear after these experiences. He even asked if we had a museum commemorating the Second World War. Unfortunately, the Museum of the Resistance didn't open until after he had left.

Hampton recorded a programme for radio during his visit in Oslo, and he was very satisfied with his stay. In England, he had been refused a work permit by the Musicians' Union, but through contacts on the Continent, I was able to arrange credentials for the rest of his tour. He recorded four albums during the course of his stay in Europe. He had already released a number of records in the United States, notably the trilogy LPs recorded in just twenty-four hours – *All Night Session* – featuring Red Mitchell on bass.

Hampton always felt at home with us and once borrowed

Hampton Hawes at the piano, 1967

Hey! Randi,
You have a lot of souls,
I hope that Some day we will
meet again and If we don't I hope
we feel like we did anyway
Your friend
Hampton Hawes

19307 Broadacres
Compton Calif.
U. S. A.
Phone NE 67663

Hampton and Jacqueline from my guest book

Christina's bicycle to ride down to Manglerud and go shopping, something my husband certainly never expected ten years earlier when he bought the bike. As soon as Hamp had a little free time, he would sit down to play the piano, or he drew. He was making a drawing that was to be a gift to me, but I was not allowed to look or to know even what it was of. He wanted to give me a picture personally drawn by himself, and he even went to town to buy crayons. When the picture was finished, he gave it to me – an SAS aeroplane – and was proud to learn that I later had it framed.

A long time after Hampton had visited me, I came across a book he had written, called *Raise Up Off Me*. I was very surprised to read of all the anguished events of his life, and even more surprised that he devoted a page-and-a-half to his recollections of his visit to Oslo. First, he remembered being amazed that I had said he and Jacqueline could simply go directly to my house, even though I wouldn't be home from work until later: the door is open and the refrigerator is full. "Who would say something like that in Los Angeles?" Hampton wrote. He also recalled that his stay in Oslo opened doors for him professionally, as well: "After only one job in Europe, things started happening. Randi made contacts, and I was met at the airport in every new city. I played, made records, and suddenly I felt important." This was surprising reading. I had thought of his visit to Oslo as our honour.

Hampton was divorced from Jacqueline after a time, and he did remarry, but it was Jacque who was with him at his deathbed. He lay in a coma for two weeks before he died on 22 May, 1977, forty-eight years old, without regaining consciousness.

JAKI BYARD

When Jaki Byard guested at Oslo with Charles Mingus one year, the Molde officials had already planned to ask him if he would like to return to the festival as a soloist in 1971, or to play with a trio. Byard was interested right away, and for once he planned to take his entire family along on the European tour – his wife, his daughter and his son. His son even sat in on drums.

During the Molde Festival, Byard even accompanied me, singing a revue number. Gunnar Bull Gundersen and Totto Osvold had set up a "festival evening" for radio, and they had asked if I would be a part of the programme.

"I only know one song," I said. "It's about 'Einar Rose', and it's a revue number. I learned it at summer camp when I was eleven years old."

I agreed to sing if I could have one of the world's best piano players to accompany me. "People have to understand that this is only a joke," I said. I was under the impression that the song would be recorded in a back room in the movie house, but as the "concert" drew nearer, I learned that I was to sing on stage and in front of an audience – not to mention that this was to be a live programme for national radio!

Naturally, I was scared out of my mind. It was too late to pull out so I asked Kenny Drew if he would play for me.

Jaki Byard and his wife Louise, with son Gerald and daughter Diane at dinner, 1971

"Can you sing?" he asked.

"No."

"Then I don't want to play for you. I don't want to make a fool of myself."

But Jaki Byard, the festival's top billing, agreed immediately. We couldn't find a piano in the whole town that wasn't already in use; everybody, Karin Krog and Dexter Gordon included, was rehearsing for the evening performances.

Without rehearsal, we went on stage, and miraculously, the number went reasonably well, once I found the right microphone and the right key to sing in. I couldn't go wrong, with Charles Mingus's super pianist as my accompanist. He even played 'Alexander's Ragtime Band' as a suitable tag to the number.

The song was unknown to everyone, including my own mother and father, who were listening intently. I never got to ask Einar Rose before he died, but he surely knew the song.

Jaki Byard definitely had not heard the song, but he was very gracious, and I am eternally grateful to him. He is also a fun person to be with. During the festival, it suddenly occurred to him that his next festival job wouldn't be for another two weeks, and he seemed worried. He wondered if he should break off the tour and take his family home?

"No," I said, "you can all live at my house."

I thereby became hostess to four houseguests. Jaki made it a point of honour to serve me dinner each day, and the Byard family were exceptionally nice people. Seldom did I hear so much beautiful piano music as I did during those fourteen days. Jaki dedicated a composition to me, too – 'Oslo To Kristiansund To Molde' – a beautiful ballad, and written at Gartnerveien.

RADIO

Many festival interviews and private conversations have been faithfully recorded over the years, and I have made use of them principally in radio programmes. The first time I broadcast for NRK – the Norwegian Broadcasting Corporation – was in 1967. Thorleif Østereng, the director of programming, had received a tape recording from Prague, and since I had been present at that festival, he hoped I would tape a programme for radio. I rehearsed and rehearsed, and I felt I knew my material from memory. After that first show, I broadcast from festivals in Poland and the Soviet Union, and eventually became one of the permanent voices of the *Jazz Club* series. I worked for NRK for twenty years, making programmes with many people there. For a long time, I had my own one-hour spot, and I think I enjoyed that most of all, but later I was given the *Novelties* show. Since 1987, I have mainly worked for local radio stations, but whatever the channel, it is always a pleasure to be able to go on the air and share jazz experiences with listeners, even without any renumeration. That's how it is with jazz. The pay is often only satisfied listeners or readers, but that is enough.

In 1973, I experienced my busiest festival season in Molde. In addition to my regular job as journalist and photographer for *Dagbladet*, I suddenly made my debut as a technical director for NRK, when the programming secretary became ill. I sat for forty hours in the radio bus, directing technicians from venue to venue. Recordings were to be made in clubs and on concert stages, several commentaries and reports were made in the bus itself, and on top of all this, I was trying to take care of Eubie Blake and his people. Upon my return to the capital, I was summoned directly to the studio to make the usual *Jazz Club* programme.

The most important task, of course, was my regular job as a reporter for *Dagbladet* and I would run from the bus to concerts, from the typewriter to the bathroom in order to develop film. It was stressful, but it was a new and exciting challenge. And this week was part of my "summer holiday" away from my main job as editor for Norsk Hydro.

CHAPTER 15

Sonny Rollins –
The Colourful Giant

I n 1968 I had the pleasure of meeting Sonny Rollins, a legend I knew
from records but whom I had never heard live. He was playing at
Montmartre in Copenhagen, and this was just before he disappeared
from the jazz scene for a couple of years. I had been at the premier
performance of a group named Savage Rose, and I made sure that while
I was in the city I would be able to hear the American saxophone giant
– the tenor player who had invented a new style of playing and who had
dominated several jazz groups with his compositions.

I was excited about the prospect of meeting Rollins, although I had
heard that he was difficult to communicate with and that if irritated by
his audience, he was known to simply pack up and leave.

He had played three weeks at Montmartre, and this was the last day.
The club was jammed with people, and there was electricity in the air.
He played intensely, with virility, and the audience was awed. We were
treated to standard tunes and his own compositions, the public
nodding knowingly, happily, as the first bars of 'St Thomas' rang out.
Rollins has so much humour and strength in his horn, and the
happiness that comes out is infectious.

At the piano sat Kenny Drew, an old acquaintance of mine who had
borrowed my piano the last time he was in Oslo. I asked Drew if he
could introduce me to Rollins, but he refused: "Talk to him yourself."
I thought this was a strange rejection, but I suppose he had his
reasons for it.

Sonny with a Norwegian/Swedish rhythm section in Kongsberg, 1971

When Rollins finished the first set, I followed him up to his dressing room. "Sonny Rollins, could I have a word with you?"

He whirled around and surveyed me quickly: "Okay, come on."

I hurried after him up the stairs. Once inside the dressing room, I asked if I might first take a couple of pictures. He obliged, posing willingly in different places around the room.

"Is this okay, or should I stand under the lamp?" he asked.

I was pleasantly surprised – my first encounter with him was absolutely trouble-free. We talked about Bud Powell and Rollins was interested when he heard Bud and I had been close friends.

He played an extra long second set, wiping the perspiration from his forehead between numbers, giving each song everything he had. At the end of the set, I remarked how wonderfully he had played.

"That's because you were listening. I could feel that that's what inspired me."

He played much longer than he had to that evening, and when he had finished, he asked me to wait for him. He wanted to take me back to the hotel. We were going to walk, but the new shoes he was wearing bothered him.

"I was just in India," he said, "and there I walked around in sandals." He had been in India to study yoga, not to play jazz.

As we walked through the quiet early morning streets of Copenhagen, he was continually impressed by the trees we passed. "I love trees."

At the hotel, we wound up sitting in the reception area and talking together. Abruptly, he asked, "What are the people like in Norway? Are they like you?"

A strange question, impossible to answer, and probably prompted by my asking him if he would like to come to Norway.

SONNY'S RETURN TO JAZZ

The following day, he flew back to the United States and I returned to Norway, still floating on a cloud after this special encounter with Sonny Rollins. I felt that there was a special bond between us, although I had relatively few notes for the interview I had planned to get with him.

Later Rollins disappeared from the jazz scene, and nobody heard anything from him for two years as he withdrew entirely from his audiences. In 1971, I gave his address to the Kongsberg Festival arrangers. They had a burning desire to bring him over, and they were willing to try to persuade him. I told them to give him my regards when they wrote.

Miraculously he agreed to come on his first visit to Norway – but only on the condition that he could perform with Norwegian musicians, not with Americans. It was nothing less than a sensation that he was coming at all. He was forty-two years old and already a legend and it was a well-known fact that he didn't accept just any kind of engagement. As an example, he had taken the job at Montmartre in Copenhagen only because the club was recommended by his good friend Yusef Lateef. Since that gig, however, his activities had been cloaked in silence.

When I arrived at the Kongsberg Festival, Rollins was already there. He had asked for me, the arrangers said, immediately upon arrival. I was flattered and proud.

As requested, he played with Bobo Stenson on piano, Arild Andersen on bass, and Jon Christensen on drums and was very pleased with the results. Why was it, though, that he had demanded Norwegian musicians?

"I figured they would give me the best backup they could – they would accompany me with enthusiasm," Rollins said. He was right, and the concert was a tremendous success.

During the rest of the festival, I spent a lot of time with Sonny. He escorted me to the other concerts, because he wanted to hear as much as possible himself. George Russell's church concert was a sensation that year and we were also at the Odd Fellow club to listen to Johnny Griffin and Art Taylor. He enjoyed meeting old colleagues, but he was especially interested in listening to Norwegian musicians. On reflection, Sonny seemed to enjoy his stay in Kongsberg. He prefers small, intimate festivals.

Every night he was driven up to the festival's mountain retreat – the Knutehytta – where he could practise the saxophone out of doors. In New York, he lived in an apartment, which meant practising was somewhat limited, but in the mountains he was able to blow the horn as loud as he liked.

Before we left Kongsberg, I asked if he would like to stay at my home in Oslo for a few days – he would be able to practise as much as he liked there, also. He accepted my offer right away.

SONNY WITH THE LAWN MOWER

It was an enjoyable week, but he didn't practise at all. His teeth were bothering him, and he was booked to see the dentist as soon as he had returned to the States. In general, the Sonny Rollins I met was very health conscious – every evening as part of his yoga exercises he stood on his head for at least ten minutes to relax. "You should try this," he said, "it's so important for you."

As he had mentioned in Copenhagen, he had been to India in 1968 to study yoga. He was astounded to find a few lines in one of my guest books written by Niranjan Jhaveri – the man who later founded the Jazz Festival of India.

"Do you know Jhaveri?" Sonny asked. "I was invited to dinner at his house, but I don't know to this day how he figured out I was in India. I was there for yoga, not as a musician. Jhaveri had a full set of drums and

Playing in the yard at Gartnerveien, 1971

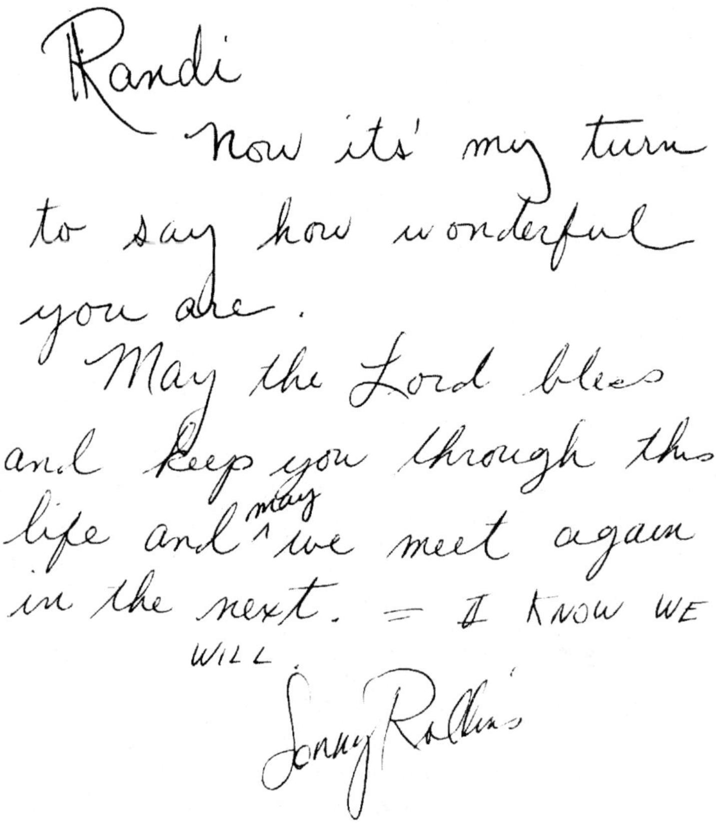

Randi

— Now its' my turn to say how wonderful you are.

May the Lord bless and keep you through this life and may we meet again in the next. — I KNOW WE WILL.

Sonny Rollins

a bass standing waiting for me, and he had even gotten hold of a tenor saxophone. I had no idea. I thought I was just going to dinner."

I pondered. Jhaveri is a very effective person, who has done great things for Indian jazz. He figures in my guest book along with Karin Krog, from the time he came to Norway to initiate us to Indian music. It was Karin who invited him, and when I heard that Jhaveri was a vegetarian, I told him that he would have to make his own dinner. He and Karin went shopping for ingredients, I put an apron on each of them and he slaved and sweated over the hot stove. This was the first time he had prepared food – at home in India, he had servants to do that for him.

"So, Sonny, while you had to play for your supper at his house, he had to cook his own food at mine!" We laughed.

Sonny was into one of his fasts when he stayed with me, eating only fruit. He would buy the fruit from the shop next door and enjoyed chatting with the shop owner while I was at work, before coming back and talking with Christina, who was home from her travels abroad. Just as he had taken to mountainside practising, Sonny liked to spend time in the yard, and for some reason took to mowing grass, even though he maintained this was the first time he had ever pushed a mower in his life.

"It's so nice to be outside," he said. "I hope you appreciate how nice it is in Norway, with the light in the evenings and the clean air. There's no pollution over here. Your yard is like a dream."

I took a picture of Sonny with the lawn mower – a picture which later graced the pages of *Down Beat*. Here people were wondering what had happened to Sonny Rollins, and suddenly they saw a picture of him in somebody's yard in Norway, at Gartnerveien 6, Oslo.

REINCARNATION

In Kongsberg that same year, Sonny was interviewed by Art Taylor, the drummer who also wrote books on jazz. Rollins was also interviewed by an African journalist who used to write for *Melody Maker*. While I was at the office, he had plenty of time to read jazz magazines, taking in everything I had in English, including an issue of *Melody Maker* where he found some articles by the same African journalist. He didn't like the articles at all, and he began to become worried.

"He was the one who interviewed me in Kongsberg, isn't he? – I should have asked to read what he wrote before it got printed. What can I do to stop the article?"

"Write a letter to the editor of *Melody Maker* as soon as possible," I suggested, "and then drop it in the mailbox at the Manglerud post office."

Sonny took my advice and made the trip to the post office, but he never received a reply to his letter. The article was printed not only in *Melody Maker*, but in other magazines, as well – even in *Down Beat*, to Sonny's dismay. He often mentioned this incident in his letters to me.

During the evenings at home, I played a lot of Norwegian jazz for Sonny, including an old record featuring the Norwegian singing group, The Monn-Keys, which he liked. I was surprised that he knew the lyrics to most of the tunes by heart. He knew all the standards. Some horn players, maybe mainly trumpet players, also sing, and they like to know the lyrical content of what they play. Sonny and Dexter Gordon had this trait in common.

Sonny whistled and sang to himself all day long, having fun on his own. We talked about doing an interview for radio, but the days went by quickly. On the last evening of his stay, he mentioned the interview himself – and we wound up talking until late into the night – not just about music, either. I asked him if he believed in life after death, because in the guest book, he had written something about meeting again in the next life.

"Sometimes you feel that a person lives on, even after death," Sonny explained. "In a way, I believe in that. That's something I felt the first time I met you, Randi. There's something about you that makes me think either that I have known you before, or that I'm going to meet you again in another life."

I remarked to him that I had been a little afraid to approach him the first time, and he found the thought incomprehensible.

"Am I difficult?"

JAZZ AND YOGA

Sonny's first inspiration was saxophonist Coleman Hawkins and later he listened to Lester Young and Dexter Gordon. "Dexter had a big influence on Coltrane, too," said Sonny. "I can hear a lot of Dexter in the way he plays. Dexter played a big role in the history of jazz." Of all Sonny's compositions, 'Oleo' was the one most often played by other musicians, and personally, he liked Miles Davis' version – the very first recording of the tune – best. But as he admitted, "I haven't heard all the versions of 'Oleo'."

"Do you compose often?"

"A lot of times I'll write new material when I'm going to make a record. But I always have music paper ready, so I can write down ideas whenever they come to me."

Enjoying the fresh air, 1971

Dear Randi,

How are you? I hope to

God you are well. Do you remem

ber taking the picture with me

in the yard. All the trees and

grass and me coming out of the

woods you know

I'm just wondering about using this on an

album cover or something. I'm just try-

ing to figure out how I should look,

maybe two little horns coming out of

the head or maybe little saxophones

I'm thinking — I'm thinking . . . .

"When you compose, do you think about writing especially for the tenor?"

"Not necessarily, but I do probably think how I want to sound myself."

"What about big band arranging?"

"It takes too long, but I would like to do that. It would be nice to be able to do it all alone – then I could get it exactly the way I want it – especially since I don't like to have to depend on other people. If I have to do that, then I'd rather not do anything."

"Do you ever go out to listen to jazz when you're not playing yourself?"

"No, I don't listen much to music. But I'm afraid I do watch too much TV!" Sonny laughed.

"Weren't you originally supposed to go to art school?"

He laughed again: "I like to paint, especially water colours, and I really get inspired from looking at pictures. Painting maybe means something for my playing. I also like sculpture – everything that has to do with art."

"How about yoga?"

"I became interested in yoga in 1960. Now there are a lot of musicians who practise yoga. When you practise your instrument, that is also a form of yoga – it has to do with discipline. Yoga helps me stay healthy, I'm convinced of that. Exercises and meditation."

MULTIPLE INSPIRATIONS

"Did you hear a lot of Indian music when you were in India?"

"Quite a bit, and I was especially fascinated by the music of South India – the instruments they use."

"You've been to Japan several times – do you have friends there?"

"I have one good friend there – my yoga teacher. He has yoga schools in several places, and he has stayed at my home in the States."

"It was in Japan that you shaved the sides of your head bald so that you looked like an Indian, right?"

"How did you know that?"

"I think it was Coltrane who asked me how I liked your new hair style."

"I can't remember why I did that, but when I went back to Japan the

Sonny liked to use my film camera

next time, I had normal hair, and people didn't recognise me. The funniest thing was that I met an artist who had copied my Mohawk haircut, but I had hair."

"You've learned a lot about Norwegian jazz – both in Kongsberg and from the records you've heard."

"I was especially impressed by those two guys who made a record for the first time when they were already pretty old."

"You mean tenor sax player Bjarne Nerem and trumpet player Rowland Greenberg?"

"Right. And I liked the other tenor player who also played with the trumpet player. Kristian Bergheim."

"Did you meet a lot of musician friends in Kongsberg?"

"I've played with most of them, and I knew the piano player Mal Waldron because he went to college with my sister. She used to brag to him about how good her brother could play."

"Do you have any other brothers and sisters?"

"One brother who was a violinist before he switched to medicine and became a doctor. He played classical music, and I used to like to listen to him."

"What made you become a jazz musician?"

"I think it was Louis Jordan. He played the saxophone and had a good blues group. They played in Harlem. I remember that I got interested when I used to go by the Savoy and saw the posters outside. And the Cotton Club. It was exciting to see the pictures of the sax players. Of course the Apollo Theatre was a big inspiration and I used to go there every week to hear bands while I was still going to school.

3. I have read some of the articles which you sent and I do feel that you are more completely qualified to write on Jazz than anyone in Scandinavia or Europe. Maybe they discriminate against you because you are a woman. They are probably jealous of your intimate understanding of the music and the musicians. I think your articles can be 'hard-hitting' as much as you want — no one can censor you, as you are obviously more knowledgeable than they. You have only your own conscience to listen to in your writing. But as I said you must be careful of their discrimination against your sex, and their jealousy of you and your rapport with musicians.

Randi - please take care of yourself - there are people who love you - like myself

Sonny

You can imagine what a thrill it was for me when I played there with my own group – but that was a long time afterwards."

FASCINATING LETTERS

Since the time Sonny Rollins stayed at my house in 1971, we have kept in touch. His interesting letters came more often in the first years and they are now mainly postcards from various places. I treasure the letters that he wrote me – they are full of warmth and wisdom, and several of them are truly historical in terms of their content.

The letters I sent back to him were reciprocally enthusiastic. I urged him to seek out new, young musicians. One time he typed a reply, saying that it would be a "round letter" – almost non-stop:

"So much of life is gone since we last talked to each other. Life Death...Pops passed away and then my dog after eleven years, and Charlie Shavers (which was bad, it happened so close to Louis...). Have thought about taking care of my Indian Obo more in the future, and my wife and people and trees and books and love and will and belief and trust and struggle...to reach something meaningful..."

He asks how Christina is and says that he felt at home in Gartnerveien. Then he wonders if the corner shop still exists. It closed shortly after Sonny left. "Write back if you can't find anything better to do," he closed.

"PLAYING IN THE YARD"

Sonny spoke in his letters of composing a melody for me, and when he later released the record with the tune 'Playing In The Yard' among the cuts, it struck me that yard really exists – at Gartnerveien. It is a hard-swinging composition which might easily reflect the way he feels as he plays in the yard with the lawn mower.

In another letter, Sonny tells about a female journalist who wants to put him in a book about black musicians. He wrote: "...as far as her idea of white and black musicians is concerned, I'm not interested. There are a lot of people who are hung up and confused about races these days. Maybe I'll give her the interview, but you remember what happened with that journalist in Kongsberg?"

FAMILY

Sonny Rollins has played in Kongsberg three times – 1971, 1974 and 1979 – and during the latter years I also met Lucille, his wife of a number of years and a sweet and intelligent lady who had her own career for a long time. Later, however, she chose to become manager for Sonny, and he is surely grateful for that. She organises the concerts, advises on the choice of musicians, and is often co-producer when Sonny does studio recordings. She also ensures that he is properly treated and that he gets the fees that he deserves – her efforts have without a doubt made him more attractive as an artist than ever before. European festivals queue up to engage him, and this is deservedly how things should be.

Sonny mentioned something on the subject in one of his many interesting letters, and clearly he is right:

"A lot of people ask me to appear at many concerts – and I am grateful to be in demand – but in order to try and be healthy and maintain some semblance of a tranquil life at home, I cannot accept many of the offers. I want to stay in top hotels, ride first class and get good money. I have stayed in enough dirty hotels, ridden on enough buses and not been paid often enough to want to enjoy these things now. And when I strive to meet these standards, I am doing so not just for myself, but for all my compatriots who had to suffer the indignities of those conditions while bringing joy to the world through their music. And even the musicians who are still alive can perhaps gain something themselves by the respect I demand in my career. Feeling as I do and being able to carry out those things, has of course made me the target of many people in the music business who do not think an artist should have any power over his own life."

Normally it is Lucille who writes letters nowadays, while Sonny prefers to call. In 1995, the same year I received the aforementioned letter from Sonny, I underwent a couple of serious operations for cancer. He called regularly to give me support and to cheer me up. I'm always in a good mood after talking to him; he has infectious laughter and a marvellous sense of humour. Not to mention an excellent memory – he still remembers names and Norwegian words from his first visit to Norway in 1971.

He and Lucille have become two of my closest friends, and it was so good to see them again in 1996, when Sonny surprised fans in Europe with a large concert tour in November. I enjoyed his concerts in Oslo and the finale in London. It was phenomenal. He played so well at the last concert in London, that you would think it was the opening of the tour. Better than ever, Lucille agreed. He gives everything he's got – and he is truly a colourful giant.

CHAPTER 16

Jazz In Eastern Europe

I n 1966, I was invited to the festival in Prague. Karin Krog and Jan Garbarek were also going there. When we had checked into the big hotel, Jan informed us that he had gotten a wonderful room – even equipped with a "footbath". We teased him a little, saying they should have at least given him two bidets – one for each foot! During dinner on the first evening, Jan bought each of us a rose, which was a gallant gesture for a young man of only nineteen.

The concerts in Prague took place in Lucerna Hall, and we noticed in the programme that several of the Czech musicians had doctorates. There was also a sizeable contingent of foreign musicians. When Karin had to select musicians to complement herself and Jan, she was a little hesitant in choosing local talent. She was offered Jiri Mraz on bass, but she took instead Swedish Kurt Lindgren, with whom she was already acquainted. Mraz later become bassist for Oscar Peterson. We were quite surprised over the quality of several of the eastern European musicians.

As a journalist, I was invited to international luncheons. It was at one of these that I met Jan Byrczek, president of the jazz society of Poland, and he invited me to go to Warsaw after the festival. Jan and Karin were eventually going to join me there, after visiting some smaller Polish towns.

Just before we were to leave, I became ill. It was thirty-eight degrees centigrade, and this was October. I caught a cold,

Fifteen-year-old Jan Garbarek winning first prize, Oslo 1962

accompanied by a nasty fever, and was confined to bed at the hotel. The luncheons ended with the closing of the festival, and I was then on my own. A colleague summoned a doctor. When the doctor arrived, I had to laugh. He crawled up onto the bed and put his ear to the middle of my back! Was this really a doctor, or was it a musician playing some kind of joke? I had never experienced an examination like this, where the doctor didn't even have a stethoscope. He made sounds like he wanted me to cough. I understood this, but little more. We were unable to communicate. I tried to tell him that I had to be well as soon as possible, because I had to write articles, and I had to be on my way. I asked if he had some tablets – or cough drops.

"You drops, I fix," he said, and a short time later, a bellboy came up from the reception desk with the medicine. The equivalent of twelve Norwegian crowns (about two dollars today) for both the doctor and the medicine.

Karin Krog and Jan Garbarek with Kurt Lindgren on bass, Prague 1966

GARBAREK IN WARSAW

I did get to Warsaw in time, and this visit became my first encounter with a long list of Polish talents. I furnished *Dagbladet* with a photo of Adam Makowicz, who I thought was especially brilliant and eleven years later, Makowicz was discovered by John Hammond in the USA. Jan Garbarek was specially invited to Warsaw because of the film music composer Krzystof Komeda, who had heard Jan in Kongsberg, but Karin was officially the leader of the group. Many people were entranced by this young Norwegian's saxophone playing, and Jan recorded his first record during the festival.

During the opening jam session in one of the jazz clubs, Jan surprised Monty Sunshine by joining him on the stage, and Karin and I must have become two of very few people to have heard Jan play in a Dixieland band. I don't even think that the members of the English band know that Norway's most famous contemporary saxophonist once played with them. Garbarek has been named musician of the year a number of years in a row by *Jazz Forum*, the international magazine that was printed in Poland, and he has guested in Warsaw several times since this first festival. There, as practically everywhere else, he is considered in a class by himself. A documentary film about Jan was made for Norwegian television during one of his visits to Poland, and in 1982 he shared the stage in the Palace of Culture with none other than Miles Davis. He played magnificently, and I witnessed several Polish musicians in the audience break into tears at the end of the concert.

As for Miles Davis, he was turning the Polish festival arrangers grey with worry. He demanded to be picked up in a private jet, and the hotel where he would be staying had to have a swimming pool. The festival officials drummed up a military plane, and the hotel began filling its pool, which hadn't been in use for years. Miles never used it during his stay either.

POLISH CULTURAL MEDAL

In Poland, they are very fond of giving awards. Twice I was honoured with a prize in competition for best media article – for a total of several thousand zloty, a sizeable sum by Polish standards. Probably the most prestigious award I have ever received was the Polish Cultural Medal. This was given to me at nine am in 1978, and it was the Minister of Culture himself who pinned the medal to my lapel. I had been informed of this honour before I left from Oslo, and I therefore came prepared to reciprocate with a small token for the minister – a doll dressed in a Norwegian national costume. The Poles looked bemused – an award recipient didn't customarily give something in return – but luck was with me, because it turned out that the Polish minister was a collector of dolls from around the world.

Warsaw has invited me each and every year they have had a jazz festival – until 1990, that is, when *perestroika* ruined the Jazz

Receiving the Cultural Medal from the Polish Culture Minister

My Cultural Medal certificate

With Jan Garbarek on the floor of the Palace of Culture, 1966

Photo: Marek Karewicz

At a press meeting in Warsaw, 1990, with (right) Willis Conover – "The Voice of America" – and Batachef, the famous Russian jazz writer. Both received the Culture Medal in 1978

Jamboree's. It had been easier to finance the festival before, as Pawel Brodowski said: "Jazz has been our *perestroika.*"

ANOTHER WEDDING

I have had many Polish musicians visit me – the first back in 1962, when saxophonist Stanislav Kalwinsky played the Metropol. Five years later I had Jan Bryczek and Adam Makowicz stay for a few days after the end of the Molde Festival.

That same year, in 1967, I happened to drop by the Grand Hotel in Oslo, and there I accidentally made more Polish friends. It was quite a musical discovery: Michael Urbaniak and his orchestra had been hired as the house dance band, and their repertoire was bejewelled with top notch jazz numbers.

Urbaniak played violin during concerts – flute and tenor sax during dance sets. Urszula Dudziak was the vocalist, at the organ sat Wojtek Karolak, and on drums, Andrew Dobrowsky. Together they were four of Poland's finest jazz musicians. By coincidence, it turned out that they were renting rooms next door to my own home, so within no time, I had invited them in. Among other things they told me that they had earlier had a gig in Skien, where Urszula played piano – she had a degree from Poland as a pianist.

Jan Garbarek plays with members of the Monty Sunshine Band, Warsaw 1966

The wedding of Urszula Dudziak and Michael Urbaniak at the Polish Embassy, 1967

I wrote rave reviews in the newspaper about the dance band at the Grand – an article which resulted in a recording contract for them, the first for the now world-famous Urszula and Michael. Jan Erik Kongshaug was the sound technician, and he has become just as well-known internationally in his field as the Urbaniaks. On the record, Michael plays groovy tenor during Charles Lloyd's 'Sombrero Sam', and Urszula sings 'Lover' and 'Dark Eyes' with a high-pitched, clear voice, often in perfect unison with Michael's flute tones. It is a fine record which has been followed by more than twenty LPs recorded in the United States since then.

I became very good friends with Ula and Michael. We held regular jams at my house, and suddenly it was announced that the two of them wanted to celebrate their wedding in my home at Gartnerveien, on 23 December, 1967. Trumpet player Donald Byrd was to be the best man but on the big day, we waited anxiously for the arrival of the American – first at the Polish Embassy, where the bridal march was played endlessly in the hope that Donald would finally come through the door. In his absence, we had to go on with the ceremony.

The other members of the band went ahead of us to my house in order to receive some Polish guests who had been invited to the reception, while I sat with the newlyweds at Fornebu waiting for the arrival of the delayed flight from America – which eventually did land, but without Donald. When we arrived at home, we got a call from him at home in the US. He had caught the flu and had turned around at the airport and gone home to bed. It was that bad.

As evening approached, the newlyweds began to ask whether or not they had to play at the Grand that same evening – maybe it's closed, since it's the night before Christmas eve? We went downtown, and we were given the entire Hall of Mirrors for our party. Among the few invited guests was Karin Krog, who sang duets with Urszula for the occasion – a wonderful wedding gift. While we were having our little private jam session, there came a knock on the door. I opened and told the couple standing outside that I was sorry, but this was a private party: "The Grand is closed."

"But we're newlyweds," they said in unison, and that changed the matter. They were invited in and treated to entertainment they will never forget. The groom turned out to be musical himself, coincidentally having once been in a singing group led by my ex-husband.

MICHAEL URBANIAK AND URSZULA DUDZIAK

Just after the wedding, the Urbaniaks took their band to Trondheim and then to Sweden. They continued playing dance music until they became tired of it and returned home. In Poland, Michael began to work with new forms of expression. He played two saxophones at the same time, and he began playing jazz on an electrically amplified violin. When I later heard them at the festival in Warsaw, Urbaniak was eager to show me his discoveries. I was disappointed, though, because Urszula was still singing 'Lover' with her classically beautiful, crystal clear voice. Why hadn't she followed up Michael's innovative thinking? She eventually did so. When I later heard them in Kongsberg, Norway, I was truly impressed. Urszula by herself was a sensation.

They finally moved to New York and took American citizenship. They also got record contracts galore. In Molde, as in Norway in general, they were extremely popular, guesting at Club 7 several times. Later they were divorced, unfortunately, and Urszula returned to Molde with the singing group Vocal Summit, also singing in Oslo Jazz House as a one woman show a couple of times. It is amazing how she has developed. She is a true star in the way she enhances her voice electronically, in perfect control of everything she does at all times, and always uniquely independent as a performer. I remember how thunderously she was received in Warsaw's Palace of Culture in 1989, as she walked out onto the stage. Whoever said one can't be a prophet in one's own land?

Both Urszula and Michael have brought something new to jazz. They are hesitant even to mention their first record from 1967 so Urszula was shocked when she once met Stan Getz in the States and he told her what he thought of it (I had just recently played it for him in Oslo). He couldn't resist the urge to tease Urszula a bit, though. Later she moaned: "Randi! I'm really upset! Stan Getz has started his own record company, and now he's bought the rights to that record we made in Norway. He's threatening to re-release it!"

TO TALLIN

In 1967, I was invited to attend the first international jazz festival in the Soviet Union – in Tallin, Estonia. I travelled with the Lloyd Quartet, Janne Johansson and Egil "Bop" Johansen. Willis Conover was present, and he was a big hit. Everyone recognised "The Voice" from America.

I listened to about thirty Russian jazz groups. This was one festival that made a strong and lasting impression on me – especially because I was so unprepared for what I heard. The place was flooded with talented musicians, and the four lengthy reviews I wrote for *Dagbladet* were duly translated and sent to the Soviet Minister of Culture, who – it was said – appreciated reading them.

On the trip home, I shared the company of Janne and the gang aboard the ship from Tallin to Helsinki. I'll never forget Janne playing my newly purchased balalaika, while Egil "Bop" danced Russian folk-style on deck, as fit and lively as he has always been.

MOSCOW

In 1990, I was invited back to the Soviet Union again, this time by the Union of Composers in Moscow. The festival was very international, but what made me most happy was being able to hear once again some of the musicians that I had written about the last time I was in the Soviet Union. It was rewarding to see that they were still among the top players, twenty-three years later, and that they obviously belonged to a favoured jazz elite. Aside from these, the majority of the players on stage were Americans. I had my own personal guide, who followed me around twelve hours a day – thank goodness, because it was difficult to find food, taxis, and the like, not to mention the concert venues. I was interviewed on a couple of Moscow's largest radio stations and used the opportunity to present some Norwegian jazz records. Mike Hennessey also invited me to participate in an international TV programme from the Moscow concerts.

AND JAZZ FROM JAPAN

Jazz festivals are popular in many parts of the world, and participants are increasingly more international. Unfortunately I have never been to Japan, where the interest in jazz is deeply special. Our own singer, Karin Krog, was named Vocalist of the Year a couple of times there. One of the first

Japan has a lot of good jazz musicians, among them Terumasa Hino, whom I first heard in Berlin in 1971

311

Japanese jazz musicians I heard was Toshiko Akiyoshi – on an LP I got from Norman Granz from the Newport Festival. It was Toshiko's debut in the United States – a brilliant pianist, and I still remember her melody 'Between Me And Myself', which actually reminded me a lot of one of Dave Brubeck's compositions. This was in 1956. It was actually Hampton Hawes who met Toshiko in Japan and helped her to come to the United States.

A Japanese evening at Gartnerveien with saxophone player Sadao Watanabe and Karin Krog, twice vocalist of the year in Japan

The first musician I heard live in concert was trumpeter Terumasa Hino, who played the Berlin Festival in 1971. Joachim Berendt was always good at presenting new nations at his festivals.

Eventually I did host several Japanese musicians on their visits to Norway – including Terumasa, who came in the company of John Scofield and Dave Liebman. Saxophonist Sadao Watanabe has also been a guest, accompanied by Karin Krog. Jazz musicians from Cuba and Russia have also been to Gartnerveien, but I have yet to have a musician visitor from China.

CHAPTER 17

Eubie – The One, The Only

In November 1972, I was invited to the Berlin Jazz Days and stayed for the occasion in one of the city's largest hotels, the same one where most of the festival musicians were staying. Every day I saw three elderly people sitting in the same sofa in the vestibule – a gentleman and two ladies. The man was very elegantly dressed and had the air of a performer, so I presumed he would be playing at the festival. I was curious about these three, because all they ever did was sit and follow what was going on in the hotel lobby.

Then came the day when he was finally presented on stage. I've never been so surprised: this was none other than Eubie Blake – ragtime composer and the only original ragtime performer from the turn of the century still living.

During his solo performance in Berlin, I was filled with a feeling of wonder and contentment like I've never felt before. This elderly gentleman with a gleam in his eye – who danced, who sang – exuded

To be or not to be
was not the question simply
Eubie as always at 90 & 12

To MRS. RANDi W. HULTiN
from Eubie Blake   aug 12th 1973

such warmth and good will. And the way he played the piano! He was magical on stage, truly amazing, and we enjoyed every second of it.

"Ladies and gentlemen, I will now play 'Charleston Rag', which I composed in 1899 – at the same time as Scott Joplin wrote 'Maple Leaf Rag'. You've all heard of Scott Joplin? He was the father of us all – the first ragtime composer."

Eubie performed and held us breathless for over an hour all by himself. As he explained the origins of the music, he would run over to the piano to demonstrate for us. He was enjoying himself, even singing excerpts from Broadway shows of the early 1920s. It was fantastic.

When he had left the stage, I couldn't resist the urge to run backstage and meet him. For the first time in my life, I had become a born-again fan. I wanted to ask for an interview – a taped interview, so that the radio listeners back home could hear this phenomenon.

Backstage already sat Willis Conover, and the world-famous music critic Leonard Feather. I was definitely not the only admirer of Eubie. He sat writing autographs for the fans and seemed to be on top of the world. I was introduced to Marion, Eubie's wife, who turned out to be absolutely the right person to meet – she arranged everything for me. I would be given an interview with Eubie the following day, she said, and sure enough, while the ladies waited in the hotel lobby, Eubie and I retired to another room for our interview.

RAGTIME IN THE BROTHELS

Eubie was born in Baltimore, Maryland, 7 February, 1883, of slave parents, and he began to play the piano at the age of only six. He spoke in a serious and formal manner into the microphone.

"I had an old organ, and a lady in the neighbourhood taught me how to play. Then I started listening to street music. I liked the way they played so much – it was ragtime music. That's how I wanted to play. I started jazzing up my piano lessons and I thought it sounded a lot better that way. But one day my mother came home a little earlier than expected, and she got mad. 'Git that ragtime music out of my house!' she yelled. Ragtime was not so well thought of at that time, you know. It was played in bars and other places with bad reputations.

'Not in good homes,' mother said. If I was going to play, it would have to be Mozart or Beethoven. Jesse Picket, who taught me how to play ragtime, was a pimp and a gambler. I was only thirteen-fourteen years old, and not long after that, I got a job at Aggie Sheldon's disreputable house. The job was paid well, but my parents couldn't find out about it, so I used to sneak out through the window of my room and go over the roof. And on the way to work, I stopped and rented a pair of long trousers for twenty-five cents a night.

"Before I knew it, I had a permanent night job. My parents slept like logs, so you could shoot a cannon and they wouldn't have heard it. But one day I was overheard by one of the neighbours. 'It couldn't have been anybody else than Eubie,' she told my mother. 'There's nobody else with a left hand like that – I recognised the boogie bass.' She had been walking by outside the whore house. Mother was furious, and when she was mad at me, she called me Mr Blake: 'We're going to have to tell this to your father, Mr Blake.' When my father heard that I played in a whore house, he thought it was terrible, but when he heard that I earned three dollars a week and even got tips on top of that, he thought about it a little bit. I invited him upstairs and showed him the money I had hidden under the rug. Almost a hundred dollars. Dad was quiet a long time, because he didn't even earn more than nine dollars a week. 'Well, I'll talk to your mother,' he said. So I kept on playing at Aggie Sheldon's all the way until 1901, when I got a job in Dr Frazier's Medicine Show, where I also tap danced. It was a travelling show: we had a horse-drawn wagon, and I used to dance up on the back of the wagon, while another guy sold hair oil. The year after that, I got a job in a minstrel show."

Eubie told about his musicals, and he sang and demonstrated for me in my hotel room. I became more and more fascinated. He had learned everything there was to know about ragtime, but he also listened to other music, including Grieg, Wagner, Strauss and Lehar. One of Eubie's pieces that I've come to love is his version of 'The Merry Widow', which became one of his classic standards when he performed on stage. The piece he preferred himself, however, was 'Eubie's Classical Rag'.

"In the beginning, I used to compose," said Eubie. "I never say that I wrote music, because I didn't know how to write music until 1915, when I met Noble Sissle. We wrote several musicals together, the first of which were *Shuffle Along* and *Chocolate Dandies*, two purely black shows for Broadway. Then we wrote *Elsie*, a show for white artists. That was the third time a white show was written by Negroes. Then I wrote Lew Leslie's *Blackbird* and *Bandana Land*. There were six shows in all, but I'd rather forget the sixth one."

YOUNG JOSEPHINE BAKER

"In *Shuffle Along* and *Chocolate Dandies*, I presented two people who would later become very famous," said Eubie. "One of them was Paul Robeson, and the other was Josephine Baker. She was just a young girl and was very successful in the show. Soon we had to pay her double as much as the others, because everyone asked to see 'the cross-eyed girl'."

I told Eubie that I had met Josephine Baker almost forty years later, when my husband was her accompanist. It's a small world. *Shuffle Along* also featured a pianist who would later become just as well-known as a singer, Nat "King" Cole.

From the shows, two melodies in particular became popular, 'I'm Just Wild About Harry', and 'Memories Of You'. The latter earned Eubie a considerable yearly sum just in Norway alone, since it was used for years as the theme song for a morning show on the radio. As for 'I'm Just Wild About Harry', there were a lot of people who thought it was specially written for President Harry Truman's campaign in 1948.

"And I let them think it was," said Eubie, "but I really wrote it in 1921."

Eubie talked and talked non-stop. It was an experience to listen to him. He was warm and lively and full of humour.

"People always ask why ragtime is only played on the black keys, and I answer, 'Well – you know that most of us started playing in the South – that's why we're afraid of hitting the white keys.'

"When I was sixty-three, I retired from showbusiness, because then I wanted to study classical music." Indeed, at the age of sixty-seven, Eubie completed his studies at the Shillinger System of Composition, with professor Rudolph Schramm.

Eubie had been married previously to a concert pianist named Avis, who died in 1939. They had had no children and he took her death very hard. In 1945, he met his second wife, Marion Gant Tyler, who had also been in showbusiness at an early age. They never had children either, but Eubie celebrated two silver wedding anniversaries in his lifetime! Marion was his impresario and secretary – a fantastic person, very intelligent and keen. He was very dependent on her.

Eubie also wrote musicals together with Andy Razaf.

"Andy was a real prince," he said. "He was a son of the king of Madagascar, and his real name was André. He was one of the most popular lyric writers I've ever worked with. I still compose, but always at night – and not at the piano, because it's downstairs on the first floor."

Eubie wrote at least a thousand compositions. About 400 of these are copyrighted.

'RANDI'S RAG'

Suddenly, Eubie said that he wanted to write a melody for me. What would I like – a ragtime or a charleston?

"I think I'd like a ragtime," I answered.

"Okay, 'Randi's Rag', that sounds good." Eubie gave the song a name even before it was written. A couple of years later, I got the music in the mail. Perfect manuscript notation, written by a composer more than ninety years old.

I had not been the only Norwegian at the Berlin Festival. Svein Erik Børja, from television, had been invited to film the event for the Germans, and two of the Molde Festival arrangers were there as well. Everyone was fascinated by Eubie and after consultation with Petter Petterson and Otto Sættem, I asked Eubie if he might like to come to Molde. He looked pensive and inquired how far it was to Norway. "I never take a plane," he said. He had sailed to Europe and had taken a train to Berlin. I told him how wonderful it was to fly, and I showed him brochures from the beautiful Romsdal mountains. Eubie and Marion decided there and then that they would fly for the first time in their lives.

When I left Berlin early the next morning, after the interview, I first went to say goodbye to Eubie and his lady entourage at the breakfast

"Randi's Rag
1974
By Eubie Blake
Mod'to Dance Tempo
A
R.H.
L.H
KING BRAND
NO. M-1 12 STAVE
1595 B'WAY, N.Y.
MADE IN U.S.A.

table. I was just as surprised as the two ladies when huge tears ran down Eubie's cheeks: "Will you promise to write to me?" he asked. Of course I would.

Our most intense correspondence began after he had been to Molde. He came in 1973 with Marion, Carl Seltzer – who was Marion's assistant and Eubie's record producer – Betty Jordan and Dorothy Coshburn. They came via Zürich and Copenhagen, where he played concerts, and then continued by plane via Bergen to Molde – the first flight of his ninety-year life. After that, it was like a new world opened up for him. He visited the Nice Festival a couple of times, and he flew from New York to Los Angeles to participate in Johnny Carson's *Tonight Show*, where he was a frequent guest.

MOLDE

It wasn't the beautiful countryside that interested Eubie most in Molde. He was most interested in meeting new people. He loved to talk, and he got up early each morning just to be able to talk to everyone he met. Musicians adored him. Clark Terry's big band stood around him attentively listening to stories from the old days. They learned where the musician jargon came from. Eubie became a popular attraction, even off the stage. One day he actually tap danced on the balcony of the Alexandra Hotel.

His first evening in Molde, we took him to the Alexandra club to hear Rowland Greenberg. Rowland played 'Memories Of You' as soon as Eubie came into the club, and Eubie looked moved. Later on that night, Eubie took the stage and was met with thunderous applause. The next night, there was a concert with the Swedish swing group, Kustbandet. Eubie didn't want to miss anything.

One day I was asked to come to the local Rotary meeting and to bring with me one of the main attractions of the festival. It had to be Eubie, I thought, and I asked if he would tell a little bit about his life. He talked and wandered around the floor, having a fine time. Eventually I had to interrupt him to tell him that the meeting was about over, but he had only gotten as far as 1905 in his life history!

Eubie's concert was a new, wonderful experience. He talked and played, walking back and forth between the microphone and the

Doctor Eubie Blake

Clark Terry with Eubie, Molde, 1973

piano, full of vigour and vitality. The crowd went wild. He was full of stories. His playing technique showed no signs of age – his long, bony fingers flew over the keys effortlessly. We heard all his classic numbers, and he flirted continuously with the audience, capturing our hearts.

Eubie also listened intently to the concerts of the other artists. For him it was unusual to have so many concerts by so many different musicians at the same time. On the eve of his early morning flight to Bergen, with a connection to catch to New York, he went out on the town, playing at the Vardestua club until two am. He was everyone's favourite at the Molde Festival.

Eubie was unique. He was honoured continually during the last thirty to forty years of his life. He had been successful throughout his lifetime, even as a pre-teen, and later, he would play at the White House and meet presidents – though he never attached a lot of importance to those occasions: "I'm always a little afraid to be around presidents. Those are the people that get shot at.

"Reagan has probably forgotten that we once played vaudeville theatre together," Eubie speculated. Eubie did, however, get an award from the Republican president – an honour he appreciated very much. Award has followed award, and Eubie has received honourary doctorates, had streets named after him, had a bronze statue dedicated to him in one of New York's museums, and – possibly his most valued recognition – been present at the declaration of 14 February as annual "Eubie Blake Day" in the town of his birth, Baltimore.

"I have to laugh," he said on receiving an honourary doctorate from Brooklyn College in Baltimore, Maryland. "I've been playing my whole life and never got any education. I didn't get a degree until I was ninety years old!"

Eubie's life was an adventure, and the adventure continued after he had reached ninety, as well. Through his letters to me, I followed his life.

HISTORICAL LETTERS

"I'll send you letters," Eubie had said, but I was sceptical. He was ninety, and it is seldom that one begins corresponding regularly at that age. But he kept his promise. The first letter came in August, 1973.

"Dear Miss Hultin," he wrote, "or should I call you Randi, maybe?" He thanked me for taking care of him in Molde, and invited me to New York: "I'll show you the city and my home."

Eubie in his Molde sweater, 1973

I began to get letters several times a month, sometimes as often as twice a week. He switched to red ink every time he wrote something he wanted to emphasise. He once wrote in pencil, starting with an apology: "I'm in the hospital, so that's why I'm using a pencil, but don't worry. It's not serious, just something that happens when you're over fifty. I have a prostrate problem." He was ninety-four at the time.

He mentioned in several letters that he would like to give a concert in Oslo. "I often think of you and wonder if you really meant that you could arrange a concert for me. I've been looking forward to it, but will it happen? I know that you aren't an agent – but please, can you use your charm on someone over there?" In his next letter, he wrote of concerts in various places around the USA, including his third performance at Carnegie Hall, "but there'll be other ones."

In between Eubie's letters, I would occasionally get one from Marion, too. I think she may have been a little jealous of our correspondence, but I explained to her how much Eubie's letters meant to me. It was like getting a shot of vitamins. When she realised that Eubie wanted to come to Oslo, she wrote that it would have to be during the summertime. Marion thought about everything. "Concerning the tour to Oslo," wrote Eubie, "remember that if you write to Marion, she'll always tell you when I can't come."

In April, 1975, Eubie wrote from Los Angeles and told me that he had made three shows with Bill Cosby. "He's a very, very funny man on stage. He is very rich. I was a guest in his house in Massachusetts. He has a house in Beverly Hills, too. Maybe this doesn't interest you, but it interests me. Now I have to go. I have to do another show – plus a Johnny Carson show. Have to go, because the car is here. Sincerely, your real, real friend."

MORTEN GUNNAR LARSEN

Three years after my first meeting with Eubie in Berlin, I was at the New Orleans Workshop club in Pløens Street in Oslo, where the young ragtime pianist, Morten Gunnar Larsen, impressed me greatly. He was twenty years old, and this was the first time I had heard him.

"You should have met Eubie Blake, whom I met in Berlin. Are you familiar with him?" I asked. I was slightly embarrassed by Morten Gunnar's reply.

"I heard your interview with him on the *Jazz Club* programme," he said. "I was really surprised. I've admired Eubie Blake since I was thirteen years old."

When Morten Gunnar was to record his third LP, including 'Randi's Rag', I sent a cassette to Eubie and asked him what he thought. I also

Eubie and Morten Gunnar at Gartnerveien, 1977

Randi & Eubie Oslo 1977

hinted that he might do the honour of writing something for the record cover. Eubie took out his red pen and declared that he was very proud that Morten Gunnar had recorded his music: "I, Eubie Blake, is very, very proud to have such a great artist as Mr Morten Gunnar Larsen to record my music.

"There are only two people in the world who can play 'Charleston Rag' the way I want it played," said Eubie. "One of them is Morten Gunnar Larsen."

TO OSLO

As the time approached for Eubie's trip to Oslo in July, 1977, I asked Morten Gunnar if he would play on the same bill as Eubie at Club 7, with his new group, Ophelia Ragtime Orchestra. Although Eubie liked to perform alone, a whole evening alone might be too much – he was, after all, ninety-four years old. Morten Gunnar said that it would be an honour.

Marion and Eubie came to Oslo in the company of Dorothy Coshburn, a former school teacher and very close friend of theirs. On the way, they had stopped for a couple of days to visit their good friends in Denmark, Lis and Kurt Andersen. At the airport in Oslo, Eubie was welcomed by Magnolia Jazzband, with Morten Gunnar among them. TV reporters were also there. Eubie was tickled pink, and he beamed when he heard the band. "Do you understand what I'm saying?" he asked, as he went around and thanked each one of the musicians individually.

I had said that they could stay at my house, and Eubie was happy to, but Marion preferred the SAS Hotel. It was probably better that they stayed there anyway, because they had a lot of luggage. They did have dinner with me the first evening, though.

First, we took a trip into the yard to see "Eubie Blake Lake," the little pond that my father had put in. It's not much more than six feet in diameter, but Eubie was impressed.

Then came the moment when we were to have dinner.

Being a terrible cook, I had cooked fricassee several days in a row, but just to be on the safe side, I also served fish fillets and sausages. It was the best I could do. "Is this typical Norwegian food?" Marion asked. I had to explain hurriedly that it was rather more typical me.

Morten Gunnar had also been invited to dinner, and afterward, they played for us and for each other. There was also a pre-concert press conference in my home. Eubie played and talked for a couple of hours. He was being the showman, and the journalists were impressed with his vitality. He told stories, joked and laughed all the time:

"I had the world's finest parents, but my mother didn't like ragtime music. She wanted me to play for Jesus, but you can't make any money doing that! Mother had eleven children, and I was the only one who grew up. Unfortunately I didn't meet up to expectations. 'You'll never amount to anything, boy,' my mother said."

During Eubie's stay in Oslo, there was also time to do a radio show with Johs Bergh. While I accompanied Eubie to the studio, Marion and Dorothy were to go on a fjord cruise. The interview went smoothly. In

July 28th 1977

I thank you for having to Visit
Your Home, I should have said
" Your Beautiful Home.
Please have me to Come Back here
And I also thank for arranging
for me to Play the Concert at
Club 7.

My Marion & ~~me~~ me or
I should said My Marion & Me

Sincerly

Eubie Blake

Greetings from Eubie, 1977

fact, it must have been the cleanest take that Johs Bergh ever had – at no time did he have to stop the tape and record over, and when he posed a question, it was like pressing a button: Eubie held forth. We finished the interview and were back at the hotel long before Marion and Dorothy returned from their cruise.

Eubie got his room key, and we went upstairs. After we had sat down to relax, he suddenly felt a pang of conscience and decided that it was not suitable to be alone in his hotel room with a woman who was not his wife. He jumped up, ran to the door, and wedged the waste basket in the entrance, so that the door was held ajar. "People think a lot of strange things, you know, so it's best that they can see what we're doing," he said.

When Marion arrived, she scolded us for not waiting down in the reception. It didn't help that I explained we were finished with the interview earlier than expected.

"I said we would meet downstairs. You have to listen to what I say!" she said. I felt like a schoolgirl being reprimanded by Marion. And to her, I was just that. She was over eighty years old at the time.

Another day, as we ate dinner at the SAS Hotel, Eubie asked if he could have my cigarette butt. I protested and said that I would go out and buy more cigarettes. "No," he said, "I've always smoked butts since I was six years old. That's how I started. Think how old I would have been if I didn't smoke!"

STANDING OVATION

In readiness for Club 7, Eubie was dressed to kill, with a silk shirt and a silk suit. Arne Dahl was master of ceremonies, and although it was not normally very formal in the club, I asked if he might request the audience to stand when Eubie came in. In several of his letters he had talked about "standing ovations", so I thought this would be an appropriate gesture.

Eubie certainly appreciated that welcome. He shone like the sun as he took the stage. After that he played and talked non-stop. The audience was wild about him.

When Ophelia Ragtime Orchestra played, Eubie sat close to the band and listened intently to every note.

That concert at Club 7 is one of the historical high points in the history of the club. It was thoroughly entertaining, packed with listeners of all ages, and marked Ophelia Ragtime Orchestra's debut, with "the master of ragtime" in attendance. Not many bands making their debut can boast such an experience.

PREDICTION ABOUT AMERICA

During his visit to Oslo, Eubie again invited me to New York: "I'm getting so old now that you can't expect me to come to Norway any more just to meet you. I don't want to hear any more about that fortune of yours."

As a young girl, I had had my fortune told by a gypsy, and believe it or not, much of what she told me has come to pass. That's why I have never travelled to the United States. "You love to travel," she had told me, "but you will never go to America." I must admit that this prediction was quite a shock, because at the time, the only thing I could think about was going to America as soon as the war was over – not to listen to jazz, because I wasn't yet interested in that, but I wanted to visit relatives in the States.

After having my fortune told by this woman, it didn't make any difference what people said after the war. I was offered free trips by several musicians, but I always refused. "Forget it!" I was adamant about not challenging my fortune.

"Baloney!" said Eubie. "You're too smart and too grown up to believe that kind of stuff. You got me to fly for the first time when I was ninety, now you owe me a return visit. We'll meet in New Orleans next year. That will be a good place to start, since you're coming to America."

Suddenly it was as if the spell was broken. Eubie was right – I owed it to him to take the chance. I was not afraid to fly, it was just the idea of flying to America that bothered me...

I did take the chance, embarking on the same plane as the Magnolia Jazzband who were going to play a festival in New Orleans. I'll never forget the feeling when I touched down in Chicago. I'd done it!

A marvellous week followed, in the company of the boys in the Jazzband – including Morten Gunnar. Eubie gave a concert and was

Eubie making tea in his own kitchen, 1979

the top billing of the festival. We had a press conference at the home of author Al Rose, who was just completing his book on Eubie. I asked if Rose had received any letters from Eubie.

"Letters?" Rose looked at me inquisitively, as if I had said something stupid. "We talk on the telephone, of course."

Poor man, he had no idea what he was missing. Eubie's letters are some of the dearest memories I have of him. Two folders full of them.

Morten Gunnar played 'Randi's Rag' during the press conference. Eubie himself never learned to play it because it is very difficult, but he did try to occasionally. In fact, in 1990, I received a surprise cassette from the Andersens in Denmark, who had recorded Eubie practising my ragtime.

One day Morten Gunnar and I were invited to a jazz brunch at the Commander's Palace, a well-known restaurant where there was a trio playing during dinner. It was led by Alvin Alcorn, and Eubie shocked Marion by putting some money in his pocket.

"You don't do things like that," she maintained.

"Maybe not," said Eubie, "but they deserve the money. They play well."

We frequented several restaurants, and at one, we heard a very talented singer. "Do you want to know her name?" asked Eubie, and before I could reply, he had jumped up and run over to the bandstand to ask for her name and address. Quite a helpful escort – at ninety-five years of age!

TO BROOKLYN

The year after New Orleans, I was invited to celebrate Eubie's birthday – 7 February, 1979. I was to stay at their home at 284A Stuyvesant Avenue, in Brooklyn. Marion met me with a chauffeur at the airport, and I was given a room on the third floor of their home, the floor on which Marion had a room.

The flowers literally streamed in. Each year, Bill Cosby, Frank Sinatra, and Dean Martin were first – all of them sent extravagant baskets of flowers. The house in Brooklyn was a four-storey brownstone and the entrance was filled with pictures from floor to ceiling. I found Morten Gunnar's hanging side by side with Dave

Eubie at ninety-nine, with Lou Jacobs, Maurice Hines, Lucille Armstrong and Eddie
Heywood, 1982

Brubeck and Bill Cosby. Further in towards the living room, where
Eubie's Steinway stood on the right side of the room, all of the walls
were covered with posters and awards. I counted a hundred in all.
Between the living room and the kitchen was Marion's writing table.
Eubie's bedroom was on the second floor, with the desk where he
often sat and composed at night. On the fourth floor, there was yet
another guest room, and the attic was full of music and documents.
On the first floor, there was a cozy kitchen, and it was here that I
would spend many a fine moment with Eubie. Each day he read aloud
from the newspaper. He was exceptionally sharp and always made
witty comments as he read. He also had a habit of making comments
in the evening while he watched television on the second floor. I
laughed constantly. One night Eubie made enough tea for the whole
week. He used a huge kettle into which he dumped a large amount of
sugar. "I like sweet tea," he said.

I was with Eubie on most of his birthdays from the time he was
ninety-six until his death at 100 years and five days. During my first

Eubie at the piano with singer Mary Louise, 1982

visit, the Broadway musical *Eubie* was playing. It presented a total of twenty-two of Eubie's melodies, with dance, song and orchestra – everything from his strong vaudeville numbers to gospel, blues and spirituals. It was an experience. We sat on the third row – Marion, Eubie and I. As soon as the show was over, the artists were grouped together with Eubie on stage. Marion nudged me: "Take your camera and go up on the stage. You'll get some nice pictures with the TV lights up there right now."

On the stage stood brothers Maurice and Gregory Hines, tap dancers and actors whose careers Eubie himself had launched. A large cake was brought out. Later we went to Windows Of The World restaurant, atop the twin towers in Manhattan where Eubie was given a specially-baked cake designed as a grand piano, and the band played 'Memories Of You'. It was obvious that all present were honoured by Eubie's presence. We were together with friends of Eubie and Marion, including Phoebe and Lou Jacobs, whom I saw more of in later years. Phoebe Jacobs was secretary to a senator, in addition to working for

Mercer Ellington, Duke's son. She was as talented as Marion when it came to doing things right.

After the visit to Windows Of The World, we went on to Luchow's – one of New York's best and oldest restaurants. Here there were more friends, including the cast of the musical, and Eubie was again greeted with a standing ovation.

TRIUMPH

About a month past his ninety-eighth birthday, Eubie fractured his femur and had to use a walker. "When we go out, we have to use a wheelchair," Marion wrote in a letter. Even in his wheelchair, Eubie visited the jazz clubs, among other places, Sweet Basil's, where they met the Norwegian ragtime pianist, Morten Gunnar Larsen. "As long as Eubie can meet people and listen to music," said Marion, "there's no danger."

Before long, he had discarded both the wheelchair and the walker. When I visited him the following year, on his ninety-ninth birthday, he

Eubie with pianist McCoy Tyner, 1982

could walk without any help. A lot of adulation was given him that year. I don't think I've ever experienced anything so fantastic in all my life. Eubie didn't know I was coming to New York, and when I walked into their living room, he sat down at the grand piano and played a whole hour for me – 'Memories Of You', 'Tricky Fingers', 'Love Will Find A Way' and other melodies that I had become so fond of listening to. It was really quite amazing, a man of that age playing the way he did.

The year was 1982, and the big party was to be held at Gallagher's, a restaurant in the heart of New York. Eubie was being filmed by a TV crew and was continuously feted. Lucille, the widow of Louis Armstrong, was invited along with all the female singers from his past, many of whom sang for him. He was one big smile as he sat at the place of honour in the company of Marion, Maurice Hines, Lucille and pianist Eddie Heywood. Usually I sat next to Marion, but at the dinner at Gallagher's, I had been placed with a Danish gentleman. I think Phoebe had some special intentions – he was just the right age, and he was a recent widower. His daughter was married to Mercer Ellington. Thinking about the consequences of this set-up – that is, if Phoebe's ploy were to be successful – I had to laugh to myself: would I become the step-grandmother of Duke Ellington's grandchildren?

To everybody's joy, Eubie was playing. In the midst of it all, while I was standing there with my camera, I was filmed for two or three minutes by several TV crews. As a matter of fact, a colleague of mine on a business trip to New York was slightly shocked when he suddenly viewed Mrs Hultin on television involved in all this commotion.

One day we went to the Songwriters Hall Of Fame where they were unveiling a bust of Eubie. I was going to take care of him alone this time – that is, with the help of an old musician, Panama Francis, as there were certain things I couldn't manage. Eubie was sitting on the stage for nearly four hours, under the TV lights, among people who were singing songs especially written for the occasion.

There were many speeches, with Eubie telling a lot of stories. All of a sudden, an old lady who looked at least 110 years old made her way to the stage and took over the piano stool. She was assisted by her niece.

"I was in Eubie's shows in the old days," she said.

"I can't remember that," retorted Eubie.

The lady was not discouraged by his interruptions and was

Children performed Eubie's last musical at a Brooklyn school, 1982

determined to steal the show. Eubie tried to get rid of her, but she started to sing and play the piano. Even I understood that her act was a little bit risqué.

THE SCHOOL PLAY

Every birthday, Eubie would receive a letter from a school in Brooklyn, written by an entire class of about thirty students making their best joint effort. When he was ninety-nine years old, and the students were about nine or ten, they told him that they had practised some melodies from one of his Broadway musicals, for a show they called *We're Just Wild About Eubie*. Could he possibly attend the opening?

"No, that would be too much for him," said Marion. "The answer is no."

"Why not?" I asked. "Imagine how happy the kids would be if he showed up!"

When the day came, we drove up in our limousine. Year after year, Marion used a driver from Brooklyn who worshipped Eubie. Accompanying us was a lady from the school neighbourhood. When

At the children's musical   **Eubie with a baby**

we arrived we were greeted by the principal and the teacher of the performing class. The American flag was waving, and the children were lined up with letters spelling out "Eubie" on their chests. I wanted to film the show and got out my camera, but I soon found it difficult to focus. It was touching, and I was misty-eyed. The children gave a marvellous performance, all dressed up in cute costumes.

Every seat in the school hall was occupied. In spite of this being an integrated school, I saw only black children, with the exception of one student. Whole families were present, and they were justifiably proud, because Eubie – the master of ragtime – was there!

Afterwards, when the principal made her speech, Eubie suddenly announced that he would play for the children. He seated himself at the grand piano and played 'I'm Just Wild About Harry'. His playing was as youthful as ever!

At the home of Carl Seltzer, the record producer and Eubie's manager, there was yet another big party. In attendance were Rudy Blesh, pianist McCoy Tyner, the ageing singer Alberta Hunter, and a number of well-known ragtime pianists. Eubie was again the centre of attention, and again he played for us. McCoy asked if he could have his autograph, which to me was a rare scene in itself. Since I first met him playing with Coltrane, McCoy and I had become great friends. To be a guest of Eubie's, he felt, was a big honour.

I asked McCoy to play something – Eubie's 'Memories Of You', for example. "I'm afraid to," said McCoy, but he sat down at the piano nevertheless. Eubie listened. "That's a clever young man," he pronounced.

It was a fantastic party, and it was also the first time I met Carl's girlfriend, Deli. She was the daughter of Marion's former secretary. The next time I met her, she was getting married to Carl around the time that Eubie was to celebrate his 100th birthday.

In the summer of 1982, Marion died. She had been afflicted with diabetes, angina pectoris and cancer all at once. In spite of all that, she had managed to keep up with her work around the house. Her secretary informed me shortly after Marion's death.

PLAYING FOR THE PRESIDENT

In 1983, Eubie's 100th birthday was to be celebrated. Two weeks before the occasion, I received a telephone call inviting me to accompany him to Washington, DC where he was to be honoured at a grand show with the President of the United States in attendance.

As I didn't have much vacation left, I couldn't join him immediately and had to wait until the day before the big event. When I finally arrived in New York, Eubie had already been to Washington and back. According to his friends, the Andersens, from Denmark, he had been given the go-ahead for this trip by his personal physician, but nonetheless still caught pneumonia. The Danes were staying with him when I arrived. Eubie's physician, who had taken care of him for many years, said that Eubie was alive only thanks to him. Many of Eubie's friends, however, believed the converse to be true: this doctor was seventy-nine years old and had for years practised with only one patient – Eubie.

My newspaper colleague, Arvid Bryne, picked me up at the airport and drove me directly to Eubie's house. We were both surprised to find Eubie lying in bed downstairs where he lay exposed to a draft each time someone entered the front door. When I came in from the cold, the nurse asked me to wait a few minutes before I went in. Eubie's physician, however, never waited. Every day he charged right in to where Eubie, now very weak, lay under oxygen.

"How are we today?" the doctor asked, pinching Eubie's sunken cheek. He never waited for the answer, but he sent a bill for sixty dollars for each visit to the patient.

I met Virginia, from Los Angeles, a friend who was there to help out, and Dee, the young maid who had been fired by Marion but rehired by Deli. Eubie also had three very nice nurses to take care of him around the clock. They loved the fine old gentleman.

Eubie was very happy to see me. I had brought presents, and I wrote a poem for him. What he appreciated most, though, was a little music box that played 'You Are My Sunshine'. His face lit up when I played the melody and held the box to his ear. He was slightly hard of hearing, but he was completely alert, and his sense of humour was totally intact.

"We're going to wash you now," said Josephine.

"You go wash yourself," said Eubie. "You're blacker than me!"

In order to help keep his respiratory passages clear and functioning, Eubie was given massages and helped up to walk a little each day. He was extremely weak, however. The Andersens told me that he'd been playing the piano right up to the day he went on that ill-fated car trip to Washington. As it turned out, the doctor was the only person to be seen on the TV broadcasts. Eubie was sitting behind him, and the President never appeared. I'm sure Eubie would have preferred to stay home.

Through several nights I sat with Eubie, keeping him company with only the night nurse present. I put together a photo album with pictures from our eleven years of friendship – snapshots from Berlin, Molde, New Orleans, New York, and his visit to the school in Brooklyn. He loved for me to go through the album with him. "Can you imagine, Randi, that we have known each other for eleven years?" he whispered. He asked for Morten Gunnar Larsen, and I said that he would be coming to New York soon and that I would try to bring him over. This wouldn't be easy to arrange, because a lot of ragtime pianists called wanting to visit, and they were refused. Journalists from all over the United States, as well as the BBC, were calling regularly. Whenever I happened to answer the telephone, I would say that Eubie was ill. After a while I was asked not to answer the phone.

After the Andersens' departure, I was the only white person in the house, and I felt that my only contact was with Eubie, the nurses, and

Carl and Deli whenever they dropped by. I still had those precious, quiet nights with Eubie, and at such moments I read to him the poem that Ruth Reese, the American singer living in Norway, had written to him. I later donated the manuscript to the Eubie Blake Theatre.

THE GREAT DAY

The day before Eubie's centennial, famous artists and jazz musicians started their celebration in St Peter's Church, an event that would last twenty-four hours. For the big day itself, a spectacular show was planned at the Schubert Theatre, featuring performances from the Amherst Saxophone Quartet, several ragtime pianists, and other well-known artists.

Tickets were hard to come by, and many people had probably hoped to catch a glimpse of Eubie at the show, but he wasn't up to attending. Without anyone knowing, though, Eubie's physician had arranged with the telephone company to have a direct line installed, so that Eubie could follow the show from his bed. This wasn't a bad idea, even if he could manage only five minutes at a time. On the other hand, plans were made to install an amplified line directly from Eubie's bed to the theatre stage. I was appalled, and wondered how any other person on his deathbed would react to such a proposal, let alone the physician of a dying patient! Eubie didn't even know about these plans. I mentioned my resentments to Deli, and fortunately she put a stop to the idea.

The performance was fantastic, with lots of famous people in the audience. To my surprise, I met old friends Iola and Dave Brubeck. Everyone in the show spoke directly into the microphone to Eubie, or so they thought. It was probably best they thought so. "Ragtime Bob" Darch was going to play 'Randi's Rag', according to the programme, but for some reason, he never showed up. The Eubie Blake Children's Theatre, under the direction of Rosetta, was also on stage.

"I MADE IT"

On the very day of Eubie's 100th birthday, Deli had invited only the people who were very close to Eubie, plus a couple of neighbours.

That was all, except for the doctor, who arrived with a small cake. After a while, we brought the doctor's cake down to Eubie's room. There were three candles on it. As we were all standing around him, singing 'Happy Birthday', he folded his hands over his head the way he always did when he received applause. Then he smiled in a way that I will never forget and said happily, "I made it!"

MORTEN GUNNAR'S VISIT

I was still trying to figure out how I could arrange for Morten Gunnar Larsen to visit Eubie because I knew it would be a nice experience for Eubie, one last time, to have Morten Gunnar play for him.

I thought the one to ask would be Deli since she seemed to make all the major decisions even though she did not live in the house. Deli immediately consented, but when I mentioned it to the young maid, she became hysterical: "Nobody is going to visit Eubie!"

Fate smiled on us, however – on Eubie, on Morten Gunnar, on me. A couple of days later, Eubie was delighted by a visit from two of his friends – Rosetta, the manager of Eubie's Children's Theatre, and Jimmy Butts, a bass player and nice fellow with a huge white wig. Butts told us that he was to perform for a group of elderly indigents at a social centre in Brooklyn the next day. It was close by, and he thought I might like to attend.

When I arrived, I learned that Butts' regular pianist had been unable to make the engagement. I immediately offered to get hold of Morten Gunnar. He was staying at a hotel, and I desperately hoped I would be able to reach him there. This was my chance. Morten Gunnar would then be able to return with me to Eubie's house after the concert – after all, nobody could prevent me from being escorted home.

Morten Gunnar was a big hit with everyone at the social centre – the audience, the staff, and Mr Butts. The manager, a former opera singer, observed that the young Norwegian pianist was undoubtedly a professional. The old people danced and applauded wildly. The atmosphere was lively.

The same atmosphere reigned later at Stuyvesant Avenue, when I brought home Eubie's favourite pianist. With the help of his nurse,

Eubie was a true inspiration

Eubie was propped up comfortably in his chair so that Morten Gunnar could start his private recital.

First he played 'Charleston Rag', followed by 'Tricky Fingers', admitting to Eubie that he was nervous about this piece. "I don't know if I dare to play it!" he said. Eubie just chuckled, but he was very attentive to his playing. When Morten Gunnar closed with 'Memories Of You', Eubie had to brush the tears from his eyelashes.

"Did Eubie really write all this music?" asked Beverly, the nurse. "Look how happy it makes Eubie! This young pianist ought to be playing for him every day!"

Eubie was happy, very happy. His fondest wish had been granted him before he died.

ONE HUNDRED YEARS AND FIVE DAYS

A couple of days later, Eubie passed away. I had gone in to Manhattan that night, because I had promised to hear a young singer, Evelyn Blakey, daughter of drummer Art Blakey. When I arrived, it had begun to snow heavily, and I had just barely made it to the club. When it snows in New York, the city becomes temporarily paralysed.

I was supposed to meet Tone Vestøl, a Norwegian artist and a friend of Evelyn. Both of them arrived, but only because we had a date. Even though the music was good, it was still a spooky evening. There were no other people in the club. The band was playing only for us. There was no service whatsoever – the waitresses had stayed home. The snow kept coming down, and strangely, it was accompanied by lightning and thunderclaps. Before long, the musicians' car was buried under a thick layer of snow.

A smiling young man approached me, asking if I was Randi. "Do you remember me? We met in Warsaw years back. You helped me to get tickets to a concert. You also took pictures of me with Thad Jones."

Of course I remembered the young Bulgarian, who had been standing on the steps of the Palace of Culture, looking somewhat lost. Little did I know that I had changed his life – I was somehow responsible for Angel Rangelov being in New York. Now he insisted on spending his last dime buying us food from a nearby restaurant.

When I got up to leave, it was impossible to get a taxi back to Brooklyn. Tone had a small apartment and was unable to put me up for the night because of lack of space, but Angel offered me a bed at his place. My thoughts, however, were with Eubie all the time.

Angel had a photo album. He wanted to show me what had happened in his life since we last met. He had been so thrilled when he got the pictures I had sent of himself with Thad Jones, that he resolved to defect and live in America.

He had been sleeping on park benches until, at long last, he was accepted at Berklee College of Music in Boston. Now he was the leader of his own big band in New York. It was strange hearing his story, and it was coincidentally strange that he should be appearing in exactly that night club on a night when I needed help.

The next day, Eubie's death was announced on the radio. He'd made it to one hundred years and five days old. His music was played the entire day. I cried and cried. It was terrible to be stuck in Manhattan, unable to be with my dear friend. At the same time, I thought of how difficult it would have been to be in the house and perhaps not be able to go near his lifeless body.

It was two days before I could return to Brooklyn. Beverly had to pick me up at Arvid Bryne's house and I dreaded coming home to the empty bed where Eubie had slept.

Naomi Alleyne, Eubie's secretary and a truly warm and wonderful person, arrived the following day. "Eubie died because you were away, Randi," she said. "We almost couldn't get a hearse because of all the snow."

"What about the doctor? What did he say?"

"He didn't show up the day Eubie died."

Deli and Carl were away on their honeymoon in Mexico. They are divorced now, however, and Deli's daughter lives in Eubie's historical home.

There is a Eubie Blake Museum in his hometown of Baltimore. I think, though, that I have more mementos of Eubie in my possession that the museum does.

I was sorry when Marion passed away the year before Eubie died. I miss both of them terribly, just as if they were close relatives.

Eubie Blake Lake, 1983

When I returned to Norway, I noticed that the lights over my little pond that I had named "Eubie Blake Lake" had burned out. A blue light burns there now. My dear father, who had made that pond, died on 7 February – a year to the day of Eubie's last birthday.

CHAPTER 18

Stan Getz –
"The Sound"

S tan Getz has been mentioned several times already in previous
chapters. I first met him at the Nordstrand concert hall in 1958
when he was only thirty-one years old. He was "The Sound In
Person" and had already been famous for a long time, achieving
prominence as a sixteen-year-old. It is fantastic the way he managed to
stay on top all of those years. His ballad playing was incredibly
beautiful, and he had a strong, personal, sense of rhythm.

Stan was not old when he became one of the famous "Four
Brothers" in Woody Herman's big band, and he was still a youngster
when he played with well-known bandleaders like Jack Teagarden,
Stan Kenton and Benny Goodman. Starting as far back as the 1950s,
Stan had a number of fine bands in his own name, and many famous
soloists made their debuts with him over the years.

Stan and I kept in touch continually, from the time he played a jam
session at Gartnerveien in 1958 until I lived at his house in
Copenhagen, met him in Paris or other places, and so on.

At Christmas in 1960, Stan called to say that he would be moving
from Copenhagen and back to the States. It wasn't long before he
made a tremendous comeback in the USA, despite the competition
from John Coltrane, who had become more and more prominent on
the jazz scene. Stan was lavishly successful with his interpretations of
Brazilian bossa nova tunes, particularly with the hit 'Desafinado'.

With Stan Getz, 1990

BACK IN OSLO

In February, 1970, Stan was to give a concert at the Chat Noir in Oslo, and great expectations abounded among the Norwegian fans. We had not heard him live in ten years, and there were long lines for tickets. He was going to play on his forty-third birthday – 2 February. When he arrived at Fornebu airport, however, we learned that he had collapsed onboard and had to be given emergency CPR before being rushed directly to the hospital. His wife Monica was with him, and I was in contact with her, as well as with the English musicians in his band, for the week he spent in Ullevål Hospital. The concert had to be cancelled.

When Stan was to be released from the hospital, Monica called and told me to come down to the Continental Hotel to say hello to him. Immediately thereafter they would be leaving for an engagement in London. Stan was still weak, and when we had eaten, he had to lie down again. I had brought along a little tape recorder and had decided to do my first taped radio interview. Previously, I had only used the tape recorder for taping music. My interview with Stan lasted just five minutes, and it was to be called – appropriately – "Bedside with Stan Getz".

Stan with Monica at the Chat Noir, 1970

349

Stan Getz at my house, 1960

Stan left for London shortly afterward, but he was too weak to play Ronnie Scott's Club. He returned to Oslo later, however, to give a concert, bringing with him my own son-in-law, Spike Wells, on drums.

Stan returned many times over the years, and he always delivered unforgettable concerts – whether they were at Club 7, on tour, in Kongsberg, Molde, or in Sandvika cinema with Chet Baker.

I also met Stan several times outside of Norway, and I will never forget our time in India in 1980. I was invited to Jazz Yatra, where Stan was playing, although he had no idea I would be attending. I went to the concert early and took a front row seat. The audience crowded into the concert hall, eager to see Stan, the main attraction. As the moment approached for Stan's entrance on stage, a woman suddenly stood in front of me complaining that I had taken her seat. She was from the media! "Well, then you should have arrived earlier," I countered, "because a lot has already happened here." I didn't budge from my seat. After all, I was from the press, too.

When Stan came out on stage, he played his opening solo, and then when the band took over, he looked out and spotted me. He came all the way out to the edge of the stage. The look on his face of happiness, mixed with perplexed amusement, was priceless. Five thousand spectators watched our little reunion, and there was no doubt that Stan was surprised. "What are you doing here?" he signalled, using finger language. "Come backstage when I'm finished." I just smiled, and basked in a certain triumph – the offensive journalist woman who had tried to take my seat must surely know now why I had chosen a front row seat. I wasn't about to give up this close contact with my good friend on stage in front of me.

After the concert, I had to introduce the Minister of Culture, Vatsala Pai, to Stan. It was she who had arranged my trip to India, and she had mentioned that she herself was a fan of Stan Getz.

ANTABUS DUPE

At the hotel, Stan asked if I was aware of the fact that Monica had tried to slip him an antabus – the tablet that causes nausea in combination with alcohol. He said she was trying to give him the tablets without telling him. "I've moved out. I don't dare to live in the house anymore."

The house he was referring to was "Shadowbrook" – a gigantic twenty-seven-room mansion on ten acres in Irvington-on-Hudson, New York. I've visited this old house myself; it dates from 1805 and once was home to George Gershwin. Monica and Stan had hosted Frank Sinatra, who sang for them privately in the music room, and they had received the king and queen of Thailand – and Randi Hultin from Norway.

I must admit that Monica had told me about the antabus tablets one time when Stan was playing in Oslo. She came to my house specially to give me some of these tablets. I protested, because I didn't want anything to do with something like that. If she was going to administer antabus, then he should at least be told about it, and she should be the one to tell him. She put up such a fuss about it that I finally did take the tablets. She gave me six of them, which I filed under "G" in my home archives. I realised that Monica only wanted to help Stan, because she didn't want him to drink. Still, I didn't like the fact that she was tricking him, and I liked even less that she was trying to get his friends to go along with the scheme.

"My brother, who is a doctor, says that Stan won't be harmed by this," Monica said. "He'll just get a little red and puffy in the face, and he doesn't like that. I always tell him it's because he's allergic to alcohol."

"You can understand why I can't live at home," said Stan.

I did meet Stan and Monica together in New York a year later, however. We met coincidentally at Fat Tuesday, where Stan's son Steven was in charge of booking. On the bandstand stood Phil Woods with his orchestra. It was the same evening I heard Kim Parker sing for the first time – the stepdaughter of both Charlie Parker and Woods. Stan did not look very happy when we met in New York. He looked much improved when we met again at the Nice festival in 1981. Together with Dexter Gordon, he gave a memorable concert, and was pleased with it himself. Every time we met in Nice, he would invite me to the beach, where he had a reserved spot. Whenever and wherever we met, Stan was always very gentlemanly and generous.

In the summer of 1984, he called from Stavanger to invite me to join him there and then later in Bergen. He was disappointed because he wasn't scheduled to come to Oslo. At the time he called, I had Chet Baker and his girlfriend staying as house guests. I never should have said that to Stan. Stan and Chet were like cat and dog.

"Get him out of the house before he sets fire to it!" bellowed Stan. I had to bite my lip not to tell him that I had, in fact, extinguished a wastepaper basket that had caught fire after Chet had thrown a lit cigarette into it.

Stan called me from Bergen later to give me a report on a concert at the Grieg Hall. "I got a good review from Mr Genius," he said, laughing about Arvid Genius, and went on to relate an incident during which a spectator at the concert threatened to leave if Stan didn't play 'Desafinado' for him. "I told him I would play it if he would promise to leave after the song was over!"

Stan was to return to Stanford University, where he had been a teacher for a time, along with Dizzy Gillespie. He called me from America several times while he was getting a divorce from Monica. He wanted me to go to the States and testify in court that I had been given antabus tablets. I can't say I was eager to get involved, although I understood that he wanted evidence – from me and other friends. But before the hearing, I got a letter from Monica and a doctor friend of hers who maintained they were involved in the treatment of alcoholics and they wanted me to testify to this effect in court.

"What can I do?" I asked. "I'll have to tell them that I was given antabus tablets to give to Stan."

Stan's favourite photo (with Dexter)

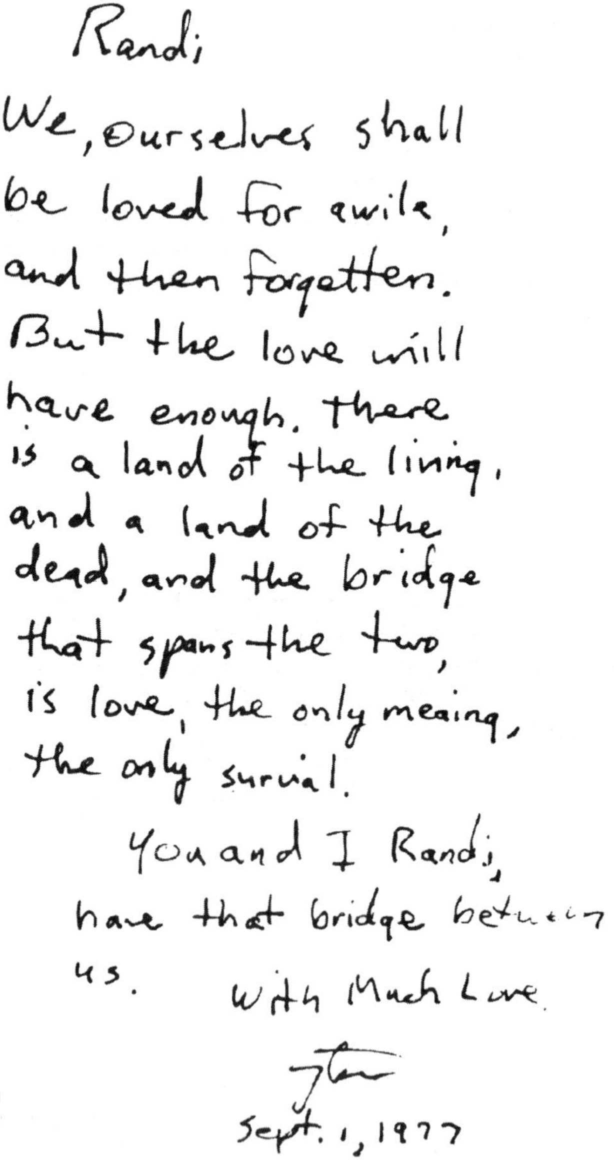

Randi,

We, ourselves shall
be loved for awile,
and then forgetten.
But the love will
have enough. there
is a land of the living,
and a land of the
dead, and the bridge
that spans the two,
is love, the only meaing,
the only survial.

You and I Randi,
have that bridge between
us.   with Much Love.

Greetings
from Stan in
my guest
book, 1977

Stan

Sept. 1, 1977

354

"All you have to say is that we all love Stan," Monica replied, "and that we only want the best for him."

Stan won the case.

ILLNESS AND FITNESS

As we lay on the beach in Nice, in 1987, Stan revealed to me how he had also found out that he had a large malignancy growing on the back of his heart and that doctors were advising an operation. The operation was scheduled for 10 August so I called him around that time to wish him good luck, but he said that he had decided to use natural medicines: "I don't want to take the chance on having an operation – maybe I wouldn't be able to play afterwards." The following month, though, Stan had to be rushed to the hospital, where they performed the operation immediately after admission. A week later, he called and was relieved because it was all over. "The tumour was as big as an orange," he said.

Five months after the operation, in February 1988, Stan came to Paris to give a concert, and I had the pleasure of being present. He played at one of the university branches outside the city because he didn't want to give an inner city concert until he was sure that the music sounded right. Stan was a perfectionist who always insisted on doing his very best. This concert was just as impressive and beautiful as usual, but it taxed his strength. After Paris, he played at the Royal Festival Hall in London before an audience of several thousands. It was probably the longest ticket line of Stan's career, and the reviews were raves. Unfortunately, he had to cancel the rest of the tour for health reasons.

He returned to California to get back into shape. "I go bicycling and I swim," he said. "I've got to get ready for a new tour, because I just can't stop playing."

JUAN-LES-PINS

The next time I met him was in Juan-les-Pins in the summer of 1989. I was at the Nice festival with my close friends – Lill, "Pastor'n", Ole Jacob, Brit and Runa – and I had heard that Stan was going to be

With Stan on the beach at Nice, 1981

playing in Antibes. I had also heard that he had cancelled a concert because he wasn't allowed to use the hotel kitchen. That was unusual – since when did Stan Getz start showing an interest in the culinary arts? When I had found out where he was staying, I called, and a short time later he called back to invite me to dinner – "macro dinner" – prepared by a Chinese cook. Stan had hired a professional cook, Donna, who prepared food for him twenty-four hours a day, so to speak, and she also gave him massages. She was a combination cook-and-nurse. Stan was convinced that she would be able to restore him to perfect health.

Stan lived at the elegant Hotel Juana in Juan-les-Pins, and the waiters and *maître d'hôtel* gladly assisted as Donna served her specially prepared meal, which consisted exclusively of vegetables. It tasted divine. Also present were Stan's girlfriend Samantha, twenty-four years old, and Stan's grandchild Christopher, nineteen. While we were eating, pianist Oscar Peterson suddenly appeared. He was staying at the hotel almost incognito; his concert wouldn't be given until much later in the festival.

"We're going to make a new record together," Stan said, and they started discussing music. Stan enjoyed working with Oscar; they had made a couple of records before, and they were among Stan's favourites. Oscar was surprised to find me at the dinner table. We are also old friends, but we normally meet only when he gives concerts, usually in Oslo.

I remember once a long time ago when I drummed up a jam session on the stage of the university auditorium. Arne Bendiksen wanted to sing scat with Oscar Peterson, because he was going to use it in a TV programme. I thought it sounded like an insane idea, but I enjoy a challenge, so after a conversation with bassist Ray Brown, I approached Oscar about going along with the idea of a jam session. To the surprise of the audience, Bendiksen got his way and was filmed in performance with Peterson. I've never seen this film clip. Perhaps it was of poor photographic quality.

The concert in Juan-les-Pins was fantastic, as usual. Stan seemed healthy and strong in spite of having undergone an operation. To sit in the park under the palm trees, a stone's throw from the Mediterranean, with Getz on the stage – what more could one desire? The audience loved Stan, and I don't think anyone has ever become bored with the fragile, lyrical tones that he plays. All my Norwegian friends were at the concert. We were all equally enraptured. Stan went back to the hotel, but we joined forces with the members of his band and went to a sidewalk restaurant afterwards. Few festivals are as quaintly comfortable as those on the French Riviera. The weather is always clear and warm, there are hundreds of places to go after the concerts, and all day long you can lounge around on the beach.

Stan was eager to return to Norway again and both the Oslo and the Molde Festivals were interested in hiring him, but the fee was quite high for them. Molde eventually raised the money and Stan had the honour of opening the festival on its thirtieth anniversary in 1990. Unfortunately I was not going to Molde, because *Aftenposten* found they could not afford to send two journalists.

TREATED BY GETZ

I had told Stan that I would not be coming, but on his way to Molde, he called from the airport and told me to get my things ready. It made no difference that I protested: "I'm telling you that you're going to Molde," Stan ordered, "and I'm paying for your flight and your hotel."

"There's probably not a vacancy in any of the hotels," I interjected, but Stan was insistent.

"I'll call you from Molde." He did. "Take the flight about noon tomorrow and meet me at the press conference. I've arranged a room for you."

Just like that, I was suddenly at the festival, and I was invited for yet another of Donna's special vegetarian meals, along with Stan's old girlfriend Jane Walsh. It was a pleasure to see them again, and a joy to hear Stan's concert.

This was to be our last meeting. Stan died 6 June, 1991, of liver cancer. He was sixty-four years old.

CHAPTER 19

Chet Baker –
The Fascinator

When Chet Baker came to Oslo to play at Club 7 in 1978, he remembered meeting me fifteen years earlier. Even then he was a living legend – a cult figure. Few can play as lyrically as Chet, and his voice has also fascinated jazz enthusiasts all over the world. He came to Club 7 with his own trio – talented musicians who had been playing in his group for several months. After Norway, they were to go to Paris.

It was in Paris that I first met Chet. He was playing at Le Chat Qui Pêche – one of the most famous jazz clubs in the French capital where a lot was happening at the time. Jazz was very much alive and well in Paris. At the Blue Note, Bud Powell and Johnny Griffin were playing; in St Germain, drummer Kenny Clarke attracted a lot of fans; and other musicians like Miles Davis, Lalo Schiffrin and Quincy Jones stopped over in Paris. I was on my way to Juan-les-Pins and after the club concerts, we would meet at the Living Room or at a place called the Calvados. Chet Baker never went to any of these after-hours places, but I did get to chat with him at the club.

At the time he was sharing the stage with a band led by Swiss trumpet player Hans Kennel. "I'm playing Kennel's trumpet," said Chet, "because mine got stolen during a break."

I thought that was extraordinary – that someone would steal his trumpet during an intermission. Later I heard that he was always losing his horn. That is, he was always selling it for dope. But he always

With Chet in Paris, 1985

had a mouthpiece in his pocket.

When we met again at Club 7 in Oslo Chet could remember our time in Paris, but little else. "My brain is dull – I've been boozed and abused," he told me.

"Do you remember that your trumpet was stolen?"

"Yeah, I remember that, because the one I borrowed, I used for seven years."

When Chet was in Paris, he took part in an American play, *The Gift*, which was performed at the Récamier Théâtre. He played trumpet and acted at the same time in the play, and people who saw it said he did a surprisingly good job as an actor. Many other trumpet players came to listen to him, among them Donald Byrd, who lived in Paris at the time.

When I arrived in Juan-les-Pins, I found that Chet was being featured there at Club 3. His name was displayed on large posters put up to attract fans to the nightclub, but Chet himself failed to appear for the opening night's performance. A couple of days later he finally showed up – at three am, carrying an infant on his arm.

"That was my son," Chet explained years later. "He's sixteen now. I've got two sons and a daughter."

The Chet who was now speaking was on intermission at Club 7 in Oslo. His concert was one of the finest I had experienced that year. He seemed so quiet and introverted, almost like his trumpet style – and his singing. Many years of suffering, both physical and emotional, had left their mark in the rugged lines of his face. Still there was something warm and charming about him, and when he smiled, his eyes had a charismatic attraction. People came in throngs to his concerts; they seemed to have a weakness for what he gave of himself. At times I felt I was being greedy – that I was taking too much from him just by listening. The vulnerable tone of his trumpet and the intensely sensitive vocal were qualities unique to him. He was the James Dean of jazz, and in his younger years he could well have passed as the famous actor's twin.

Chessney Baker, born 23 December, 1929, in Oklahoma, showed a dazzling talent for the trumpet at an early age. In 1940, he moved to California, where his mother still lives. He was in the military from 1946, and he played in a military band until 1952, when he got his break with baritone saxophone player Gerry Mulligan and his quartet. He also joined jazz legend Charlie Parker on the West Coast, serving as a replacement for Red Rodney. In addition, he had his own group. He suffered some hard times during the 1950s, despite rising high in the jazz polls. For a time he lived in Italy, then Germany, then France, but problems with narcotics always complicated his residency in Europe. He eventually moved back to the United States and remained inactive for a long time. In 1968, he was beaten up by street hoods, and the future looked grim, especially since he had his teeth knocked out. He made a comeback, however, despite having to relearn to play the trumpet. In 1973, he was back for good. Just how many records he made is unknown. He was very productive, partially due to his constant need for cash.

AT THE HOSPITAL

After the concert at Club 7, I invited Chet home for a snack. He was hungry and readily accepted the invitation. This was right in the middle of the Christmas party rush, and there were long lines at all the taxi stations. Chet was freezing in the winter air. His face and hands were turning blue.

"My illness has ruined my blood circulation," he explained. "My hands get like ice when I go out in the cold."

I felt so sorry for him that I had the urge to throw my arms around him and warm him like a little child against myself. I was cold myself, and after a time, we simply returned to the club. There we found someone who was willing to drive him back to his hotel.

"Let me have a rain check on that dinner," he said to me as he left. He would be leaving the city at six forty-five am the next day.

After Oslo, he was to play in Volda, Molde, and Kristiansund, respectively, but he didn't show up for any of these performances. He did catch his train, but when he arrived in Lillehammer, he must have asked to get off there. I pieced this theory together later, when saxophonist Carl Magnus Neumann called and asked if I knew how Chet was doing.

"I've heard that he's in a hospital in Lillehammer," said Carl. "Can you check that out, Randi? I'd like to send him some flowers."

When I called the hospital, I was told that Chet Baker had been there. "But he didn't stay the whole night," the woman informed me. "He had so much pain, poor man, from kidney stones, so we gave him a shot." After that, he had gone directly to Paris, where he spent a lot of time. In both Paris and Italy, he had a lot of friends. He had no permanent place to live, but he used the address of hotels or good friends. One of his really good friends was saxophonist Jacques Peltzer in Belgium. We could always call there if we wanted to get hold of him Jacques always knew where Chet was.

Chet became a popular guest in Norway. He played the Kongsberg Festival and different clubs – the Hot House, Jazz Alive, and at a very intimate concert at the home of Emma Hjorth – also known as "Emma's Jazz" – where there were only staff and patients present. Chet also played at Club 7 when the Norwegian Jazz Society celebrated its thirtieth anniversary, and he combined forces with Stan Getz for a concert at the Sandvika theatre. He had a loyal public in Norway, played with several Norwegian musicians and recorded an LP with Norwegian pianist Per Husby. One of his favourite bassists was Terje

Chet Baker's thanks in my guest book, 1983

Venaas, and he enjoyed working with drummer Ole Jacob Hansen. In fact, Ole Jacob was with him when Chet came to Vadsø in 1983 to play the festival there. Chet arrived in the chilly arctic north wearing a cowboy hat and sandals on his feet – without socks. The only luggage he had was his trumpet mouthpiece. No trumpet even. But he played brilliant concerts, and he reaped nothing but wonder from respectful critics. The same year, he visited my home for the first time, returning the following year as well, while on tour, but this time he came as a house guest.

WITH DIANE

When Chet came to Norway, he brought Diane with him. She was his true love during the later years of his life. She was from California, as was Chet, and she played soprano saxophone and was unusually talented. She was also pretty, and when Chet was in a bad mood, he was known to become rather jealous. He never had any cause for his jealousy, though, because Diane loved him – I could see that. Chet played at the Hot House, and it was hard to get hotel rooms in the city at the time, so the club asked if Chet and Diane could stay with me starting the following day. It wasn't a problem, so I arranged for Chet to meet me at Norsk Hydro after closing hours, so that they could come home with me.

363

Norwegian musicians Ole Jacob Hansen, Terje Venaas and Erling Aksdal with Chet and Diane

The next day I had to do some food shopping in the morning before attending, around noon, the funeral of a colleague. That was the plan, but just as I was about to leave the office, I was told by the reception desk that a visitor would like to speak with me. In the reception area stood a crowd of women who were getting ready to leave for the funeral; and at the desk stood Chet Baker. He didn't look very well groomed, but he smiled radiantly and gave me a nice hug.

"Hi, darling," he said. "We've just been out to your house, but there wasn't anyone there."

Diane was waiting outside in the taxi. I tried to explain to them that I really would have to stay in town until closing time at the office, but eventually I decided it was easier to drop everything and accompany them back to my house, delivering my groceries at the same time. The personnel manager – who was an amateur jazz violinist – walked over to me and asked discretely if this wasn't the famous trumpet player Chet Baker standing in the reception?

"It is," I said, "and that's why I can't go to the funeral."

At home, I served a meal to Chet and Diane out on the veranda. The weather was lovely, and I left a happy couple in love, in the midst of a flower garden in bloom. I managed to get back to work and eventually returned home several hours later, where I was met by the slightly embarrassed smiles of the neighbours. I understood the cause of this immediately upon entering the kitchen. Diane was sitting at the table, and in front of the refrigerator stood Chet with a satisfied smile on his face. He was wearing only a scanty hand towel, which kept sliding down his hips.

HOT HOUSE AND JAZZ ALIVE

Before Chet played the Hot House on opening night, he had to take a quick trip down to Amsterdam to buy "necessities". He arrived a little late for the concert in Oslo, but he played marvellously. What he had bought in Holland must have been potent stuff, but obviously he hadn't begun using any of that until the next day. At *my* house. He became very unbalanced, and got angry and jealous of Diane for no reason. She asked me to go with her to the Hot House that evening as well.

"When he's like this, I don't know what he's going to do," she said. "He does everything he can to get me upset." She thought it might help if I was along.

We arrived a little late and had to sober Chet up on plenty of black coffee. His playing was not, unfortunately, what it could have been, although he did complete the last set.

The next morning I had to go in to work again. That same day Chet was to record for radio, and I made him promise to take it easy. Diane borrowed the washing machine, and I took two suitcases of clothes downtown to be dry-cleaned. They hadn't washed anything in two months.

Chet and Diane went to the NRK radio studio early, but they still hadn't returned to my home by the time I arrived. It was obvious that Diane had done the laundry, because I found the yard and the driveway full of blue jeans. It's a good thing the weather held out.

The radio recording had gone very well and Chet expressed deep appreciation to me when they left. As he said his goodbyes, he turned

Chet's admission card from when he visited me at Norsk Hydro, 1984

to me with a radiant smile on his face and said, "I think I just might write letters to Randi, even though I never do that kind of thing."

I never got a letter, but it's the thought that counts. I felt that I had found good friends in both Diane and Chet. I do have one written memento from him, though. While he was waiting in the reception area for me at the company where I work, he had filled in the registration form that is required of all walk-in visitors. In the box asking for "length of stay" Chet had answered "short as possible".

The next time Chet and Diane came to visit was in June of the same year. He and the Norwegian musicians had been on tour and were returning to play at Jazz Alive. During the tour, however, Chet had again become jealous of Diane. The sidemen said that he had been so angry with her that when she threatened to go home, he threw a roll of money into the ocean.

"How am I going to get home now?" cried Diane.

"Swim!" said Chet.

For his next visit – to the new Jazz Alive, which was located in Rådhus Street – Chet arrived alone. He was to play three evenings, but he didn't show for opening night. This was not his fault, as someone had mixed up the times of his connecting flights. Chet was sorry when he heard that I had waited for him at the club, so when I came in on the last evening, he played an extra hour just for me.

That was the kind of thing one might expect from Chet. He was always thoughtful towards his friends. It took time before he accepted people, but once he had made a friend, he was every loyal.

In 1985, at the time I was in Paris for the filming of *Round Midnight*, I met Chet Baker again at New Morning. He was, as usual, surrounded by lots of friends, including Peltzer. After the concert Chet invited all of us to a restaurant.

"BLÅMANN"

The next time I met Chet was at a club called Musikkflekken, in Sandvika, in 1988. This was to be the beginning of our last memorable encounter with one another. The Norwegian "jazz poet", Jan Erik Vold, had called me to pass on a request. Vold had always dreamed of being able to make a record with Chet – would he agree if I proposed the project? Chet knew that Jan Erik had made a record with bassist Red Mitchell, but to Jan Erik, approaching Chet personally seemed difficult. I gave Chet the letter Jan Erik had written and when I asked if a recording session would be possible, Chet had an immediate reply: "Between 17 and 20 February, in Paris. If they are ready, I'm ready." It sounded too good to be true.

Chet played in Sandvika with Terje Venaas and his Italian friend Nicola Stilo on flute, guitar and piano. Terje had come expressly from Sognefjorden, and once again we enjoyed the pleasant company of Chet.

I looked forward to calling Jan Erik in Stockholm, because it now looked like his dream would be fulfilled. There was no guarantee, though, until we were sitting in the studio. Guitarist Jon Larsen, on behalf of his own Hot Club Records label, had obtained a grant from

Chet with Jan Erik Vold, 1988

the state royalties fee fund, and it was now important to locate a studio in Paris.

"It would be nice if you could come along," Chet said to me. "It would make it extra nice."

It turned out I was in fact invited to go along, partially because it was thought that my presence might guarantee that Chet would honour his agreement. Chet was happy because Terje would be playing bass, and I assured him that Egil Kapstad's piano playing would be a pleasant surprise. As for Jan Erik, he had done poetry readings to jazz accompaniment many times before. One of his first records was with Jan Garbarek.

The recording sessions were scheduled for 17 and 18 February during the daytime. Jon had rented Studio Sysmo – a small, cosy place far from the centre of Paris. All that remained was to make sure Chet kept his promise. We had mentioned that we would be coming a day in advance, but when we called Chet's hotel, he was not there.

"He's supposed to start playing tomorrow, but nobody knows if Chet is coming," answered the man at the reception desk. "He usually lives here, but we never know. You can speak with someone who knows more. I'll ask him to call you when he comes in."

The man was referring to guitarist Philip Catherine. I asked Jon and Jan Erik if we could take along Philip, too. At worst, we wouldn't have rented a studio for nothing. Philip called later in the evening and was surprised to find me in Paris. He was a good friend, and I felt now that we were in good hands.

"Maybe you would agree to join us on a record?" I asked. "We don't have a lot of money to offer you – just great musicians."

Philip would definitely enhance the record. He's one of the world's finest guitar players. Besides that, he was to play with Chet at the New Morning, so collaboration on the record would be natural. Not even Philip could say for sure whether Chet would show up or not, but I asked him to drop in at the hotel the next morning. When he arrived, he was exhilarated: "Chet is on his way! He just got in by train from Rome." We almost couldn't believe it. Jan Erik had a look of relieved salvation in his eyes.

While the boys tried to hail a taxi for Terje's huge bass, I was supposed to get hold of Chet. When I called the hotel, he answered right away. "Hi, Randi! You can pick me up in an hour." He was ready and he had not forgotten our agreement.

Jon, Philip, Chet and I came to the studio first, because Terje had problems with his bass – no ordinary taxi would agree to transport it. We drank coffee while we waited in the place that was to become our regular "break" café, located across the street from the studio.

Egil and Jan Erik had selected a number of fine jazz compositions to accompany the poems, but in their luggage they had also brought along Anne Haavie's children's lullaby 'Blåmann, Blåmann, Bukken Min'. It was a natural backdrop for Chet's fragile blue notes.

I'll never forget the instant Chet put the trumpet to his lips and sight-read 'Blåmann, Blåmann'. He played the melody all the way through – straight – and then came his improvisations. The melody was created for Chet, it seemed, and all of us were transfixed. Chet was in great form, joking and smiling, but he kept checking his watch: "The tape is rolling. Let's get going."

Chet in Paris, 1967

THE TAPE IS ROLLING

Chet insisted on hearing a translation of the poems, even though he was able to feel the atmosphere. He had absolutely no difficulty fitting right in with Egil's piano style, including some of Egil's own compositions. Like 'Blåmann', many of Egil's works could have been written especially for Chet – particularly 'Children's Waltz'. Philip functioned superbly in the group, and the whole studio was swinging. In a room by himself, Jan Erik stood swaying to and fro, shifting his weight from his toes to the balls of his feet, as he read his poetry. He was immersed in the event, and it was like going to church each time we went into the technician's room to hear a playback. Most of the material was perfect on the first take. There was a special atmosphere, almost as if everyone was personally honoured and happy to be there. Everything was working out.

There was not enough time to translate all the poems for Chet, but he seemed to feel the poetic content instinctively. The poem '6-Hekt' ("Six Links"), where six poems were linked together, is a good example of his intuitive playing. The music cooked unrestrained on the standard 'Love For Sale'. 'I Går Ja' is another mini-poem which was explained briefly to Chet, and the music he improvised freely to accompany it was filled with expressive feeling.

The next day we were just as excited about continuing the session in the studio. Chet asked me to come and pick him up again, but when I got to the hotel, he had left a message: "Meet me at the café up the street on the corner." I found him there, sulking angrily.

"What happened to Nicola?" he fumed. "He took my trumpet."

I began to have my suspicions about this, and I waited nervously in the taxi. Chet got in beside me and scanned the streets around him.

"There he is! But where's the trumpet?"

I began to despair. Had he sold his trumpet last night? Fortunately, it was not Nicola at all. He showed up shortly afterward – with the trumpet. I think maybe Nicola wanted to go along to the studio with us and that was why he took the trumpet.

While Chet sat in the studio, he suddenly started talking about his grandfather, who had come from Norway. "His name was Mosier, or something like that – I have to ask my mother," said Chet. In the studio, he also took out the mail that had been waiting for him at the hotel. He showed us a beautiful photo of himself and Diane and smiled lovingly as he gazed at the photo: "This was taken in Amsterdam. Diane is there now. I'm going to see her later."

As usual, I had both my snapshot camera and my film camera with me, and I got some good footage both in the studio and at New Morning. We went to the club when the studio sessions were over. Chet invited everyone, and even asked if Terje and Egil would sit in with him during the evening. During the intermission, he went around looking for them. Egil went on stage, and Chet announced to the audience that he had just finished making a record with Norwegian musicians. He said he now had the pleasure of introducing Egil. Egil's playing was greatly admired by the audience as he accompanied Chet on 'Solar' and 'Just Friends'. The rest of us sat in the room and felt pride.

When the concert was over Chet treated all of us to dinner at his favourite restaurant. He was a great conversationalist and proved to have a deep social conscience. We were so happy because this trip to Paris had been so rewarding in so many ways. Jan Erik's dream was now safely preserved on the master tapes.

"Maybe we should make a copy of the master and send it by another plane?" Jan Erik suggested.

This was the last time we saw Chet Baker. On 13 May, he fell from a hotel window in Amsterdam, three months after our recording session with him in Paris. No one knows what really happened.

We were deeply grieved over the tragic loss of a person who had meant so much to us.

For all of us who experienced that magic week in Paris, Chet Baker has become synonymous with 'Blåmann'. We can't listen to the melody without hearing Chet's trumpet at the same time. Sorrowful, blue notes.

CHAPTER 20

Jazz And Fate

"I am interested in making a TV programme about you," said Jan Horne. "You could tell a little about what has happened in your house, use your own pictures, films and private recordings."

Of course I was interested, especially since it was Jan who asked. I knew that he would handle the material correctly. He is also a talented drummer, and that would be a plus, in terms of making a jazz programme. I had just seen a programme he had made about Egil Kapstad and Bjørn Johansen, and if there is someone who can make people be themselves in front of a camera, it is Jan.

At the end of January, 1984, he paid a visit to Gartnerveien and looked at guest books, pictures and other memorabilia. He also took with him a pile of old reel-to-reel tapes containing private interviews and recordings of private jam sessions.

My father was ill in the hospital at that time, admitted just after we had celebrated his eighty-ninth birthday. He was very weak but he managed a smile as I played him a cassette of his favourite accordion music. He knew the melodies and faintly hummed along. A few days later he was gone.

When we started taping for television, my thoughts were with my father, although I smiled for the camera. We had invited people to a jam session, and trumpet player Joe Newman was the natural main attraction since he was in town. It was thirty years since he had been

Norsk Hydro's intrepid reporter on the platform of Treasure Seeker

in the house for the first time, along with the Basie band. Several Norwegian musicians showed up, and there were spectators, too. Outside the house stood two large TV buses, and the neighbours were curious about the goings on. The electrical capacity of the house was inadequate for the television equipment, and the temperature indoors dropped as windows had to be opened for cables to be drawn into the house. When the jam session was at a boiling point, the electricity went. But Jan didn't lose his head; his crew of seven were people who knew what they were doing.

Later on, Jan would come home to take close-up footage of books and pictures. He was always full of ideas, and he was meticulous about his work. It is no wonder he has won so many international prizes for his jazz documentaries.

CANCER

In May I was afflicted with unbearable stomach pains. I decided that I had eaten too many fibre tablets without taking enough water with them. The pains subsided, but to be on the safe side, I contacted the company doctor where I worked, and she advised me to have a physical examination. She found traces of blood, and I was sent for x-rays. First, though, I was determined to go to the Kongsberg Jazz Festival.

The x-ray session scared me a little, because it was so incredibly thorough. I didn't wait for the results, but instead flew off to the Nice Festival. I was somewhat worried, even though I was not experiencing any pain. When I returned to work, Sidsel Sjølyst, the company doctor, stood solemnly waiting for me:

"You have to report to Ullevål Hospital right away. No more jazz festivals for you for the time being. We've found a tumorous growth."

I asked if it was malignant, and she said yes. In the letter from the hospital, it said in two separate places that this was probably cancer. My world collapsed. The professor at Ullevål told me that I had a fifty-fifty chance and that they couldn't give a prognosis until they operated.

Oslo Jazz
Festival's "Ella" statuette
by Marianne Hazeland, 1995

I asked if I could postpone the operation a few days – I had to go to the Molde Festival. I explained that the television crew wanted to shoot the last footage for a programme and, besides, I felt sorry for the TV team – they had really been looking forward to going to Molde. I didn't want to let them down.

"It's up to you," the professor said. I decided to go, but I was nervous about it.

In Molde I found Elvin Jones and his Keiko. To enhance the programme, Jan Horne wanted to tape some of the yearly soccer match between the musicians and the journalists at the festival. I was to be a linesman, and Elvin was to be referee.

It turned out that Elvin was a born soccer referee. He had a great time on the field, and I laughed and laughed directly into the camera.

Inside, though, I was thinking constantly about the upcoming operation and I wondered if I would ever see any of the TV programmes.

The operation went well. I was in the hospital for only one week and one of the first visitors I had was Jan Horne. During the course of the months we had been making the TV programmes, we had become very close friends. Actually, I had been worried that he would become sick and tired of me altogether, considering all he had to put up with in order to make the shows. But he called me constantly and talked about new ideas he had. Eventually, I did get to see the finished result. My mother saw them also, fortunately, just a few months before she died. "Your father should have been here to share this," she said. My mother was fantastic.

The concept of making one documentary had grown to four individual programmes. First *Jams At Gartnerveien*, followed by *The Saxophonists Are Coming*. Then the programme about pianists, and finally the last one dedicated to the media and festivals. My beloved Eubie was featured, contributing a humorous touch to proceedings and it was in this last programme that Elvin ran around like a wild man on the soccer field in Molde – I didn't regret that I had decided to go to Molde and put off my operation for a short while.

After I came home from the hospital, I was nursed back to health with help from my daughter Wivi-Ann, who had come from England with her two daughters to stay with me. I sat in the yard, happily enjoying the sun. When my daughter had to return to England, the company I worked for sent meals-on-wheels three times a week, and that was a big help. I asked them to send work for me to do at home, too. My column in *Aftenposten* continued to appear regularly, even on the very day of my operation, 6 August. During the first days of convalescence, I dictated the next column to my daughter Wivi-Ann.

ON A JAZZ CRUISE

In October, I was invited on a jazz cruise on board the SS Norway to the Caribbean. I travelled in the company of Hege Schøyen and Arild Andersen and their little daughter Line. Arild helped me to carry my camera equipment around since I was not totally recovered from the operation, but I couldn't miss this new and exciting jazz experience.

The luxury liner was a floating jazz festival, with trumpet players Dizzy Gillespie and Clark Terry, singer Joe Williams and several top names among a couple of hundred established jazz musicians. There were seven grand pianos on board and over forty different activities to choose among. Jazz was plenty enough for me by itself.

I was given permission to invite the jazz stars to a special private cocktail party on board, and of course I was asked to sit at the captain's table. He was startled by my request to see the engine room – but the burner had been specially manufactured by the company I worked for. I decided to write articles both for the company magazine and for my jazz column while on the cruise.

One day we all met up on the bridge for little Line's baptism ceremony – we were just off the shores of St Thomas so I wrote the baptismal song based on Sonny Rollins' standard of the same name. Later, I got Sonny to send a special greeting to Line. Arild assisted with the baptismal anointment, in the presence of the ship's captain, and Stein and Arne, from Kloster – the men who had invited me on this sensational adventure cruise.

VICISSITUDES OF LIFE

My life has been filled with chance happenings, and I can thank jazz for most of them. It was jazz – much more than my artistic talents – that fostered my debut exhibition in 1976. Frode Holm, who had his own gallery, had dropped by to talk about music. When he saw all the jazz drawings on the wall, he asked if I would like to exhibit them in his gallery. I hesitated at first, but Leif Brandt, who was a graphic artist at Norsk Hydro, helped me get things ready.

The exhibition ran for four weeks. Jazz drawings, paintings, collages and sculptures were displayed, and eighty musicians came to the opening. We held a jam session and sipped red wine. The jam was so successful – though sales were not – that we arranged a second opening two weeks later, also with more musicians invited to play.

Since my debut, I have had exhibits in Kongsberg, Molde, Bergen,

Trondheim, Sandvika, the American Embassy in Oslo and New York City. In 1997 I showed my jazz portraits in Moss, at a music seminar. Jazz gets the credit for all of these.

TO INDIA WITH JAZZ

One of the most exciting places to hear jazz has been, surprisingly, India, and twice I've been to the festival there, in 1980 and 1990. Niranjan Jhaveri, who started Jazz Yatra, invited me along to Bombay the first time. What impressed me most was all the classical musicians we heard each day; we could listen to hours of improvisations played by India's foremost musicians. In the festival park, Ravi Shankar played with Indian jazz performers, and we were treated to a classical interlude by TV Gopalkrishnan – singer and expert on the mridangam, a two-headed Indian drum. He was also my interpreter when I interviewed a saxophonist, and afterwards he invited me to Madras, where he and his family lived.

Gopalkrishnan was a guru with almost forty students and I was

introduced to one of his former pupils, who is now a successful composer of film soundtracks. Forty musicians were in the studio but before each take, they all had to be blessed over a flame in a coconut shell. This was interesting. When I left Madras, I stopped in Delhi to greet the Minister of Culture, and I visited the branch office of the company I worked for. People there received me generously, and gave me a guided tour of the city.

When I was invited back to India, Niranjan asked if I could bring along a good jazz group, preferably with a saxophonist. I suggested instead Magni Wentzel and Egil Kapstad, who I knew had a fine group, with Terje Venaas on bass and Tom Olstad on drums.

There were no Indian classical musicians giving concerts this time, as they had a decade earlier, but at the Bombay airport, I was lucky to run into flautist Chaurasia. He was on his way to New Delhi, and he

Dear Randi,
I'll try harder next time with the "chapatis". Perhaps they will come better when I see you in Bombay.
Best — Niranjan Jhaveri
(ਅੰਜਨ ਝਵੇਰੀ)   30-Sept 197

Visit from India – chief of Jazz Yatra Niranjan Jhaveri with Karin Krog, September 1970

TV Gopalkrishnan and Gopaluat in Bombay, 1980, at the second Jazz Yatra

invited all of us to a concert. Gopalkrishnan also came there, and that was an additional pleasant surprise. The day after, he attended our Norwegian concert and was deeply impressed.

We visited Bombay, New Delhi, Goa, Bangalore and Calcutta. I would never have believed, as a fledgling fan in the 1950s, that jazz would one day lead me to India.

JAZZ AT NORSK HYDRO

I also never would have believed that I would one day be named editor of Norsk Hydro's internal newspaper because of my jazz articles written more or less as a hobby. In fact I was editor for the last twenty-two years of my time with the company.

In 1989 I had the exhilarating experience of staging a company jazz concert for a thousand of my colleagues. Haugesund had its yearly Herring Jazz Festival, so the festival was expanded with a "Foundry

Jazz" addition. Karmøy Factories cleared the foundry floor to make room for festival musicians. On stage were several New Orleans artists and Magnolia Jazzband. The foundry swung – just as Oslo swung at about the same time, since the two festivals overlap.

FATE REVISITED

Jazz in Oslo has changed since the time we first opened our home for private jam sessions. Not only have we inaugurated a number of jazz clubs over the years, but we have our own annual jazz festival. It was first arranged in 1986, and in a way, the festival would become a part of my fate. There are many people to whom the festival owes its start – not the least of these being Aage, Mona and Lisbeth, who sacrificed so much but succeeded in making the capital swing during the month of August each year. As sure as rain, ninety-five-year-old Benny Waters,

born in 1902 and a member of the world's earliest jazz band, has gone on stage with his saxophones. He has won many fans with his strong tone and sense of humour, not to mention his annual proposals of marriage. Always anxious to play music, always a flirt, he will be deeply missed the day he decides he is too old to return to Norway.

Anthony and Mona at Gartnerveien, 1953

Benny made a recording in Oslo, together with Christiania Jazzband, in 1983. On the cover, I wrote that he was "the Eubie of the horn". It looks like I was right. The last time he played in Oslo was in 1996, with a singer friend from Paris, Polya Jordan, "a youngster of sixty-six", as he said. They had also recorded a CD together. When he celebrated his ninety-fifth birthday in January 1997, at the new "Birdland" in New York, the party lasted for three days, and he was recorded live. "Sax gets better with age," says Benny, always in good spirits, even though he has lost his sight in the autumn of his years.

On the subject of recordings, several other festival musicians have

Anthony Ortega and Mona Ørbeck back in Oslo after thirty years, meeting Ivar Børsum, Scott Lunde, Einar "Pastor'n" Iversen and Arnulf Neste – old musician friends, 1984

recorded in Oslo – American artists in collaboration with Norwegian musicians. One of them, Ellington's former saxophonist Harold Ashby, actually made a comeback with his LP *The Viking* for Gemini Records. The producer was Bjorn Petersen, usually found standing in the reception line when musicians arrive at Fornebu; Petersen has secured many a fine tune for his record label. The Oslo Jazz Festival has become one of the joys of life for many people. Bebop, swing orchestras and Dixieland bands abound during the season, and there are ticket lines everywhere.

On several occasions I have had the pleasure of hosting musicians at garden parties. At one of these, someone got the idea to wander around looking for four-leaf clovers in the back yard. Following the others, Benny Waters was found peering into the grass, head down, bottom up. In fact, the whole yard was filled with guests walking around bent over. What must the neighbours have thought? One of them did ask me if it was really Joe Williams sitting on my porch eating a hot dog. Yes, of course, that tall figure was indeed the former Basie vocalist. It had been thirty-two years since his first visit to Gartnerveien.

Benny Waters, still swinging at ninety-five (left) and wearing his Hydro cap

In 1987, I showed the tapes of the television programmes, *Randi's Jazz*, to some of the festival musicians. Two of them, Anne Phillips and Bob Kindred, were so impressed that they suggested they be shown on a full cinema screen in New York. Bob played tenor sax in the Pan Am orchestra his wife Anne is a composer, arranger and producer who has planned and produced several large jazz-related performances in the United States. Before I knew what had happened, I was sent first-class tickets for my flight to New York.

Bob was one of the many who played for me, and the show was called *Randi's Jazz*. For three unforgettable days, I experienced being the centre of attention in the world of Manhattan jazz. Once again, fate and chance happenings had brought this on me.

UNDER THE SIGN OF JAZZ

The year after, I took part in another big event in New York. NYU

Ernie Wilkins, Basie arranger and tenor player, trying on one of my "guest wigs"

dedicated an evening to *Randi's Jazz*. Students from across America attended, and Anne and Bob had gotten hold of arrangements to several of the melodies that various musicians had dedicated to me. These were performed, between showings of the Norwegian television programmes on a wide screen, by big bands, smaller ensembles, and a guitarist. The latter played Jon Eberson's composition 'Randi, The Grand Old Lady', arranged for solo guitar, without accompaniment. This is a melody that I adore. I heard it for the first time in Molde, and I'll never forget how beautifully it was played by Jon on guitar and Tore Brunborg on tenor sax.

If Jon's father Leif – who frequented Gartnerveien in the early years – could have known that his son would dedicate a song to me, he would certainly have been a proud father. But unfortunately, he died very young.

MANY COMPOSITIONS

Many fine compositions have been written and dedicated to me in the course of my life with jazz, including several tunes from Norwegian musicians. Clarinettist Gustav Kramer, for example, has written a tribute to 'Gartnerveien 6', pianist Sigurd Haugen has written 'Randi's Home' and Jon Eberson has written one of my favourites, 'Randi, Grand Old Lady', a beautiful ballad recorded in Oslo and played live in Molde and New York.

But the very first melody written to me was 'Theme For Randi', composed by saxophonist Nathan Davis. Musicians who have played the piece have been very pleased with it, but I have never heard it myself. I asked for a copy when Nathan lived in Paris, but he had so many other recordings on the same tape that he found it difficult to meet my request. Today audio copying is much simpler than it was in 1965, but now Nathan has so much to do as professor at Pittsburgh University, that I have lost hope of ever hearing it. He leads Pitt Jazz with annual seminars, concerts, and their Hall Of Fame, and has also toured in Europe. A very fine musician, he played at the first Kongsberg Festival.

That same year – 1965 – Donald Byrd titled one of his compositions 'Randi', arranged for NRK's big band. Jørgen and Italo in Sweden have written tunes for me, as well as bassist Anatoly in Moscow. From Clifford Jordan I got 'Impressions Of Scandinavia', and Jaki Byard has also dedicated a beautiful ballad: 'Oslo To Kristiansund To Molde'. Tenorist Tad

The Bird's Nest

Shull composed 'Randi's Rondo', and Mona Ørbeck wrote 'Randi Lives'. Another tune I hope to hear again, is the pearl 'Waltz For Randi' that Adam Makowicz played for me in New York 1988, and later in Copenhagen. Many years ago he wrote 'Ballad For R', as well as creating 'Randi And Bamse' with Urszula Dudziak in 1972, a really avant-garde composition, on their LP *Newborn Light*, which in fact became the record of the year in Europe. 'Randi's Rag' by Eubie

Jon Eberson's 'Randi, Grand Old Lady'

Twenty compositions dedicated to me

With Nathan Davis in Kongsberg, 1965, and, below, his entry from my guest book

Blake has been recorded, as has Sonny Rollins' 'Playing In The Yard'. Both of these evoke good memories: Sonny loved to mow the grass in my yard, and Eubie enjoyed the dedication of "Eubie Blake Lake" in my garden a few years later. Of course I am also very proud of Bud Powell's 'In The Mood For A Classic', which he dedicated to me at the Blue Note in Paris in 1964.

The most well-known is undoubtedly Phil Woods' ballad, 'Randi', performed by many big bands throughout the world. The most recent reference to it that I

Nathan Davis - etter Kongsberg

This short trip to Oslo has been a great historical event in my life and I shall never forget your sweetness and hospitality during my short stay. You shall always hold a warm place in my heart. May God Bless you & yours.

(P.S. Don't let Wini stop dancing)

Yours always
Nathan Davis

June 1965

heard, was that it had been used in a show in the United States, led by Frank Sinatra Jr. Phil also wrote the lyrics, and Kim Shaw sang this for me together with a big band at the New York University evening in 1989.

CANCER AND ANOTHER JAZZ CRUISE

My retirement from Norsk Hydro in February 1993 coincided with the departure from Norway of United States Ambassador Loret Miller Ruppe, who was exceptional. She had shown a great interest in the Oslo Jazz Festival, just as she showed a genuine interest for everything happening in Norway. I arranged a farewell jam session for her and her husband Philip, and the ambassador even sang at the session. She also surprised me with a framed certificate of appreciation on behalf of the United States for having opened my home to so many American musicians.

Some months later, I visited Loret and Phil in Maryland, and we drove to the Eubie Blake museum in Baltimore, where he was born in 1883. Unfortunately there had been a fire in the building, so there was not much to see. Very little of what Eubie's wife Marion had intended to give the museum had come into their possession. She died a year before he died.

Before I returned to New York, we went to a jazz club in Washington and heard Stanley Turrentine. Loret had obviously become a jazz enthusiast and even asked for addresses of New York jazz clubs.

What neither of us knew was that both of us had cancer. Loret learned of it in the summer of 1994 and was operated upon immediately. As for myself, I took some tests shortly after that, but I

With Loret Miller Ruppe at the American embassy in Oslo, 1992

389

no longer had my attentive doctor, Sidsel, at the Hydro Corporation, to follow up for me. As I heard nothing from my new doctor, I assumed that all was well, and I even comforted Loret by letter, saying that I had recovered even though I had had cancer ten years earlier. But in 1995 the hospital told me that I had got cancer again in my colon, and I learned then that the tests taken seven months previously, had actually revealed bad news. "But you didn't call and ask" was the doctor's only defence. The disease had spread to the liver, requiring two operations. Fate brought me the very same professor who had received me at the hospital eleven years earlier: Morten Ræder, one of our best.

Loret and I consoled one another by letter, but I also had my jazz. Between operations I caught the Mulligan concert in Oslo, and after the last operation, I was asked to be present at the opening of the Oslo Jazz Festival. The directors wanted to give me the very first "Ella Statuette" – a sculpture I have come to love – which was a superb encouragement for me.

In November, I once again got the urge to go on a jazz cruise with the SS Norway, and through that received another sign of fate. On board the ship I met Ernie Jackson, an American who had jazz programmes on the radio. When he saw the Norwegian version of my book *Born Under The Sign Of Jazz*, he asked me to contact his friend Ken Vail, in England, who was the author of many fine books on jazz. Thanks to Ken, we are both colleagues for the same publishing company in London.

Loret should have lived to see this. She had hoped that the book would come out in English, but tragically, she didn't live to see it. She died in August 1996 on the exact day that the Oslo Jazz Festival opened to celebrate its tenth anniversary.

I hope what I have been privileged to experience can be shared with many. The jazz music form has rewarded me with a full and exciting life and, although it took me quite a while to realise it, there can be no doubt that I was born under the sign of jazz.

I thank my stars for that.

CHAPTER 21

Rare Moments

Like most musicians, bass player Ray Brown also plays the piano, 1980

Drummer Billy Higgins, a frequent visitor, loves singing and playing guitar Brazilian style, 1977

Milt Jackson, famous for his vibraphone in the MJQ, surprises us here with his singing and piano playing in 1965. He actually started on piano with Dizzy

**Donald Byrd was another frequent visitor. In September 1965 he stayed a week and
arranged music for the radio big band**

Teddy Wilson and George Russell met at the Down Town Keyclub in Oslo, in the early seventies

Drummer Max Roach playing and making up his own bebop lyric, 1977

Index